A SHORT COMMENTARY

ON THE

BOOK OF DANIEL.

A SHORT COMMENTARY

ON THE

BOOK OF DANIEL

FOR THE USE OF STUDENTS

BY

A. A. BEVAN, M.A.

FELLOW OF TRINITY COLLEGE, CAMBRIDGE.

CAMBRIDGE:

AT THE UNIVERSITY PRESS

1892

CAMBRIDGE UNIVERSITY PRESS
Cambridge, New York, Melbourne, Madrid, Cape Town,
Singapore, São Paulo, Delhi, Mexico City

Cambridge University Press
The Edinburgh Building, Cambridge CB2 8RU, UK

Published in the United States of America by Cambridge University Press, New York

www.cambridge.org
Information on this title: www.cambridge.org/9781107669949

© Cambridge University Press 1892

First published 1892
First paperback edition 2013

A catalogue record for this publication is available from the British Library

ISBN 978-1-107-66994-9 Paperback

PREFACE.

THE main object of this work is to assist those who are entering upon the study of the language and text of the Book of Daniel, by affording them such philological information as they are most likely to need. Since however philology can never be separated from history, I have found it necessary to devote considerable space to the treatment of historical questions. In the history of religion the Book of Daniel occupies a very important, perhaps a unique, position, but the working out of this subject belongs rather to the historian than to the commentator. Hence the relation in which this Book stands to the Prophets on the one hand and to the later Apocalypses on the other could not here be examined at any great length. Discussions upon speculative theology or philosophy I have studiously avoided, as I cannot but think that when introduced into exegetical works they serve rather to obscure than to elucidate the real matters at issue.

It is scarcely necessary to say that this work contains very little that is new. As to the character and general meaning of the Book of Daniel all sober critics have long been agreed, and I have therefore, in the great majority of cases, contented myself with stating, as concisely as possible, the views of former investigators. It has been my endeavour to collect, not only from Commentaries but from all other sources accessible to me, whatever appeared to be of real value for the purpose of interpretation. In a book intended for ordinary students an

exhaustive treatment of the subject is, of course, out of the
question. Hence it did not seem to me desirable to fill my
pages with bibliographical details interesting only to the curious.
It would indeed have been easy to supply much fuller lists of
names and references, but had I attempted to give anything
like a history of the interpretation of each passage, my book
would have been swelled to many times its present bulk. Only
now and then have I thought it worth while to say something
about the views of the Rabbins and of the Christian Fathers.
In citing modern writers I have generally confined myself to
mentioning those whose works are the fruit of original research,
passing over in silence the crowd of imitators and imitators of
imitators. I ought here to state that I have unfortunately not
been able to consult the essay of J. W. van Lennep, *De* 70
jaarweken van Daniel (Utrecht, 1888). Still more have I reason to regret that Prof. Driver's *Introduction to the Literature
of the Old Testament* did not appear till my book was in the
press, and has thus been used only to a very limited extent.
Some persons may perhaps think that I have not examined at
sufficient length the arguments brought forward by Hengstenberg and English writers who belong to the same school. But
the fact is that in a great number of cases these arguments are
based upon assumptions which all scholars now agree in reject-
ing. Of what use would it be, for example, to refute such
arguments of Hengstenberg as rest upon the theory that the
First Book of the Maccabees was originally written in Greek,
or to point out the numerous statements of Pusey, respecting Aramaic philology, which are now universally regarded as
erroneous ?

On many questions, as might have been expected, I have
found it impossible to form a definite opinion. Though the
Book of Daniel is by no means one of the more difficult books
of the Old Testament, it nevertheless contains a considerable
number of passages of which the meaning is still uncertain, and
some which will perhaps remain for ever unintelligible. Where

doubt or obscurity exists I have never sought to disguise the
fact, and in offering explanations of my own I have been careful to indicate that they are mere suggestions to be accepted or
rejected by the reader as he thinks fit. One principal cause of
difficulty seems to me to be the corruption of the text. During
the last fifty years the opinion that the text of the Old Testament is well-nigh faultless, has been constantly losing ground.
The common maxim that the difficulty of readings raises a pre-
sumption in favour of their genuineness, is true only if understood to mean that no scribe *consciously* substitutes a difficult
reading for an easy one. But when readings owe their origin
to carelessness or to the external damaging of a manuscript,
the above maxim is obviously inapplicable. In very many
cases the text of the Old Testament can be explained only by
means of conjecture, and our task consists in deciding which of
several conjectures is the most probable. When I have proposed conjectural emendations I have done so in the full
consciousness of the fact that very few emendations have any
claim to be regarded as certain. The Hebrew of Daniel, as
compared with that of other Old Testament writings, has
so many marked peculiarities that it would be altogether a
mistake to ascribe every anomaly to textual corruption. The
business of the true textual critic is to distinguish those
anomalies which are characteristic of the author's style from
those which are not, in other words to distinguish linguistic
peculiarities from linguistic impossibilities. The practice of
rash and arbitrary emendation cannot of course be condemned
too severely, but the old-fashioned school, who tortured grammar and syntax in order to extract a meaning from obscure
passages, must appear equally unscientific.

In all that relates to Aramaic philology I have been guided
chiefly by the works of Professor Nöldeke, of Strassburg, in
particular by his *Mandäische Grammatik* (Halle, 1875), and his
"Beiträge zur Kenntniss der aramäischen Dialecte" in the
Zeitschrift der deutschen morgenländischen Gesellschaft, Vols.

XXI. XXII. and XXIV. By far the best work on Biblical Aramaic is Prof. Kautzsch's *Grammatik des Biblisch-Aramäischen* (Leipzig, 1884). If I have occasionally ventured to express disagreement with Prof. Kautzsch, this has been done solely from the conviction that his work is likely long to remain a standard book of reference, so that it is particularly necessary to point out those statements in it which are open to criticism. The older Grammars are very untrustworthy, since they were written at a time when a scientific classification of the Aramaic dialects had not yet been made, and when Biblical Aramaic (or, as it used to be called, Chaldee) was commonly believed to be a dialect learnt by the Jews in Babylonia during the Exile. That it is, on the contrary, a *West*-Aramaic dialect, has now been conclusively proved. I have endeavoured throughout to call attention to the close resemblance between the Aramaic of the Bible and the dialects afterwards spoken in Palestine and the neighbouring countries. In order the better to illustrate that resemblance I have published, in an Appendix, some specimens of the Palmyrene inscriptions, which have hitherto been practically inaccessible to most English students. Very similar is the dialect represented by the Nabatean inscriptions, which may best be studied in Prof. Euting's *Nabatäische Inschriften aus Arabien* (Berlin, 1885). The dialect of the Palestinian Christians is known chiefly from the Lectionary published at Verona in 1861—1864 by the Count Francesco Miniscalchi Erizzo, under the title of *Evangeliarium Hierosolymitanum*. In referring to the Samaritan dialect I have always quoted from Nutt's *Fragments of a Samaritan Targum* (London, 1874), of which the text is generally admitted to be more correct than that contained in the Polyglot Bibles.

Of Assyriology I possess no independent knowledge. My principal authority is Prof. Schrader's work *The Cuneiform Inscriptions and the Old Testament*, which I have used in the English translation (published by Williams and Norgate, 1885 —1888), since it contains the latest corrections by the author.

In my citations I have followed the paging of the German
edition, which is given in the margin of the English text, so
that possessors of either work will be able without difficulty to
verify my references.

The transcription of Oriental words is notoriously a matter
about which scholars still differ, and here I have found it
impossible to be strictly consistent. Quotations from Phoenician and Aramaic inscriptions, from the Samaritan Targum
and from the Christian Palestinian Lectionary have been printed
in ordinary Hebrew letters. Syriac has usually been printed
in the Old Syriac character, without vowel points, but when
it was necessary to indicate the vocalization, I have, for the
convenience of those who do not read Syriac, followed the
method of transcription adopted by the late Prof. Wright in
his article "Syriac Literature" (*Encyclopaedia Britannica*, 9th
ed.)—a method which in spite of some disadvantages is perhaps
the best that has yet been proposed. Assyrian and Babylonian
words are generally spelt as in Prof. Schrader's work, but for
š, which is liable to perplex English readers, I have written
sh, and the guttural which corresponds to the Arabic ﺡ has
been represented by *kh*. It is perhaps not superfluous to add
that the real pronunciation of the Assyrio-Babylonian language
is still very uncertain, since even on points so important as
the number of the vowels Assyriologists are not yet agreed,
some maintaining and others denying that *e* and *i* are distinguished in the cuneiform character.

In a work compiled from so many scattered sources and
touching upon so many different subjects, errors will naturally
be found. Some of these have, I hope, been rectified in the
"Addenda et Corrigenda", but others no doubt remain. If
in any place I have failed, through inadvertence, to acknowledge obligations to previous writers, I beg to offer them my
sincere apologies. It remains for me to express my thanks
to those personal friends who have aided me in the revising
of this book. Prof. Robertson Smith has been so good as to

read through the greater part of it, either in manuscript or in proof, and to him I owe many valuable suggestions. I am also greatly indebted to Mr E. A. Wallis Budge, of the British Museum, who has on several occasions supplied me with information on Assyriological matters.

TRINITY COLLEGE, CAMBRIDGE,
Dec. 1891.

ADDENDA ET CORRIGENDA.

Page 3—That the original Pĕshīṭtā did not contain the apocryphal additions to Daniel may be inferred from the fact that Polychronius, who lived early in the 5th century, says with reference to the Song of the Three Children, Εἰδέναι δὲ δεῖ ὡς οὗτος ὁ ὕμνος οὐ κεῖται ἐν τοῖς Ἑβραϊκοῖς ἢ ἐν τοῖς Συριακοῖς βιβλίοις.

p. 9—Since the above was written, a posthumous edition of Prof. Delitzsch's *Messianic Prophecies* has appeared.

p. 17, line 30—For *Nabūnāid* read *Nabūnāid;* the same mistake occurs again on p. 18 and in the note on p. 19.

p. 36—The suffix הם " their " appears frequently in Nabatean inscriptions, most of which are post-Christian.

p. 37—As specimens of the Passive formed by internal vowel-change may be mentioned the word עבידת " was made " in a Nabatean inscription of the year 39 A.D. found at Madabah (see the *Zeitschrift für Assyriologie*, Vol. v. p. 290), and the Palmyrene נבי " has been taxed " (cf. נלי Dan. ii. 19, 30) in the Fiscal Inscription, where it is said טעון קרם די בלמא גנם כלה לארבעא טעונין די נמלין מכסא נבי, " a cart-load of whatsoever kind has been taxed as much as four camel-loads."

p. 39, line 19—For *'ălayk* read *'ălaik.*

p. 41, note 2—It should be noticed that in this passage of Polybius the κεράτιον corresponds to the קרנא of Dan. iii. 5, 7, 10, 15. The reading κεραμίου is evidently a mistake.

p. 70—With regard to the phrase כל־קבל די "because", I should have cited the remarks of Luzzatto in his *Elementi grammaticali del Caldeo biblico*, p. 52, "La voce כל non ha quì alcun valore, e sembra che le due voci כָּל־קֵבֵל formassero primitivamente una sola voce כְּלֵקֵבֵל eguale al Rabbinico כְּלַפֵּי, כְּלַאפֵּי. Da כל־קבל sembra nato il corrispondente כָּל־עֻמַּת di Koheleth". This explanation appears to me decidedly preferable to the ordinary one.

p. 74—On אֲלוּ "behold!" see Prof. Driver's note (*Introduction to the Literature of the Old Testament*, Addenda, p. xxv), where the word הלו in an Aramaic inscription of Egypt (*Corpus Inscr. Sem.* Pt. 2, Nº. 137) is explained as being probably a variant of אֲלוּ.

p. 83, last line—For *Lehnwörter* read *Fremdwörter*.

p. 86, line 16—For (and תִּכָּל chap. v. 16) read (and תִּבּוּל chap. v. 16, *Ḳĕrī*).

p. 120, line 17—For *Chald. Wörterb.* read *Wörterb. über die Targumim*.

p. 146—The method of interpreting Scripture by the artificial combination of different passages is so strikingly set forth in a fragment of Origen's Commentary on the Psalms that it may be worth while to quote it. "In entering upon the interpretation of the Psalms, let me first cite a tradition of singular beauty which has been handed down to me by my Hebrew teacher as applying generally to all Holy Scripture. This Hebrew used to say that all divinely-inspired Scripture, by reason of its uncertain import, might be compared to a number of chambers in a single building, all locked. At the door of each chamber there is a key, but not the key which fits it; and thus the keys have been scattered over the chambers, none being adapted to the chamber where it is found. Hence it is a work of enormous difficulty to find the keys and to fit them to the chambers which they are capable of opening. The Scriptures then can be explained only when they receive one from another the first hints towards their explanation, since they contain in themselves

scattered up and down the principles of their exegesis". (See
Delarue's edition, Vol. ii. pp. 526, 527.) For this reference I
am indebted to the kindness of the Rev. J. A. Robinson of
Christ's College.

p. 148, line 5—The date 588 B.C., for the destruction of Jerusalem,
is that given by Schürer (*Gesch. d. jüd. Volkes*, ii. p. 616) and
by Driver (in the Chronological Table at the beginning of his
Isaiah, his life and times). But the latter scholar has since
adopted the view that Jerusalem was destroyed in 586 B.C. (*Introduction*, pp. 232, 233).

p. 183, line 21—It is possible that וֹבַת הנשים is a corruption of
וֹבתו בנשים, i.e. "*and he shall give him his daughter to wife*"
etc. The phrase בנשים "to wife", "in marriage", does not
seem to occur elsewhere in Hebrew or Jewish Aramaic, but
ܟܢܫܐ often has this meaning in Syriac; cf. *The Chronicle of
Joshua the Stylite*, ed. Wright, p. 19 of the Syriac text, line 8—
ܝܗܒܬܗ ܠܗ ܒܟܢܫܐ "she gave her to him in marriage".

CONTENTS.

PROLEGOMENA.

COMMENTARY.

N.B. *Citations from the Old Testament are always made according to the chapters and verses of the Hebrew Bible.*

Καί μοι δοκεῖ μεγίστην θεὸν τοῖς ἀνθρώποις ἡ φύσις ἀπο-
δεῖξαι τὴν Ἀλήθειαν καὶ μεγίστην αὐτῇ προσθεῖναι δύναμιν.
πάντων γοῦν αὐτὴν καταγωνιζομένων ἐνίοτε καὶ πασῶν τῶν
πιθανοτήτων μετὰ τοῦ ψεύδους ταττομένων, οὐκ οἶδ᾽ ὅπως αὐτὴ
δι᾽ αὑτῆς εἰς τὰς ψυχὰς εἰσδύεται τῶν ἀνθρώπων, καὶ ποτὲ
μὲν παραχρῆμα δείκνυσι τὴν αὑτῆς δύναμιν, ποτὲ δὲ καὶ
πολὺν χρόνον ἐπισκοτισθεῖσα τέλος αὐτὴ δι᾽ ἑαυτῆς ἐπικρατεῖ
καὶ καταγωνίζεται τὸ ψεῦδος.

POLYBIUS, Fragm. of Bk. XIII.

PROLEGOMENA.

GENERAL INTRODUCTION.

The Text and the oldest Versions.

THE Palestinian Jews, as is well known, divided their Scriptures into three parts, the Law, the Prophets, and the Hagiographa (Heb. כְּתוּבִים). The Book of Daniel was never, so far as we know, included among the Prophetical Books, but occupied a place in the Hagiographa. In our present Hebrew Bibles, Daniel stands between Esther and Ezra; in ancient times, however, the order of the books in the Hagiographa was not rigidly fixed.

The received Jewish or Masoretic text of Daniel is written partly in Hebrew (chaps. i.—ii. 4 a, viii.—xii.), partly in the Aramaic dialect spoken by the Jews of Palestine (chaps. ii. 4 b—vii.). At what time this text assumed its final shape, cannot be positively stated, but it is now agreed that the present Jewish Bible, leaving out of account the vowel-points, accents etc., is virtually identical with that which was used in the latter half of the second century after Christ. Many scholars believe the Masoretic text to have been fixed much earlier, though few would venture to go further back than about the beginning of the first century—the date assigned by Nöldeke (*Die alttestamentliche Litteratur,* p. 241). It is in itself probable that the text of some books was fixed earlier than that of others. Since the Book of Daniel, like most of the writings included in the Hagiographa, does not appear to have been used in the public services of the Synagogue, it was presumably one of the latest books to assume a stereotyped form.

Daniel and Ezra-Nehemiah are the only books of the Old

Testament which are lacking in the collection of Aramaic versions or paraphrases known as the Targums. Whether this be due to the fact that parts of the books in question are already written in Aramaic, is uncertain. In the Mishnah (*Yādayim* IV. 5) the Aramaic portions of Ezra and Daniel are called Targum, but they are expressly distinguished from other Targums, since they always "defile the hands" (i.e. they are of Canonical dignity).

The so-called Septuagint version of Daniel is generally believed to have been made rather more than a century before the Christian era. An examination of this version reveals at once two facts, firstly that the text used by the translator, or translators, differed in numerous *details* from the Masoretic text, secondly that the version contains an unusual quantity of later additions and alterations. To this work a separate chapter will be devoted.

The Greek versions of Aquila and Symmachus have been preserved only in fragments, as in the case of other Old Testament writings. On the other hand, Theodotion's version has been handed down to us entire. According to some Theodotion was a Jew, according to others an Ebionite Christian. It was formerly supposed that he lived about the middle or end of the second century after Christ, but Schürer has lately brought forward arguments to prove that his date may be somewhat earlier (*Geschichte des jüdischen Volkes*, II. p. 709). Theodotion's version of Daniel is to be regarded as a revision of the Septuagint for the purpose of making it agree more closely with the Masoretic text, or at least with a text differing from the Masoretic only in a very small number of minute details. The apocryphal additions (Susanna, the Song of the Three Children, Bel and the Dragon) were retained by Theodotion, though with some changes.

Whether Theodotion's translations were ever used among Greek-speaking Jews, is not known; but in the Christian Church his translation of Daniel rapidly became so popular as almost entirely to displace the old Septuagint version. Yet, as might have been expected, reminiscences of the Septuagint soon found their way into Theodotion's text, while the Septuagint in its turn became interpolated from Theodotion. One striking proof of the popularity of Theodotion's Daniel and of the obscurity into which the Septuagint text fell, is that Porphyry, writing about 270 A.D., based his criticism of the Book of Daniel upon Theodotion's version, which he believed to be the original[1]. In the time of Jerome this version alone was in official use among Greek-speaking Christians, and so long had the Septuagint been set aside that the reason of the change had been forgotten (*Praef. in Vers. Dan.*).

The Coptic version published, with a Latin translation, by Tattam in his *Prophetae Majores* (Oxford, 1852), is evidently based upon Theodotion[2], though it contains occasional interpolations from the Septuagint. It may be remarked in passing that the Coptic text has a long additional chapter which was composed centuries after the Mohammedan conquests, probably in the reign of the Fatimite Caliph Al-Ḥākim (996—1020 A.D.). It is a *naïf* attempt to bring the prophecies of Daniel down to date. The author, like most other apocalyptic writers, displays great ignorance of the remote past, while as he approaches his own time his descriptions gradually become more minute and more accurate.

The Old Syriac Version, the so-called *Pĕshīṭtā*, almost invariably follows the present Jewish text—the apparent divergences being generally due to the paraphrastic style of the translator or to later corruption. Only in a very small number of cases does it appear at all probable that the text used by the translator differed from the Masoretic. The apocryphal pieces are found even in the oldest MSS. of the Pĕshīṭtā, but seem not to have belonged to it in its original form.

---

[1] That Porphyry believed the Greek text to be the original is expressly affirmed by Jerome (*Prol. Comm. in Dan.*), and that the Greek text used by Porphyry was Theodotion's appears from Jerome's commentary on Dan. xi. 38, "*Deum MAOZIM ridicule Porphyrius interpretatus est, ut diceret in vico Modin, unde fuit Mathathias et filii ejus, Antiochi duces Jovis posuisse statuam, et compulisse Judaeos ut ei victimas immolarent, id est, deo Modin.*"

[2] The same would seem to be the case with the Coptic text edited by Joseph Bardelli (Pisa, 1849), as far as can be gathered from the Latin preface, for my ignorance of the Coptic language makes it impossible for me to speak from personal investigation.

Ancient and medieval interpreters.

The ancient Jewish interpretation of the Book of Daniel is known but imperfectly, since it was not till the Middle Ages that the Jews began to compile systematic commentaries, and we have therefore to gather our information from stray allusions in the Talmud, the Midrashim, and other works. The statements of Josephus on this subject are of little value, as his acquaintance with the book was very superficial[1]. Much Jewish tradition as to the book of Daniel may be found embedded in the works of the Christian Fathers. Among the writers who are of most value in this respect may be mentioned the Persian Christian Aphraates (who lived in the middle of the 4th century, and whose *Homilies* have been edited, in the original Syriac, by Prof. Wright), Aphrēm of Nisībis (commonly known as Ephraim Syrus), of whose *Commentary* on Daniel excerpts have been published in the Roman edition of his works, and, above all, Jerome.

One writer, who was neither a Jew nor a Christian, the Neo-Platonic philosopher Porphyry (233—304 A.D.), a native of Tyre, occupies a prominent place in the history of the interpretation of Daniel. He wrote a *Treatise against the Christians*, in 15 books, of which the 12th was intended to prove that the Book of Daniel had been composed by a Palestinian Jew in the time of Antiochus Epiphanes, that the supposed prophecies of Daniel relate the history correctly as far as the time of the real author, and that beyond that point they are mere guesses[2]. For the purpose of his work Porphyry had studied various Greek historians, among whom were several

[1] See *Antiq.* x. 11. 7, where the vision in Dan. viii. is confused with other parts of the book in a manner which shews that Josephus was writing from vague recollection.

[2] "Contra Prophetam Danielem duodecimum librum scripsit Porphyrius, nolens eum ab ipso cujus inscriptus est nomine esse compositum, sed a quodam qui temporibus Antiochi, qui appellatus est Epiphanes, fuerit in Judaea, et non tam Danielem ventura dixisse quam illum narrasse praeterita. Denique quidquid usque ad Antiochum dixerit veram historiam continere, si quid autem ultra opinatus sit, quia futura nescierit, esse mentitum." Jerome, *Prol. Comm. in Dan.*

now lost[1]. His treatise has, of course, perished, but considerable fragments are cited by Jerome and other writers.

The theory of Porphyry, as may well be imagined, met with no favour. It was "refuted," before the time of Jerome, by Methodius, Eusebius of Caesarea, and Apollinarius, and appeared to have been swept away for ever. But it was to be heard of again.

In the 9th century the Jews, influenced by the Mohammedan schools of learning, began to give the exegesis of the Old Testament a scientific form. Of the medieval Jewish commentaries on Daniel one of the earliest was the work of Saadia (892—942 A.D.), the Gāōn, or head of the academy, of Sūrā in Babylonia. This work is quoted by Ben-Ezra, and a fragmentary copy of it exists in the Bodleian (see Neubauer's Catalogue, No. 2486); the commentary which appears in the Rabbinic Bibles under the name of Saadia is the work of a much later author[2]. Shĕlōmōh ben Yiṣḥāk (commonly known as Rashi, 1040—1105), and Abraham ben Mēīr ben Ezra (commonly known as Ben-Ezra or Abenezra, 1090—1168), are the most important of the medieval commentators. Ben-Ezra is incomparably superior to Rashi in acuteness and originality, but for that very reason less valuable as a depositary of Jewish tradition. The Commentary of Yepheth ibn 'Alī, a Karaite Jew, who wrote about 1000 A.D., has lately been edited in the original Arabic, with an English translation, by Professor Margoliouth.

Modern interpreters.

Modern Christian commentators on Daniel were, until the latter part of the 18th century, almost entirely dependent on Jewish and Patristic tradition. Occasionally doubts were expressed, for example by Spinoza and Hobbes, as to whether

---

[1] " Ad intelligendas autem extremas partes Danielis multiplex Graecorum historia necessaria est: Sutorii videlicet Callinici, Diodori, Hieronymi, Polybii, Posidonii, Claudii, Theonis, et Andronici cognomento Alipii, quos et Porphyrius esse secutum se dicit." *Ibid.*

[2] The statement on this subject in Smith's *Dictionary of the Bible*, Art. "Daniel," is incorrect.

Daniel had actually put in writing the whole of the book ascribed to him, but as a rule the authenticity and integrity of the work were confidently assumed. Sir Isaac Newton gave it as his opinion that "the last six chapters contain prophecies written at several times by Daniel himself; the first six are a collection of historical papers written by others" (*Observations on the Prophecies of Daniel and the Apocalypse of St John*, p. 10). This theory, however, was not intended to call in question the absolute veracity of the book, and Newton expressly declared that to reject Daniel's prophecies "is to reject the Christian religion. For this religion is founded upon his Prophecy concerning the Messiah" (p. 25).

Some approach to a critical examination of Daniel was made by J. D. Michaelis, who had doubts as to the antiquity of certain chapters (see his *Deutsche Uebersetzung des Alten Testaments*, Vol. x., Anmerkungen zum Propheten Daniel, p. 22). The first modern writers who ventured to dispute the authenticity of the whole, were Corrodi and Eichhorn. But the commentary of Bertholdt, *Daniel neu übersetzt und erklärt*, 1806—1808, was the first serious attempt to grapple with this historical problem. Bertholdt, however, adopted the unfortunate hypothesis that Daniel is the work of nine distinct authors. Gesenius clearly recognized that the whole book was written under Antiochus Epiphanes, and protested against Bertholdt's theory of a composite authorship (see the *Allgemeine Literaturzeitung*, 1816, No. 57, and also the *Ergänzungsblätter* of the same, No. 80). Gesenius was followed by Bleek and De Wette, who in the most important points agreed with him.

During the last sixty or seventy years almost all writers unbiassed by dogmatic prejudices have maintained both the literary unity of Daniel and the theory of its Maccabean origin. Even as to the interpretation of details there has been little disagreement. Of the commentaries the most valuable are those of Von Lengerke (1835), Hitzig (1850), and Ewald (in the 3rd Vol. of his *Propheten des Alten Bundes*, 2nd ed. 1867 and 1868).

It was not to be expected that the critical theory of the Book of Daniel would be accepted without a contest, for all the partisans of ecclesiastical tradition, both Catholics and Protestants, had an obvious interest in withstanding it. The history of the controversy is particularly instructive. At first the so-called "defenders of Daniel" endeavoured to maintain the traditional opinion in all its integrity. Of concession or compromise they would hear nothing. They argued that if the Christian religion be true, the book of Daniel *must* be authentic, and consequently that all arguments urged against its authenticity must be worthless. They spent enormous labour in seeking to shew that the impugned statements in Daniel were not only not disproved but were signally confirmed by the testimony of history, and they confidently predicted that further research would justify their position. Of these apologists the most eminent were Hengstenberg (*Die Authentie des Daniel und die Integrität des Sacharjah*, 1831) and Hävernick (*Commentar über das Buch Daniel*, 1832). The apologetic works of Auberlen, Kliefoth, Keil, Pusey, and others, are, in the main, reproductions of Hengstenberg and Hävernick; as a specimen of the tone adopted by these writers, the following extract may suffice. "The book of Daniel is especially fitted to be a battle-field between faith and unbelief. It admits of no half-measures. It is either Divine or an imposture. To write any book under the name of another, and to give it out to be his, is, in any case, a forgery, dishonest in itself, and destructive of all trustworthiness. But the case as to the book of Daniel, if it were not his, would go far beyond even this. The writer, were he not Daniel, must have lied on a most frightful scale, ascribing to God prophecies which were never uttered, and miracles which are assumed never to have been wrought. In a word, the whole book would be one lie in the Name of God." (Pusey, *Daniel the Prophet*, p. 1.)

Of late years however a great change has taken place in the policy of conservative theologians with respect to this book. When the critical theory was still new, it was easy to denounce it and to proclaim that it would soon be universally abandoned, but when the theory, so far from being overthrown, was confirmed by a long and important series of discoveries, some of the apologists began to suspect that they had slightly overstated the absurdity of "half-measures." The "middle path," which, as long as it was not needed, had appeared so contemptible, now acquired a strange fascination. Accordingly there commenced a succession of attempts to reconcile the results of criticism with orthodoxy. Concession after concession was made. Instead of labouring to "defend Daniel" from beginning to end, the apologists of the New School freely admitted that many things related in the book were unhistorical. But these things, it was explained, are interpolations, and do not in any way interfere with the truth of the rest. Thus Lenormant accepted the latter part of the book as genuine, but thought that the earlier chapters had been garbled by the scribes. The very first verse of Daniel contains, according to Lenormant, "a gross error." M. Babelon, in the new edition of *Histoire ancienne de l'Orient*, expresses himself thus. "Au reste, quand il s'agit des données historiques contenues dans le livre de Daniel, il ne faut jamais oublier ce fait capital que si ce livre est parfaitement authentique et incontestablement écrit à Babylone, nous n'en possédons plus le texte original dans un état intact, mais seulement un remaniement écrit en partie en syro-chaldaïque, et fait vers le IIIe siècle avant l'ère chrétienne, par un transcripteur assez ignorant de l'histoire, qui a commis des interpolations et plusieurs confusions manifestes dans les noms des rois babyloniens" (Vol. IV. p. 438, note). Unfortunately neither Lenormant nor any other apologist of the New School has pointed out a criterion whereby to distinguish the "undeniably authentic" portions of Daniel from the "interpolations." Hence we find that scarcely any two of these apologists are agreed as to which pieces should be "defended" and which should be abandoned. The latter part of Daniel, which Lenormant pronounced genuine, is, according to some conservative theologians, manifestly quite late (see the *Handbuch der theologischen Wissenschaften*, herausgegeben von Otto Zöckler, 2nd ed. 1885, Vol. I. pp. 171—173).

Thus the "defenders of Daniel" have during the last few years been employed chiefly in cutting Daniel to pieces. But to pass all these theories in review is quite unnecessary, for the discordance between them is a sufficient proof of their arbitrariness.

Of modern monographs on Daniel the following are the most important :

BLEEK—" Die messianischen Weissagungen im Buche Daniel, mit besonderer Beziehung auf Auberlen's Schrift," in the *Jahrbücher für deutsche Theologie,* 1860.

CHEYNE—Art. " Daniel," in the 9th edition of the *Encyclopaedia Britannica.*

CORNILL—" Die Siebzig Jahrwochen Daniels," in *Theologische Studien und Skizzen aus Ostpreussen,* Vol. II. 1889.

FRANZ DELITZSCH—Art. " Daniel," in Herzog's *Real-Encyclopädie,* 2nd ed. 1878. [For Prof. Delitzsch's rejection of the theory of the antiquity of Daniel, see his *Messianic Prophecies,* translated by Curtiss, 1880, p. 90, and his *Old Testament History of Redemption,* 1881, p. 153.]

DE WETTE—Art. " Daniel," in the *Allgemeine Encyclopädie* von Ersch und Gruber, 1832.

GRAETZ—" Beiträge zur Sach- und Worterklärung des Buches Daniel," in the *Monatschrift für Geschichte und Wissenschaft des Judenthums,* 1871.

GRAF—Art. " Daniel," in Schenkel's *Bibel-Lexikon,* 1869.

HOFFMANN—" Antiochus IV. Epiphanes, König von Syrien," publ. by Alfred Lorentz, Leipzig, 1873.

KUENEN—" Historisch-critisch onderzoek naar het ontstaan en de verzameling van de Boeken des Ouden Verbonds," 2nd ed. 1887—1889, Vol. II. pp. 446—508.

LENORMANT—" La divination et la science des présages chez les Chaldéens," 1875, pp. 169—227.

NÖLDEKE—" Die alttestamentliche Litteratur," 1868, pp. 216—234.

REUSS—" Die Geschichte der heiligen Schriften Alten Testaments," 2nd ed., 1890, pp. 592—604.

SCHRADER—"Die Sage vom Wahnsinn Nebuchadnezar's," in the *Jahrbücher für Protestantische Theologie,* 1881.——— "Cuneiform Inscriptions and the Old Testament," 1885—1888, Vol. II. pp. 124—136 [pp. 428—438 in the German edition].

SCHÜRER—"Geschichte des jüdischen Volkes," 1886—1890, Vol. II. pp. 613—616. [Transl. in Clark's Foreign Theological Library.]

Those who wish to see the controversy as to the date of Daniel stated in a short and popular form may consult a Tract entitled, " Notes on the Defence of the Book of Daniel, addressed to the Clergy, by a Clergyman," London, Simpkin and Marshall, 1878.

THE ORIGIN AND PURPOSE OF THE BOOK OF DANIEL.

THE evidence as to the origin of the Book of Daniel is of two kinds, external and internal. The external, as being the less complicated, may first be considered.

It has already been mentioned that in the Hebrew Scriptures Daniel has never occupied a place among the Prophetical Books, but is included in the third collection of sacred writings, called the *Kĕthūbīm* or Hagiographa. Of the history of the Jewish Canon very little is known with certainty, but there is every reason to believe that the collection of Prophetical Books, from which lessons were read in the Synagogue, was definitely closed some time before the Hagiographa, of which the greater part had no place in the public services. That the collection of Prophetical Books cannot have been completed till some time after the Exile, is obvious, and on the supposition that Daniel was then known to the Jews, the exclusion of this book is wholly inexplicable[1]. The reasons assigned for it by the later Rabbins are evidently mere guesses. Thus when Maimonides tells us that there are *eleven* kinds of inspiration, and that Daniel is placed in the Hagiographa because his inspiration was inferior in quality to that of the Prophets, this is nothing but a theory intended to account for the present arrangement of the books. Hengstenberg and others have

[1] In the prologue to Theodoret's Commentary on Daniel there is a very curious passage in which that writer inveighs fiercely against the Jews for not including Daniel among the prophets.

maintained that Daniel was not a "professional" prophet, but only a person possessed of the prophetic gift, and therefore could not be classed among the Prophets properly so called. This explanation, however, is refuted by the fact that Amos emphatically disclaims being a professional prophet (Amos vii. 14), yet his book was nevertheless placed among the prophetical writings. Hence it must be admitted that the exclusion of Daniel from the Prophetical collection is, to say the least, not very easy to reconcile with the theory of the antiquity of the book.

Still more important are the arguments which are drawn from the allusions to Daniel in other writings. The prophet Ezekiel, it is well known, speaks of a certain Daniel, who was proverbial for wisdom and righteousness (Ezek. xiv. 14, 20, xxviii. 3), but the phrase "Though Noah, Daniel and Job were in it," certainly seems to imply that this Daniel was not a contemporary of Ezekiel, just as the very similar phrase of Jeremiah "Though Moses and Samuel stood before me" (Jer. xv. 1) would naturally have suggested to our minds that Samuel was not a contemporary of Jeremiah, even if we had possessed no direct evidence on the subject. Ezekiel, like other Old Testament writers (see, for example, 1 Kings v. 11), occasionally alludes to traditions of which nothing is known to us, and it is therefore impossible to decide who the Daniel was to whom reference is here made. Presumably Ezekiel believed him to be, like Noah and Job, a person of the remote past. Ewald's dictum that the Daniel of Ezekiel *must* have lived in the Assyrian captivity has found few, if any, adherents (*Geschichte des Volkes Israel*, Vol. IV. p. 347, *Propheten des Alten Bundes*, Vol. III. p. 313). Nor can we safely conclude, with Smend (*Der Prophet Ezechiel*, p. 218), that the legend of Daniel was one of those ancient myths which the Israelites had in common with their heathen neighbours. Thus the passages in Ezekiel afford no means whatsoever for fixing the date of the book of Daniel.

On the supposition that the narrative in Daniel is historical, it is marvellous that it should be passed over in utter silence by all extant Jewish writers down to the latter half of the 2nd century B.C., that it should have left no trace in any of the later prophetical books, in Ezra, Chronicles, or Ecclesiasticus. It is, of course, possible in each particular case to imagine some reason for the omission of the subject, but the *cumulative* evidence derived from such omissions is not so easily set aside. Thus it has often been said that nothing can be concluded from the silence of Ben-Sīrā in Ecclesiasticus xlix. But in order to realize the true state of the case we should consider how easy it would be to refute, from Jewish literature, any one who asserted that the book of Isaiah or that of Jeremiah was composed entirely in the Maccabean period. That the absence of external testimony to Daniel has been felt to be a real difficulty by the apologists themselves is shewn by their desperate efforts to discover "traces of Daniel" in pre-Maccabean literature. But Hengstenberg is obliged to confess (*Authentie*, p. 277) that of these "traces" none is really conclusive[1].

An attempt has often been made to compensate for the lack of external testimony, by arguing that if Daniel had really been composed in the Maccabean period, it could not possibly have been received into the Jewish Canon. But this is a mere begging of the question. For the theory that the Jewish Canon was closed before the Maccabean period rests upon no evidence whatsoever.

The earliest passage which can, with any probability, be regarded as an allusion to the book of Daniel, is found in the collection of Sibylline Verses III. 388 ff.

"Ἥξει καί ποτ' [ἄπυστ' εἰς] Ἀσσίδος ὄλβιον οὖδας
ἀνὴρ πορφυρέην λώπην ἐπιειμένος ὤμοις
ἄγριος, ἀλλοδίκης, φλογόεις· ἤγειρε γὰρ αὐτὸν
πρόσθε κεραυνὸς φῶτα· κακὸν δ' Ἀσίη ζυγὸν ἕξει
πᾶσα, πολὺν δὲ χθὼν πίεται φόνον ὀμβρηθεῖσα.
ἀλλὰ καὶ ὣς πανάιστον ἅπαντ' Ἀίδης θεραπεύσει.
ὧν δή περ γενεὴν αὐτὸς θέλει ἐξαπολέσσαι,
ἐκ τῶν δὴ γενεῆς κείνου γένος ἐξαπολεῖται·

[1] That Ecclesiasticus xvii. 17 is not an allusion to Daniel, but a quotation from Deut. xxxii. 9 (see the LXX.), hardly requires to be stated. The importance which many apologists have attributed to this passage is a sufficient proof of the straits to which they were reduced.

ῥίζαν ἴαν γε διδούς, ἣν καὶ κόψει Βροτολοιγος
ἐκ δέκα δὴ κεράτων, παρὰ δὲ φυτὸν ἄλλο φυτεύσει·
κόψει πορφυρέης γενεῆς γενετῆρα μαχητήν,
καὐτὸς ἀφ' υἱῶν, ὧν ἐς ὁμόφρονα αἴσιον [ἄρρης],
φθεῖται· καὶ τότε δὴ παραφυόμενον κέρας ἄρξει.

It is impossible here to enter upon an examination of this obscure passage, especially as it is more than probable that the text is in part corrupt. But it would appear that the piece in question dates from about 140 B.C., and that it contains allusions to Antiochus Epiphanes and to the " ten horns " of Dan. vii. 7, 20, 24. See Schürer, *Gesch. d. jüd. Volkes* II. 797—799.

The next allusion occurs in I. Macc. ii. 59, 60, where the dying priest Mattathias is represented as mentioning, among several other instances of the triumphs of righteous men, how Hananiah, Azariah, and Mishael were saved from the fire, and Daniel from the mouth of the lions (Dan. iii. vi.) To urge, as has often been done, that these words were actually uttered by Mattathias, is of course illegitimate, for with the historians of antiquity, both Greek and Oriental, it was a regular practice to invent speeches for their characters or at least to amplify and embellish the meagre reports of speeches handed down by tradition. That this was the practice of the author of I. Maccabees, is unquestionable, for to suppose that such speeches as that in chap. ii. 7—13 (to cite no others) are reported *verbatim*, would be the height of absurdity. But the reference to Daniel no doubt proves that the book existed in the time of the author of I. Maccabees (i.e. about 100 B.C.), and also that it was generally believed.

Subsequent references are so numerous and varied that it would be vain to specify them. One passage only, to which apologists have frequently appealed, calls for special notice. Josephus tells us (*Antiq.* XI. 8. 5) that Alexander the Great, after the capture of Gaza, came to Jerusalem, and was shewn the Book of Daniel by Yaddua the High Priest. From this no deduction can be drawn excepting that Josephus believed the book to be ancient. The whole account of Alexander's journey to Jerusalem has long ago been recognized as a fiction. It has been abundantly proved that as to the history of this period Josephus was extremely ill-informed, and it is no less certain that where genuine records failed him, he borrowed without scruple from untrustworthy sources and even from his own imagination.

In the New Testament, Daniel is mentioned once only, Matt. xxiv. 15, but the influence of the book is apparent almost everywhere, particularly in the Apocalypse. Dr Westcott (in Smith's *Dictionary of the Bible*, Art. "Daniel") has pronounced that no writing in the Old Testament had so great a share in the development of Christianity as the book of Daniel. The common argument that the book must therefore be genuine, may appear quite satisfactory to the dogmatic theologian, but is not of a nature to convince students of history. For the more we realize how vast and how profound was the influence of Daniel in post-Maccabean times, the more difficult it is to believe that the book existed previously for wellnigh four centuries without exercising any perceptible influence whatsoever.

We now pass from the external to the internal evidence. I shall of course confine myself, as far as possible, to those parts of the book of which the meaning is clear, reserving obscure details for the Commentary.

When we endeavour to confront the statements in Daniel with the known facts of history, we cannot but be struck by the extreme paucity of the allusions made in this book to the political events of the period in which Daniel is represented as living. Even occurrences which must have seemed most important to a devout Israelite, such as the captivity of king Jehoiachin, the destruction of Jerusalem by Nebuchadnezzar, and the Return of the Exiles under Cyrus, are either passed over in complete silence, or mentioned only in the vaguest terms[1].

[1] It is interesting to observe what ingenious attempts have been made to discover in Daniel hidden allusions to the politics of the time. Thus, when Nebuchadnezzar is troubled by his dream, this is because his mind had been preoccupied with the fear of a Persian invasion: when Daniel fasts for three weeks, this was due to his distress about the intrigues which were being carried on at the Persian court, in order to hinder the rebuilding of the Jewish Temple, etc., etc.

How different in this respect are the writings of Jeremiah and Ezekiel! Nor is the silence to be explained by the hypothesis that Daniel was a recluse or a man indifferent to the fate of his people. On the contrary, he lives in the midst of the world, at the courts of successive kings, and his zeal for "his people and his holy city" is intense (see chap. ix.).

This would in itself be very surprising, but the difficulty is greatly increased by the fact that of the small number of allusions to the political events of the period, the majority cannot be reconciled with known history.

At the very outset we are told that Nebuchadnezzar, king of Babylon, besieged Jerusalem and plundered the Temple in the third year of Jehoiakim, king of Judah. Even if we suppose Nebuchadnezzar to be here called king by anticipation—for, according to Jer. xxv. 1, his first year coincided with the fourth year of Jehoiakim—the difficulty remains that of a siege of Jerusalem in Jehoiakim's third year, Jeremiah, a contemporary, says nothing. It was not till after the defeat of the Egyptian army at Carchemish on the Euphrates in the fourth year of Jehoiakim (Jer. xlvi. 2) that there could be any question of Nebuchadnezzar's invading Palestine, where for some years the Egyptians had enjoyed undisputed supremacy. Hengstenberg endeavours, as usual, to save the veracity of the book of Daniel by forcing the meaning of the text. He maintains that the statement "Nebuchadnezzar came to Jerusalem in the third year of Jehoiakim" means that Nebuchadnezzar set out on his expedition in that year, and that he did not reach Jerusalem till the year following, after the battle of Carchemish. Such an interpretation is, of course, no less contrary to Hebrew than to English usage. In order to prove that Nebuchadnezzar invaded Judah in the fourth year of Jehoiakim, Hengstenberg appeals to the authority of the Babylonian historian Berossus, who lived soon after Alexander. Berossus, according to Hengstenberg, relates that Nabopalassar, on hearing *that the governor whom he had set over Syria and Phoenicia had fallen away to the Egyptians,* sent forth his son Nebuchadnezzar with an army. "In this campaign," says Hengstenberg, "the Egyptians were defeated at Carchemish, and Phoenicia and Syria came under the dominion of the Babylonians ; the campaign was ended by the news of Nabopalassar's death" (*Authentie*, p. 55). Here Hengstenberg has been guilty of a serious misquotation. What Berossus really says is that when Nebuchadnezzar's father heard *that the satrap who had been set over Egypt* and the regions of Coele-Syria and Phoenicia, *had rebelled against him*, he sent forth his son Nebuchadnezzar, etc. (Josephus, *Antiq.* x. 11. 1 and *Contra Ap.* I. 19). Berossus here assumes that Egypt, as well as Coele-Syria and Phoenicia, had already been conquered by the Chaldeans before the death of Nabopalassar and the battle of Carchemish—a notion contrary to all evidence. The passage is therefore altogether untrustworthy; in order to conceal its unworthiness Hengstenberg misquotes it, and then argues that it confirms the statement in Daniel. That Jehoiakim was a vassal of the Chaldeans during the latter part of his reign, is certain, but of a *siege of Jerusalem and a plundering of the Temple* in the reign of Jehoiakim, neither Jeremiah nor the book of Kings says a word, and in such a case the argument from silence is very strong, if not absolutely conclusive. The statement in II Chron. xxxvi. 6, 7 proves only that the idea in question existed among the Jews when the Chronicler wrote, i.e. long after the Exile, and thus agrees perfectly with the theory of the late origin of the book of Daniel.

The only Babylonian kings mentioned in Daniel are Nebuchadnezzar and his "son" Belshazzar, upon whose death the empire passes over to the Medes. As a matter of fact, Nebuchadnezzar was followed by Evil-Merodach (*Amil-Maruduk*) in 561, *Nergal-shar-uṣur* in 559, *Lakhabbashi-Maruduk*[1] and *Nabūnāïd* in 554. This last king, who was not a descendant of Nebuchadnezzar, but belonged to a different family, reigned until 539 or 538, when Babylon was taken by Cyrus[2]. There is therefore no room for a king Belshazzar, who, according to

[1] The name of this king, who reigned for a few months only, is very doubtful. He seems to be called Λαβοροσοάρδοχος by Berossus (Josephus, *Contra Ap.* I. 20). See Tiele's *Babylonisch-Assyrische Geschichte*, p. 424.

[2] The *exact* date is uncertain. Nöldeke places the surrender of Babylon in the autumn of 539; see his *Aufsätze zur persischen Geschichte*, p. 22.

Daniel viii. 1, must have reigned considerably over a year, on the most moderate computation. Recent "defenders of Daniel" have accordingly identified Belshazzar with *Bīl-shar-uṣur*, Nabūnāīd's eldest son, who is mentioned in the inscriptions of his father, and who seems to have held a command in the Babylonian army (Tiele, *Gesch.* p. 463. Schrader, *Cuneif. Inscr.* pp. 433, 434). It has been asserted that Bīl-shar-uṣur ruled conjointly with his father until the fall of Babylon, and in proof of this certain Babylonian tablets, found in 1876, have been confidently cited. Some of them are dated from the reign of *Maruduk-shar-uṣur*, who, it is argued, was identical with Bīl-shar-uṣur. But Mr Boscawen, who carefully examined these tablets, very soon discovered that the above theory was untenable, since Maruduk-shar-uṣur, whoever he was, must have reigned *before* Nabūnāīd[1]. Mr Boscawen therefore identifies him with Nergal-shar-uṣur. Hence we have no proof that Bīl-shar-uṣur, son of Nabūnāīd, ever bore the title of king, still less that he was supreme ruler. Cyrus, in his inscriptions, speaks of Nabūnāīd alone as king at the time of the taking of Babylon. But the Belshazzar of Daniel is evidently supreme ruler, for documents are dated by the year of his accession (Dan. vii. 1, viii. 1), which certainly does not agree with the theory that his father was still alive and at the head of the state. Many apologists have sought to evade this argument by urging that in chap. v. Belshazzar offers the place of "third ruler in the kingdom" to any one who will explain the inscription on the wall. This, it is said, proves that Belshazzar was himself second ruler, not first. But the word translated "third ruler" occurs nowhere else, and its meaning is altogether uncertain. And even if it meant "third ruler," the argument based upon it

---

[1] Mr Boscawen's words are, "I at first considered that Marduk-šar-uzur was Belshazzar. I have gone through a great number of tablets and checked them carefully, but I do not find that I can now hold to that idea." (*Transactions of the Society of Biblical Archaeology*, Vol. vi. p. 108, publ. in 1878.) Yet M. Babelon, in the *Histoire Ancienne de l'Orient*, Vol. iv. p. 438 (publ. in 1885), not only states in the most positive manner that Maruduk-shar-uṣur was identical with Belshazzar, but actually has the boldness to allege, as his authority, the very work in which Mr Boscawen has pronounced the identification to be impossible ! !

would be worthless. For a man who can of his own authority make any one he pleases "third ruler in the kingdom" must obviously be supreme in the state, not a mere heir apparent ruling under his father[1].

The above difficulties are sufficiently serious, and would in the case of any ordinary book be thought decisive, but they shrink into insignificance in comparison with the statements as to "Darius the Mede." It need scarcely be said that of a Median king Darius reigning over Babylon before the accession of Cyrus, there is no trace whatsoever in history. Both Greek and Oriental sources agree in testifying that Cyrus put an end to the Median dynasty and annexed Media to his dominions several years before the taking of Babylon. Accordingly the "defenders of Daniel" are here reduced to the most desperate expedients. Thus Hengstenberg, who is followed by Pusey and others, brings forward a passage in the Greek lexicon of Harpocration, compiled, it would seem, long after the Christian era. Here it is said that "the daric was named not after Darius the father of Xerxes, as most men suppose, but after an older king." Later authors, for example the medieval lexicographer Suidas, have borrowed the passage. But such indefinite statements, made by late Greek writers and unsupported by the citation of any ancient authority, have no historical value. The "older king" of Harpocration is, in fact, a mere shadow, nor would any one who had not a hopeless cause to defend, think of invoking the aid of such a being. Equally wild is the theory which identifies the Darius of Daniel with Xenophon's Cyaxares the Second—of whose existence there is no proof, for the narrative in the Cyropaedia is obviously not intended to be taken as history. In order to justify the book of Daniel for bringing a king Darius upon the scene immediately after the overthrow of the Babylonian Empire,

---

[1] The older apologists, who lived before any one had heard of Bīl-shar-uʂur, had no difficulty in identifying the Belshazzar of Daniel. Some, as for instance Zündel, pronounced him to be Evil-Merodach; others, with equal confidence, maintained that he was the Nabonnedus of Berossus (i.e. Nabūnāïd). It would be interesting to know who is destined to be the Belshazzar of the apologists twenty years hence.

apologists have taken refuge in the hypothesis that the Darius of Daniel is not an independent sovereign, but a viceroy appointed by Cyrus. In support of this it is urged that Darius is said to have " received the kingdom " (chap. vi. 1), and to have been "made king" (ix. 1). But these phrases mean simply that he was "made king" by God, and that he "came into possession of the kingdom"[1]. To argue (as Hengstenberg, Pusey, Keil and countless other apologists have done) that Darius is here represented as a viceroy, is not only absurd in itself but is flagrantly at variance with the rest of the book. Thus, when Darius has signed the interdict, he is reminded that " it is a law of the Medes and Persians that no interdict nor statute which *the king* establisheth may be changed " (chap. vi. 16). When Darius issues a command "to all the peoples, nations, and languages, that dwell in all the earth" (chap. vi. 26), he is claiming precisely the same authority that is claimed on a similar occasion by Nebuchadnezzar (chap. iii. 29). Finally, as if to remove all possible doubt on the subject, we are told that "Daniel prospered in the reign of Darius, and in the reign of Cyrus the Persian " (chap. vi. 29).

After this it is needless to enumerate minor difficulties, for the above statements amply suffice to shew that the narrative is unhistorical, and cannot have been composed in the period of the Exile.

Innumerable attempts have been made to outweigh the historical difficulties in Daniel by bringing forward proofs that the author was minutely acquainted with the customs of ancient Babylon; but these proofs will be found, on examination, to be either irrelevant or purely imaginary.

Thus Lenormant (*La Divination*, pp. 169, 188) lays special stress upon Dan. ii., where Nebuchadnezzar consults the diviners on the subject of his dream; for this, we are informed, was a

---

[1] The use of passive verbs, such as הָמְלַךְ, with the implied notion of God as the agent, is especially common in Daniel; thus it is said, in chap. v. 28, "thy kingdom *is divided and given to the Medes and Persians*." As for קַבֵּל מַלְכוּתָא "he received the kingdom," it is enough to say that the very same words are used by a Syriac writer to describe the accession of the Emperor Julian (see Hoffmann's *Julianos der Abtrünnige*, p. 5, line 10).

Babylonian custom which could not have been known to a later Palestinian writer. It is strange that Lenormant should have forgotten—what has often been remarked—that the custom in question, far from being peculiar to Babylon, appears already in Gen. xli., a chapter which, in some respects, bears a striking resemblance to Dan. ii. That the same custom continued in the East long after the Christian era, is well known.

Lenormant likewise claims for the author of Daniel great knowledge as to the details of the organization of the learned and sacerdotal caste (*La Divination*, p. 189). But in reality no details are given. That diviners, magicians, etc., attend upon Nebuchadnezzar, in the book of Daniel, is no matter for surprise, since magicians formed part of the regular *personnel* of an Oriental court, and the magic arts of Babylon, in particular, were celebrated throughout the ancient world. The allusions to these subjects in Daniel imply no special knowledge, but rather the reverse. Thus the learned men of Babylon are in Daniel repeatedly called "*the Chaldeans*," whereas in the cuneiform inscriptions, as in the historical parts of the Old Testament, this is the name of a nation, not of a learned caste[1]. And how are we to explain the assertion that Daniel, a strict Jew, was made chief of the heathen sages of Babylon (chaps. ii. 48, iv. 6)? It is amusing to observe that while Pusey has proved to his own satisfaction the credibility of this statement (*Daniel*, pp. 424 ff.), Lenormant, whose acquaintance with ancient Babylon was unquestionably superior to Pusey's, tells us that the position here assigned to Daniel is *evidently* impossible, and he proceeds to get over the difficulty by the usual expedient of supposing that the passages in question are interpolations (*La Divination*, p. 219).

It has also been stated that the presence of women at feasts (Dan. v. 2) is a custom characteristic of Babylon. This may be perfectly true, but it is a custom which survived for centuries

---

[1] As to the term "Chaldeans" Prof. Schrader observes, "The signification *wise men* that we meet with in the Book of Daniel, is foreign to Assyrio-Babylonian usage and did not arise till after the fall of the Babylonian empire. This is in itself a clear indication of the post-exilic date of the Book of Daniel." *Cuneif. Inscr.* p. 429.

after the overthrow of the old Babylonian Empire, as is proved by the testimony of Quintus Curtius (v. 1). And if the custom was known to a Roman writer who probably lived under Vespasian, why should it not have been known to a Palestinian writer who lived centuries earlier?

Another Babylonian practice mentioned in Daniel is the punishment of burning alive (chap. iii.). But since, in Jer. xxix. 22, Nebuchadnezzar is described as *roasting* offenders *in the fire*, and since this very chapter is elsewhere quoted by the author of Daniel (chap. ix. 2; cf. Jer. xxix. 10), there can be no difficulty in explaining whence his knowledge was derived.

Thus it will be seen that one proof after another breaks down, and it would be a waste of time to discuss arguments still more fanciful, of which a large and varied collection has been made by Mr Fuller in the *Speaker's Commentary*.

The result of this chapter has hitherto been mainly negative. We have seen that there is no external testimony to the Book of Daniel before the middle of the 2nd century before Christ, and that the narrative of Daniel is seriously at variance with the history of the period in which Daniel is represented as living. But it is fortunately possible for us to advance from negative to positive conclusions. It can be shewn that external evidence and internal evidence both point in the same direction, or in other words that the first half of the 2nd century before Christ—after which period the external testimony begins —is the only period which will explain the contents of the book.

The Book of Daniel is divided into two parts; the first consists of a series of narratives, the second of a series of prophetical visions. In the narratives Daniel is always mentioned in the third person, whereas in the visions he is himself the speaker. The narratives are evidently intended to be consecutive, in point of time, but they are very loosely connected with each other. Their most marked feature is the didactic purpose which appears throughout. In every one of these stories we see the righteous rewarded or the wicked signally punished, as the case may be. On the one hand Daniel and his three friends, the servants of the True God, though apparently helpless in the midst of the heathen, triumph over all opposition, while on the other hand the mightiest Gentile potentates are confounded and humbled to the dust. This would in itself suffice to indicate that the book was intended for the encouragement of the Jews at a time when they were being persecuted by Pagan rulers. And when we pass from the narratives to the visions, we find that this view is confirmed. For in the visions the final victory of the "Saints" over the Gentile powers is repeatedly insisted upon. Further examination shews that this victory of the Saints is to take place in the days of a Gentile king who will surpass all his predecessors in wickedness. He will arise out of the Fourth Gentile Empire, the Empire of the Greeks, and after cruelly persecuting the Jews he will be destroyed by a divine judgment. Thereupon God will set up an everlasting kingdom. It is especially important to observe that in these visions very little is said about the first three Gentile Empires, while the history of the Fourth is described at great length, and with increasing minuteness as we approach the time of "the king" whose crimes are so vividly set before us. Thus everything combines to shew that the Book of Daniel is, from beginning to end, an exhortation addressed to the pious Israelites in the days of the great religious struggle under Antiochus Epiphanes[1].

It is however necessary to guard against a possible misconception. Though the author of Daniel has everywhere the

---

[1] One of the latest commentators, Prof. Meinhold, in the *Kurzgefasster Kommentar*, has endeavoured to shew that while chaps. i. and viii.—xii. were composed in the time of Antiochus Epiphanes, chaps. ii.—vi. are the work of a Jew who lived about 300 B.C., and have as their object the conversion of the Gentiles to Judaism. Prof. Meinhold discovers various "contradictions" between the two sets of chapters, but his arguments are extremely fanciful. His theory is examined and, in my opinion, completely refuted by Budde in the *Theologische Literaturzeitung* for 1888, No. 26 (see the review of Meinhold's *Beiträge zur Erklärung des Buches Daniel*). Here it is enough to say that Prof. Meinhold commits the fundamental error of assuming that a writer of the Maccabean age would necessarily make the situation of Daniel and his companions similar *in every detail* to the situation of the Jews under Antiochus.

circumstances of his own time in view, we cannot regard Nebuchadnezzar and Belshazzar, still less Darius the Mede, simply as
portraits of Antiochus Epiphanes. The author is contending
not against Antiochus personally but against the heathenism
of which Antiochus was the champion. He justly considers the
struggle between Antiochus and the faithful Jews as a struggle
between opposing principles, and his object is to shew that
under all circumstances the power of God must prevail over
the powers of this world.

    That the author does not address his contemporaries in his
own name, after the manner of the ancient prophets, but
clothes his teaching in the form of narratives and visions, is
perfectly in accordance with the spirit of later Judaism. The
belief that no more prophets were to be found among the
people of God seems gradually to have established itself during
those ages of Gentile oppression (Ps. lxxiv. 9). Loathing the
present, the pious Jews naturally idealized the past. In their
grief and humiliation, their minds continually reverted to the
time when great signs and wonders had been wrought for
Israel, when God did not keep silence but spake to His people
by the mouth of His chosen messengers. In proportion as the
distress increased, it seemed more and more certain that the
long-promised deliverance must be close at hand, nor could it
be doubted that the prophets of old had foreseen how and when
that deliverance would be brought about. This idea is at the
basis of all the apocalyptic literature which played so important
a part in the history of Judaism and of which the Book of
Daniel is the earliest known example. The genesis of this
literature offers, it is true, a very difficult psychological problem. Some at least of the apocalyptic writers may have believed that they were inspired to reproduce lost revelations;
but however we may account for the fact, it is certain that age
after age men whose sincerity cannot be questioned put forth
writings in the name of ancient prophets and sages. This is
not the place to discuss apocalyptic literature in general; it
may, however, be remarked that the production of these works
continued till far down into the Middle Ages. I have already
mentioned a Christian apocalypse of Daniel which apparently

dates from the earlier part of the 11th century (see p. 3). There is also a Jewish apocalypse of Daniel, probably composed in the 9th century. It has been preserved in a Persian translation, which Zotenberg has published in Merx's *Archiv für die wissenschaftliche Erforschung des Alten Testaments*, Vol. I. (1869).

With regard to the sources used by the author of Daniel little can be known with certainty. The name Daniel was probably suggested by the book of Ezekiel, and some details of the story are unquestionably borrowed from the narrative of Joseph in Genesis. Jewish and perhaps Babylonian traditions may also have been employed to some extent. But it is altogether a mistake to class the story of Daniel with popular myths which grow up unconsciously in the course of ages. The strongly marked didactic character of the book must make this clear to all persons accustomed to historical investigation.

The literary form which the author has chosen is in every way suited to his purpose. The division of the work into sections more or less independent of each other—a division which gave rise in modern times to the false hypothesis of a composite authorship—is evidently intended to facilitate the diffusion of the book. In those days it was by being read aloud in public that books became known, and a series of separate narratives and visions is obviously better adapted for reading aloud than a continuous history. This explains also why the author so often seems to ignore events already narrated. It has been asked, for example, why in chap. ii. 2 and still more in chap. iv. 3 Nebuchadnezzar summons the Chaldean sages, instead of summoning Daniel whose superior wisdom had been so clearly proved. The real answer is that in each case the author constructs his narrative with a view to inculcating a particular lesson, and does not care to make the narratives strictly consistent. But the general spirit and tendency of the book are everywhere the same.

THE LINGUISTIC CHARACTER OF DANIEL.

THE literary and historical unity of Daniel, which I have endeavoured to set forth in the preceding chapter, appears at first sight to be strangely at variance with the fact that the book is written in two different languages. Nor is this all. The author of a book may have some special reason for employing different languages according to the nature of his subject, but no reason can be imagined for a writer abruptly passing from one language to another in the midst of a narrative, as is the case in Dan. ii. 4. The suddenness of the transition sufficiently refutes the theory that the author intended the Hebrew portions of the book for the learned, and the Aramaic portion for the common people; for how could the common people understand a narrative beginning in the middle of a dialogue? Nor can we admit that the author here introduces the Aramaic language because he believed it to be the court language at Babylon or the language of the Chaldean sages as distinguished from Daniel and his friends[1]. If this were the case, the author would surely not represent Nebuchadnezzar in chap. ii. 3 as addressing the Chaldeans in Hebrew, and in *v.* 26 as addressing Daniel in Aramaic. Why moreover, on the above theory, should Aramaic be the language in which Daniel records the first of his visions—a vision, be it observed, which he did not promulgate to the world, but "kept in his heart" (vii. 28)? Thus it will be seen that all attempts to explain the change of language on internal grounds, prove to be failures. The answer to the difficulty must be sought in the circumstances under which the book was produced and transmitted to us.

[1] The word אֲרָמִית "in Aramaic," in Dan. ii. 4, appears to be an interpolation; see the Commentary on this passage.

All that we know of post-exilic Judaism favours the assumption that a Palestinian Jew of the Maccabean period, writing in the name of an ancient seer, would naturally employ the Hebrew language. That the Book of Enoch was originally written in Hebrew is at least probable; that the somewhat later Book of Jubilees was so, is quite certain. The same may be said even of works which made no claim to antiquity, such as the Book of Ben-Sīrā, and the so-called Psalter of Solomon. Hence the hypothesis that Daniel was originally written in Hebrew throughout, is quite in accordance with analogy. At the same time we have to remember that the author lived in a time of intense excitement, and his book was evidently meant, not for a small circle, but for all "the holy people" (see especially xi. 33, xii. 3). His object was to produce an immediate and a powerful effect. Since however the Hebrew language was then unintelligible to the vulgar, or very imperfectly understood by them, the need of a translation would at once be felt. We cannot therefore regard it as improbable that the author himself, or one of his associates, issued an Aramaic version of the book, or at least of some parts of it. In any case the style of the Hebrew and of the Aramaic portions is so similar that we may confidently pronounce them to be products of the same school, if not of the same pen. But if the book was originally written throughout in Hebrew, why, it may be asked, has it reached us in its present form? The most plausible supposition is that a portion of the Hebrew text having been lost, a scribe filled up the gap by borrowing from the Aramaic version. This view, which is that of Lenormant, is strengthened by a consideration of the fact that under Antiochus Epiphanes a systematic attempt was made to destroy copies of the Pentateuch— an attempt which would almost necessarily entail the destruction of vast numbers of other Jewish writings, for no one can suppose that the Syrian soldiery employed in the work of extirpation were careful to distinguish copies of the Torah (of which they could not read a line) from other manuscripts found in the possession of Jews. Thus at the time when the book of Daniel was still new, when it existed only in a few copies, within the limits of a single district, it was exposed to peculiar perils. Its author and those who had first propagated it may have "fallen by sword and by flame, by captivity and by spoil," within a very few weeks of its completion, and shortly afterwards none but fragmentary copies may have been procurable. Out of these, it would seem, our present text was constructed. But no critic has been able to bring forward a satisfactory reason for believing the *substance* of the book to have undergone any extensive change, either by mutilation, displacement, or the introduction of extraneous matter. The Septuagint translator, at all events, had before him a manuscript in which the Aramaic portion began and ended precisely where it begins and ends in the Masoretic Text. This certainly appears to prove that the arrangement of our present text took place at a very early period. The mistakes of later copyists, in matters of detail, have, of course, nothing to do with this question.

The Hebrew of Daniel.

The history of the Hebrew language, as exhibited in the Old Testament, falls into two principal divisions—the period during which the language was in full vigour, and the period of decline. As long as there was a national kingdom the language remained comparatively free from foreign influence, but when Israel ceased to be a nation and became a religious community surrounded by peoples of alien speech, the pure Hebrew began, after a generation or two, to undergo change. Finally, about the 4th century B.C., Hebrew was superseded, in ordinary life, by Aramaic, and thenceforth survived only as the language of literature and religion. It must however be constantly kept in mind that all the post-exilic writers were more or less familiar with the ancient literature and often strove to imitate it. But since some were much more successful imitators than others, the later writings in the Old Testament vary greatly with respect to purity of style. Hence in assigning a date to Hebrew works, we have to remember that while the *presence* of late phrases is always an argument in favour of a late date, the *absence* of such phrases is no proof whatsoever of antiquity.

That the Hebrew of Daniel is, in its main features of style, quite unlike that of pre-exilic times, requires no demonstration. Nor does it bear any real resemblance to the language of Ezekiel or of the post-exilic prophets, as may be seen by comparing the visions of Daniel with those of Zechariah—in spite of the similarity of subject the difference of language is most marked. With Esther, of which the date is unknown, but which can scarcely have been written before the 3rd century B.C., Daniel has some peculiarities in common ; nowhere in the Old Testament excepting in these two books do we find the Persian word פַּרְתְּמִים (Dan. i. 3. Esth. i. 3. vi. 9) and the Aramaic תֹקֶף (Dan. xi. 17. Esth. ix. 29. x. 2). But of all the Old Testament writings that which has most linguistic affinity with Daniel, is without doubt the Book of Chronicles—a work which was probably compiled about the middle or end of the 3rd century B.C. The resemblance in point of language is the more noteworthy because the matter and the plan of the two books are wholly different. The following are among the distinctive phrases which are found in both :—

עָצַר כֹּחַ (*to have power, be able*), 3 times in Daniel and 4 in Chronicles—Dan. x. 8, 16. xi. 6. I Chr. xxix. 14. II Chr. ii. 5. xiii. 20. xxii. 9.

הֵיךְ (*how ?*) Dan. x. 17. I Chr. xiii. 12[1].

הִתְחַזֵּק עִם (*to help*) Dan. x. 21. I Chr. xi. 10. II Chr. xvi. 9.

---

[1] The word is doubtless borrowed from the Aramaic dialect of Palestine, and bears the same relation to the Hebrew אֵיךְ that the Bibl. Aram. הֵן (*if*) bears to the Hebr. אִם (Syr. *en*, Arab. *in*). הֵיךְ appears frequently in the Christian Palestinian Lectionary (see below), e.g. page 331 היך און יתמלון כתביא, *How then should the Scriptures be fulfilled?*—p. 437 היך אמרין ספריא דמשיחא הו ברה דדויד, *How do the scribes say that the Messiah is the Son of David?* Sometimes it is written הך, e. g. p. 339, והך את אמר אודע לן אבא, *And how sayest thou, Shew us the Father?*—p. 433 הך תערוקון מן דינא דגהנא, *How shall ye flee from the judgment of Gehenna?* See also the Palestinian Targum (so-called Pseudo-Jonathan) Gen. iii. 9. והיך אנת סבר בלבך לאיטמרא מן קדמי *And how thinkest thou in thy heart to hide thyself from my presence?* The commoner form in this Targum is היכדין.

הִתְחַבֵּר (*to associate oneself*) Dan. xi. 6, 23. II Chr. xx. 35, 37.

נָתְנוּ עָלָיו הוֹד מַלְכוּת Dan. xi. 21, cf. וַיִּתֵּן עָלָיו הוֹד מַלְכוּת I Chr. xxix. 25.

כָּל־אֱלוֹהַּ (*any god*, with a negative) Dan. xi. 37. II Chr. xxxii. 15.

The Hebrew of Daniel contains moreover a certain number of words or roots which occur nowhere else in the Old Testament, but which are used more or less frequently in the later Jewish literature. The principal of them are

גִּיל (*age, generation*) Dan. i. 10.

חִיֵּב (*to render guilty, condemn*) Dan. i. 10.

זֵרְעֹנִים (*herbs*) Dan. i. 16.

הִתְמַרְמֵר (*to be moved with anger*) Dan. viii. 7 ; xi. 11.

נֶחְתַּךְ (*to be decreed*) Dan. ix. 24.

רָשׁם (*to write*) Dan. x. 21.

מִכְמַנִּים (*hidden things, treasures*) Dan. xi. 43. This word, which occurs only in Daniel, is from a root unknown in Biblical Hebrew, but common in Aramaic and in the Hebrew of the Rabbins.

אפדן (*palace*) Dan. xi. 45.

To these may be added one or two *grammatical* peculiarities, e.g. the form מַלְכֻיּוֹת Dan. viii. 22. It is well known that though abstract nouns in *ūth* are common in the Old Testament, especially in the later books, they never have plurals of this form[1]. In Rabbinical Hebrew, on the contrary, we find not only מלכיות from מַלְכוּת but עֵדִיּוֹת from עֵדוּת, גָּלֻיּוֹת from גָּלוּת and some others. I may mention also the construction אֶחָד קָדוֹשׁ (instead of the usual קָדוֹשׁ אֶחָד), which occurs twice in Dan. viii. 13. For this there is no analogy in Biblical Hebrew, but in the Mishnah we occasionally find such phrases as מֵאַחַת יד Peāh iii. 3; see also Geiger's *Lehrbuch zur Sprache der Mischnah*, p. 53.

---

[1] חַנְיוֹת, or according to some edd. חֲנֻיוֹת, in Jer. xxxvii. 16, is too obscure and uncertain to be regarded as an exception to this rule. Whatever the word may mean, it can scarcely be the plural of an *abstract* noun. The LXX. reads χερέθ.

Another feature which is characteristic of Rabbinical Hebrew and which appears in the Book of Daniel, is the using of Old Testament words in new and peculiar senses—a very natural thing at a time when the Hebrew language had ceased to be spoken and when the meaning of many uncommon words was therefore no longer distinctly remembered. The author of Daniel, like some of the later Rabbins, often inserts into his prose rare or exclusively poetical phrases borrowed from the ancient literature. Sometimes he gives them a meaning of his own, and it may be remarked that in a considerable proportion of such cases the expression seems to have been suggested by the story of Joseph in Genesis—an indirect but significant corroboration of the theory that the narrative of Daniel was to a certain extent modelled upon that of Joseph. The following are the terms which should specially be noted. It will be observed that most of them occur more than once in Daniel; they must therefore be regarded as *characteristic*.

כַּשְׂדִּים Dan. i. 4; ii. 2—in all other Old Testament writings this is the name of the Chaldean *nation*. The author of Daniel uses it also for "wise men" or "members of the priestly caste." See p. 21, note.

זֹעֲפִים Dan. i. 10. Gen. xl. 6 (nowhere else in the Old Testament). In Genesis the word means "sad, troubled in mind." The author of Daniel applies it to physical unhealthiness produced by insufficient food.

חַרְטֻמִּים Dan. i. 20; ii. 2. Gen. xli. 8, 24. Exod. vii. 11, 22; viii. 3, 14, 15; ix. 11. The word is believed to be of Egyptian origin, and in the Pentateuch is used only of the magicians of *Egypt*. In Daniel it means magicians in general.

בְּשַׁלְוָה Dan. viii. 25; xi. 21, 24. The substantive שַׁלְוָה (Sing. and Plural) occurs nowhere else in the Old Testament but in Jer. xxii. 21. Ezek. xvi. 49. Ps. cxxii. 7. Prov. i. 32; xvii. 1, where it means "peace," "security." In Daniel בְּשַׁלְוָה is "unawares," like the Syriac *men shelyā*.

עַל־כַּנּוֹ Dan. xi. 20, 21, 38, cf. עַל־כַּנֶּךָ Gen. xl. 13 and עַל־כַּנִּי Gen. xli. 13. In Genesis the phrase is used of restoration to a former *status* or *position*; in Daniel it must be taken in the vaguer sense "instead of him," as chap. xi. 38 proves.

חֲלַקְלַקּוֹת Dan. xi. 21, 34. In Jer. xxiii. 12 and Ps. xxxv. 6, the only other passages where it occurs, this word means "slippery, dangerous places." In Daniel it is applied to "guile," "treachery."

הַתָּמִיד Dan. viii. 11, 13; xi. 31; xii. 11. Other Biblical writers call the daily burnt-offering עֹלַת הַתָּמִיד (Num. xxviii. 10 ff. Neh. x. 34), but in Daniel the simple הַתָּמִיד is used instead—so also in the Mishnah (e.g. Ta'anīth iv. 6).

הַיְאֹר Dan. xii. 5, 6, 7; cf. Gen. xli. 1, 2, 3. It is well known that in old Hebrew יְאֹר, יְאֹרִים always refer to the Nile and its streams, either literally or as a figure of rhetoric (Is. xxxiii. 21. Job xxviii. 10). Nowhere but in Daniel is any other river called יְאֹר. This general use of the word appears again in Rabbinical literature.

In conclusion therefore it may be said that the Hebrew style of Daniel differs widely from that of exilic and pre-exilic times, and agrees, in its main features, with the latest historical prose in the Old Testament, while in some important details it approximates to the Hebrew of the Mishnah and the Talmud. At the same time the author borrows many isolated words and phrases from the Pentateuch and the Prophets, and this is precisely what we might expect to find in a book written by a Jew of the Maccabean age in the name of an ancient seer. It was natural that the work should appear in an antique garb, in "the holy language," but the idea of closely imitating the style of the prophetical writings would by no means necessarily occur to the author. He avoids indeed the wholesale introduction of modern words, such as we find in the Mishnah, but is far from being a purist. In fact among the Jews of those times a delicate perception of the differences of Hebrew style was not to be expected. The belief, for example, that Ecclesiastes was a genuine work of king Solomon could have arisen only among a people incapable of distinguishing between the infancy and the decrepitude of the Hebrew tongue.

The Aramaic of Daniel.

The Aramaic language, one of the principal branches of the Semitic stock, includes a multitude of dialects, which have at various times been spoken in Syria, Mesopotamia, Babylonia, and some of the adjacent provinces. The Aramaic dialects are divided into two principal groups, the *Eastern* (including the dialects of Mesopotamia and Babylonia, i.e. Syriac, the Aramaic of the Babylonian Talmud, and Mandaitic) and the *Western* (including Biblical Aramaic, as also the dialects of the Jewish Targums, of the Samaritan Targums, of the Christian Palestinian Lectionary, of the Palestinian Talmud, and of the Palmyrene inscriptions). This distinction between the Eastern and Western dialects corresponds entirely to the geographical features and political history of the countries in question. Western Syria, intersected by numerous chains of hills, has from time immemorial been a land of small independent states, nor has it ever been politically united excepting when subjugated by some foreign power. On the other hand the countries upon the Euphrates and the Tigris were marked out by nature to be the seat of great centralized empires; intercourse with non-Semitic peoples was here unavoidable, and it is therefore not surprising that the Eastern dialects are, on the whole, less primitive than the Western.

The distinctive feature of the Eastern Aramaic dialects is that in the Imperfect Tense they form the 3rd pers. sing. masc. and the 3rd pers. plur. of both genders by prefixing *n* or *l*, whereas the West-Arameans, like all other Semites, here prefix *y*. The formation with *n* is universal in classical Syriac (i.e. the ancient dialect of Edessa in Western Mesopotamia) and is usual in Mandaitic, a dialect which was spoken, some 12 or 13 centuries ago, in Lower Babylonia. The Aramaic of the Babylonian Talmud sometimes uses *n*, but more commonly *l*, which appears to have arisen out of *n* by phonetic corruption[1]. Now when we consider the vast geographical separation between the dialect of Edessa and that of Lower Babylonia, and furthermore the impossibility of one dialect having *borrowed* from another its inflexions of the Imperfect, we can hardly doubt that this peculiar grammatical formation with *n* must have originated at a very early period, in any case many centuries before the Christian era, though the West-Aramaic formation with *y* is certainly older still.

Of West-Aramaic the most ancient documents, of any considerable extent, are the Aramaic portions in Ezra and Daniel. As to the date of the Aramaic portions of Ezra there is some difference of opinion, but that they do not all date from the time of Ezra himself is certain. According to Prof. Nöldeke, *some* of these pieces may perhaps have been composed in the Persian period, though in that case they were doubtless remodelled by later scribes (*Die Semitischen Sprachen*, p. 30). Thus the Aramaic in Ezra may be taken as representing, in the main, the dialect spoken by the Jews of Palestine in the 3rd century B.C.[2] This Jewish Aramaic cannot have differed greatly from the contemporaneous dialects of heathen Syria, for the Palmyrene inscriptions (the oldest of which date from about the Christian era) bear a striking resemblance to the Aramaic of the Bible.

The language of the Jewish Targums is a slightly modernized form of Biblical Aramaic; more modern still is the Aramaic of the Palestinian Talmud, commonly called the Talmud of Jerusalem. The Samaritan dialect (represented by the Samaritan Targums) and the Christian Palestinian dialect (represented by the Palestinian Lectionary) are also very nearly akin to Biblical Aramaic, though they are both decidedly less primitive[3].

---

[1] It is, of course, conceivable that the *n* may here have arisen out of *l*, but this is very unlikely, since the *l* appears only in the Babylonian dialects, which *in the matter of phonetics* are certainly less primitive than classical Syriac.

[2] The once popular notion that the Jews of Palestine derived their Aramaic dialect from Babylonia, is now wholly abandoned. See Prof. Wright's *Comparative Grammar*, p. 16.

[3] Neither the Samaritan Targums nor the Palestinian Lectionary can be

Between the Aramaic in Ezra and that in Daniel the difference is very slight, much slighter than the difference which
often exists between the language of authors living in the same
age and country. This similarity may be due, in part at least,
to corrections made by scribes, but such corrections, though
they may seriously have affected certain details, cannot have
altered the fundamental character of the dialect. The constant
variations in orthography and the use of different grammatical
forms with precisely the same meaning are in themselves a
guarantee that there has been no general and systematic modification of the language. In one point only does a considerable
change appear to have been made. It is well known that both
in Ezra and Daniel the verb הֲוָא (הֲוָה) invariably forms the
Imperfect להוא (in Dan. iv. 22 להוה), pl. להוין להון, according
to the *Babylonian* fashion, whereas every other verb uses the
West-Aramaic prefix י. It is impossible to believe that this
anomaly really existed in the spoken language, the more so
as we have positive proof that the other West-Aramaic dialects, Jewish, Christian, and Pagan, employed the prefix י in
the Imperfect of הֲוָא, just as in other verbs[1]. As the forms
להוא etc. are found both in Ezra and Daniel we cannot ascribe
them to a caprice on the part of the author. Nor are they due
to the carelessness of scribes, since in that case the forms with
l and those with *y* would occur promiscuously, as the prefixes *n*
and *l* are used in Mandaitic and the Babylonian Talmud. The
only remaining supposition is that the Jewish teachers deliberately altered the old forms יהוא, יהון, and יהוין, into forms with
ל. Why they did so cannot be discovered with certainty, but it

dated with certainty. They seem to
have originated between the beginning
of the 4th and the end of the 6th century after Christ.

[1] The Targum of Onkelos usually
has יהי (Gen. ix. 11, 25 ; xvi. 12), much
more rarely the full form יהוי (Gen.
xviii. 18); pl. masc. יהון (Gen. i. 29 ;
ix. 15; xv. 5, 13) ; pl. fem. יהוין (Gen.
xli. 36 ; xlix. 26. Exod. xxii. 23). The
Samaritan Targum has יהי (Lev. xxv.
28, 40 ; xxvii. 12, 15, 21, 25); pl.

m. יהון (Lev. xxv. 44, 45); pl. f. יהי
(Lev. xxvi. 33. Num. xxxv. 29; xxxvi.
4). The Palestinian Lectionary has
יהוא or יהא; pl. m. יהוון or יהון; pl.
f. יהין or יהי. The Palmyrene inscriptions have יהוא (*Fiscal Inscr.* I. 10,
11); pl. m. יהון (*id.* II. 3rd column, 24).
The very rare use of להוי in the Palestinian Targum (e.g. Exod. xxii. 24) is
either a corruption or else a mere imitation of Biblical Aramaic.

may be guessed. It is known with what awe the later Jews regarded the Divine Name יהוה; not only did they avoid pronouncing it, but even the number 15 must be written טו, not יה, because יה is an abbreviation of יהוה. Now the pronunciation of the Imperfect of הֲוָא was probably very similar to the Divine Name. It is therefore not impossible that the Aramaic portions of the Old Testament were revised in later times for the purpose of changing יהוא (יהוה) into the harmless Babylonian form להוא (להוה). In the course of such a revision the plurals יהון and יהוין might easily have been altered likewise.

The differences between Ezra and Daniel appear mostly in the pronouns; the chief variations may be seen from the following table—

	Forms common to both	Only in Ezra	Only in Daniel
They	אִנּוּן Ezra v. 4. Dan. vii. 17 Kĕthîb.	הִמּוֹ *once, v. 11.*	
them (*after a verb*)		הִמּוֹ	הִמּוֹן / אִנּוּן *once, vi. 25.*
this, *masc.*	דְּנָה		
this, *fem.*			דָּא
these			אִלֵּין *or* אִלֵּן
that, *masc.*		דֵּךְ	
that, *fem.*		דָּךְ	דִּכֵּן *for both genders.*
those	אִלֵּךְ		אִנּוּן *once, ii. 44.*

Another grammatical difference is that in Daniel the suffixes of the 2nd and 3rd persons plural are always כוֹן and הוֹן respectively, whereas in Ezra these forms interchange with the older כם and הם. But from these phenomena no certain conclusion can be drawn as to date, for, not to mention the possibility of alteration by later scribes, it frequently happens that when two equivalent grammatical forms are in use at the same time, some writers employ one only, while others employ both indifferently. Still less is it allowable to found arguments, as to the priority of Ezra or of Daniel, upon any of those Babylonian or Persian words which happen to occur in the one but not in the other.

The principal points in which Biblical Aramaic differs from the Aramaic of the Targums are these—

1. The Causative and Reflexive conjugations of the verb (Haphel, Hithpeel, Hithpaal) have ה instead of the later א. There is one exception in Ezra (אֶחַת chap. v. 15), and nine in Daniel (chaps. ii. 45; iii. 1, 19; iv. 11, 16; v. 12; vi. 8; vii. 8, 15). In the Targums some forms with ה occur, but forms with א are very much commoner.

2. Passives are sometimes formed by internal vowel change, both from the Peal (e.g. יְהִיב, יְהִיבַת, יְהִיבוּ), and from the Haphel (e.g. הֻעַל, הֻקִימַת, הֻעַלּוּ, הָנְחַת). Similar Passives were still used in Syria in the 2nd century after Christ, as appears from the Fiscal Inscription of Palmyra[1].

3. Some common particles have other forms, e.g. הֵן *if* (Targ. אִין); אִתַי *there is* (Targ. אִית); תַּמָּה *there*, only in Ezra (Targ. תַּמָּן, as in Syriac); לָהֵן *but, except*, after a negation (Targ. אִילָהֵין).

4. The Imperfect is sometimes used in describing the past, e.g. Dan. iv. 2, 17, 33; v. 6; vi. 20; vii. 16. Similar cases appear in Hebrew, but the usage in Daniel is not necessarily a Hebraism, for we find the same thing in Arabic, mostly in writings of the early period. That the later Jewish Aramaic did not employ the Imperfect in this sense may, I think, be concluded from the fact that the Targums, though generally inclined to imitate the Hebrew closely, render an Imperfect by a Perfect or a Participle, where it is obviously a question of the past, e.g. Exod. xv. 1, 5; Deut. xxxii. 10 ff.; 1 Kings x. 16; 2 Kings iii. 25.

[1] With respect to the use of the ancient passive forms, Biblical Aramaic very nearly resembles the modern Arabic, in which isolated passive forms are still sometimes employed, although the passive has, in general, been supplanted by the reflexive (see Spitta, *Grammatik des arabischen Vulgärdialectes von Aegypten*, p. 193).

5. There is a considerable difference in the vocabulary. We must however be careful not to draw hasty conclusions from this fact, for it is obvious that the Aramaic parts of the Bible, owing to their limited extent, contain only a small proportion of the words in use at the time of the authors. The same thing is true, in a less degree, of the Targums, for though the Targums are very much more voluminous, they are written in a peculiarly stiff and artificial style, and moreover seem to have undergone later revisions. A single instance will shew what caution is here necessary. The particle יָת appears once only in Biblical Aramaic (יָתְהוֹן Dan. iii. 12), whereas in the Targums it is extremely common, both with and without pronominal suffixes. But we have no right to argue from this fact that יָת was very much more usual in later times than at the period when Daniel was written. Its rarity in Biblical Aramaic may be accidental, while its frequent occurrence in the Targums is doubtless due to a pedantic imitation of the Hebrew use of את. In this case the "difference" between Biblical Aramaic and the Targums is illusive, and proves nothing as to the relative antiquity of the writings in question. Hence it is clear that lists of the particles, pronouns etc., which happen to appear in Biblical Aramaic but not in the Targums, and *vice versâ*, would give a very false impression if taken as a criterion of the changes which the language actually underwent.

If we leave out of account those peculiarities of the Targums which belong, not to the language, but to the *method* adopted by the translators, we shall find that in reality the difference between the Aramaic of the Bible and that of the Targums is certainly not greater than the difference between the English of Shakespeare and that of Pope, or between the French of Calvin and that of Bossuet; yet in these cases the interval of time amounts to little more than a century.

A very difficult and much debated question is how far Biblical Aramaic was influenced by Hebrew. As a rule, philologists were formerly inclined to go very far in assuming the existence of Hebraisms, but many of the linguistic phenomena which were so regarded have been proved by recent discoveries

to be genuine Aramaic. Thus the distinction between שׂ and ס
is regularly kept up in Palmyrene, as in Biblical Aramaic, and
though this does not necessarily prove that the two letters
were still distinguished in pronunciation, it certainly proves
that the use of שׂ in Biblical Aramaic is not due to Hebrew
influence, as Prof. Kautzsch has maintained (*Gramm.* p. 24).
There remain, however, some undeniable Hebraisms, e.g. יוּכַל
Dan. ii. 10 (contrast יִכַּל iii. 29), מְרוֹמֵם iv. 34, הִתְרוֹמַמְתָּ v. 23.
The following words also seem to be of Hebrew origin — קֵצַף
Dan. ii. 12, אַחֲרֵי ii. 29, מִנְחָה ii. 46, נִיחֹחִין ibid., חֲנֻכַּת iii. 2, הַצָּלָה
iii. 29, רַעֲנַן iv. 1, הֲזָדָה v. 20, מֹאזַנְיָא v. 27, נֵזֶר vi. 11, עֶלְיוֹנִין vii.
14, הַשְׂמָדָה vii. 26. Whether the interrogative prefix הֲ is a
Hebraism appears doubtful, and the same may be said of the
prohibitive אַל.

When and by whom the present vocalization was introduced
into the Aramaic parts of the Bible, cannot of course be known.
But it is evident that in many cases the *Kĕthīb* represents
a much more primitive pronunciation than the *Kĕrī*, e.g. אנתה
(*antā*), *Kĕrī* אַנְתְּ — עליך (*'ălayk* or *'ălayikh*), *Kĕrī* עֲלָךְ — תליתיא,
Kĕrī תְּלִיתָאָא. Sometimes grammatical inaccuracies which probably were found already in the primitive text, have been cor-
rected by the later vocalizers; thus הן, the suffix of the 3rd
pers. pl., was used indifferently for the masc. and for the fem.,
but has been marked with the vowel *ē* whenever it refers to
a feminine noun. Similarly, in the 3rd pers. pl. of the Perfect
of the verb, the termination ו is used for both genders, but has
been treated as *ā* by the vocalizers, when the subject is feminine. In many other respects the pronunciation represented by
the vowel-points may differ from that of the authors themselves. One phenomenon which deserves special notice is that
in several cases an originally long *ā* is expressed by *Pathaḥ*, in
a closed or half-closed syllable (e.g. מְטַת, שַׁעֲתָא), whereas the
word מן *who?*, which certainly had a short vowel, is vocalized
מָן. Hence we may plausibly conjecture that at the time
when the vocalization was finally settled, the Jews, like the
modern Nestorians, pronounced *ā* short in closed and half-
closed syllables, and therefore in such syllables were liable
to interchange *Ḳāmeṣ* and *Pathaḥ*. Similar confusions are

found in Nestorian manuscripts (Nöldeke, *Syr. Gramm.* p. 28).

Foreign Words in Daniel.

Both the Hebrew and Aramaic portions of Daniel contain a considerable number of words which are undoubtedly neither Hebrew nor Aramaic. These foreign words have been held by some writers to be a strong argument in favour of the antiquity of the book, by others they are regarded as proving that the author cannot have lived before the rise of the Macedonian Empire. The subject is in any case worthy of careful examination.

If the book, or any considerable part of it, were really composed at Babylon in the 6th century B.C., we might reasonably expect that a large proportion of the foreign words employed would be borrowed from the language of Babylonia, which, as is well known, was a dialect closely resembling Assyrian. But, as a matter of fact, *Babylonian* words are extremely rare in Daniel. Besides a few proper names (one of which, בֵּלְטְשַׁאצַּר, the author evidently misunderstood), we find the words— סְגְנַיָּא (rulers), פַּחֲוָתָא (governors), בִּירָה (citadel, royal residence), זִיו (brightness), שֵׁיזִב (to deliver), and אָשַׁף or אָשֵׁף (magician)[1]. Of these the first three occur repeatedly in some of the later books of the Old Testament, זִיו and שֵׁיזִב are used in the Targums, and אָשַׁף appears, with a slight variation of form (*ashōpha*), in Syriac writings composed centuries after the Christian era. In no case therefore do the Assyrio-Babylonian words in Daniel indicate that the author had any personal knowledge of ancient Babylon.

Much larger is the number of words derived from the *Persian*. It is remarkable that these are employed, not with any special reference to Persian affairs, but quite promiscuously.

[1] Two or three words, of which the Babylonian origin is uncertain, are here omitted. The Babylonian proper names in Daniel prove nothing as to date, for some old Babylonian names were still in use a century before the Christian era; see the *Zeitschrift für Assyriologie*, Vol. III. pp. 129 ff.

Thus in the list of king Nebuchadnezzar's officials (chap. iii. 2) we find two undoubtedly Persian titles. It must of course appear in itself highly improbable that Persian titles were then used at the Babylonian court. On the other hand, the long domination of the Achaemenidae introduced Persian words into all the Aramaic-speaking countries and not least into Palestine. Of these words many must have continued in use during the ages after Alexander, though as time went on and as intercourse with the remote East became less frequent, some of them fell into desuetude. The numerous Persian words which we find in Syriac writers, were likewise, no doubt, borrowed mostly during the Achaemenian period. More than half of the Persian words in Daniel are common in Syriac also, although the oldest extant Syriac works are later, by some three centuries, than the time of the Maccabees.

That Daniel contains *Greek* words has long been recognized, even by orthodox commentators. In order to reconcile this fact with the theory of the antiquity of the book, it has been maintained that the names of the musical instruments קיתרס (κίθαρις), פסנתרין (ψαλτήριον), and סומפניה (συμφωνία) may have been borrowed from the Greeks by the Babylonians as early as the 6th century B.C. Such a supposition, if not absolutely impossible, is at least extremely precarious and wholly unsupported by the evidence of the cuneiform inscriptions[1]. Even if this negative argument be set aside, there remain the positive considerations that one of the terms in question, viz. συμφωνία, as the name of an instrument of music, is peculiar to *late* Greek, and that the συμφωνία is specially mentioned by Polybius as a favourite instrument with Antiochus Epiphanes[2]. This is an "undesigned coincidence" which may be recommended to the attention of apologists.

Some of the foreign words in Daniel are of unknown, or at

---

[1] "The musical instruments that are here mentioned," says Prof. Schrader, "are Greek, and hence their names are looked for in vain among cuneiform documents." (Schrader, *Cuneiform Inscr.* p. 431.)

[2] "῞Οτε δὲ τῶν νεωτέρων αἴσθοιτό τινας συνευωχουμένους, οὐδεμίαν ἔμφασιν ποιήσας παρῆν ἐπικωμάζων μετὰ κερατίου καὶ συμφωνίας, ὥστε τοὺς πολλοὺς διὰ τὸ παράδοξον ἀνισταμένους φεύγειν." Fragm. of Bk. XXVI. p. 1151, ed. Hultsch.

least of very uncertain, origin, e.g. מְלַצַּר, נְבִזְבָּה, הַדָּבְרַיָּא, תִּפְתָּיֵא;
of such words, however, the majority are probably Persian.
That they are unintelligible to us may be due partly to our
imperfect knowledge of the ancient Persian language, and
partly to the phonetic corruption which they underwent before
they reached the author of Daniel.   In a few cases, moreover,
the spelling may have been altered by later scribes.

THE SEPTUAGINT VERSION.

It is usually admitted that the so-called Septuagint Version of the Old Testament, being the work of various translators and of several successive generations, is by no means of equal value throughout for purposes of textual criticism. It is therefore necessary, before entering upon the discussion of particular passages, to investigate the general character and history of the text in question.

In the study of the Septuagint text of Daniel we are met at once by the difficulty that this version has reached us in one manuscript only, the Codex Chisianus, which cannot be older than the 9th century, and is perhaps very much later. The best edition is that of Cozza, in his *Sacrorum Bibliorum vetustissima fragmenta graeca et latina*, Pars Tertia (Rome, 1877). Besides this direct witness, we have the Syriac Hexaplaric Version (a slavishly literal rendering of Origen's Hexaplaric text) made at Alexandria, in the years 616 and 617, by Paul, the Monophysite Bishop of Tellā-dhĕ-Mauzĕlath, who is commonly called Paul of Tellā. A great part of this Syriac version of the Old Testament has been preserved in a MS. now at Milan; according to Ceriani, it probably dates from the 8th century (*Codex Syro-Hexaplaris Ambrosianus photolithographice editus*, 1874, see p. 140). A separate edition of Daniel, according to this Codex, was published, with a Latin translation, by Bugati in 1788.

In comparing the Greek with the Syriac text, we are immediately struck by their close resemblance to one another. This is most apparent in hopelessly corrupt passages, such as ix. 24—27, where they agree almost to a word. Even if we ignore the slighter clerical errors of the Codex Chisianus (such as *ἐμβηθήσεσθε* for *ἐμβληθήσεσθε* iii. 15—*ἐπήκουσε* for *ἐπήχουσε* vi. 21—*ἀνα λὰς* for *ἀνατολὰς* viii. 4), there can be no doubt that on the whole the Syriac text is the purer of the two. Firstly, a small number of the additions, borrowed chiefly from Theodotion's version, which have crept into the text of the Chisianus, are not found in the Syriac. Such are, *εἰς γῆν Σεναάρ* i. 2—*καὶ οὐ διέλιπον οἱ ἐμβάλλοντες αὐτοὺς ὑπηρέται τοῦ βασιλέως καίοντες τὴν κάμινον* iii. 46—*ἔτι τοῦ λόγου ἐν τῷ στόματι τοῦ βασιλέως ὄντος* iv. 28. On the other hand, there seems to be no certain case in which one of Theodotion's renderings is found in the Syriac text but not in the Chisianus.

Secondly, the Syriac has preserved several words and phrases, which have been omitted in the Chisianus through mere inadvertence. E.g.

ii. 28, 29. ܡܠܟܐ ܠܥܠܡ ܚܝܝ. ܚܠܡܐ ܘܚܙܘܐ ܕܪܝܫܟ
ܕܝܠܟ ܥܠ ܡܫܟܒܟ. ܗܢܐ ܐܝܬܘܗܝ. ܐܢܬ
ܡܠܟܐ ܟܕ ܫܟܝܒܬ ܥܠ ܥܪܣܟ ܕܝܠܟ. ܚܙܝܬ
ܟܠܗܝܢ ܐܝܠܝܢ ܕܗ̇ܘ̈ܐ ܠܡܗܘܐ ܒܫ̈ܘܠܡܬܐ ܐܚܪ̈ܝܐ

ii. 41. ... ... ܡܢ ܚܡܪܐ ܕܦܚܪܐ ܢܗܘܐ

iv. 15. ... ... ܥܡ ܚܝ̈ܘܬ ܒܪܐ ܕܐܪܥܐ

v. 1. ... ... ܘܥܡ ܪ̈ܘܪܒܢܐ ܕܝܠܗ

vii. 6. ... ... ܘܠܫܢܐ ܐܬܝܗܒ ܠܗ̇

vii. 18. ... ... ܘܥܕܡܐ ܠܥܠܡܐ

(that is, the Chisianus has *ἕως τοῦ αἰῶνος τῶν αἰώνων*, instead of *ἕως τοῦ αἰῶνος καὶ ἕως τοῦ αἰῶνος τῶν αἰώνων*)

viii. 5. ... ... ܘܠܐ ܢܓܫ ܗܘܐ ܒܐܪܥܐ

ix. 23. ... ... ܘܐܬܒܝܢܬ ܒܗ ܒܦܘܩܕܢܐ

xi. 16. ... ... ܕܨܒܝܘܬܐ

On the other hand, there are but very few cases in which words wrongly omitted in the Syriac have been retained in the Chisianus; e.g. ἐν αὐτῷ ᾤκουν καὶ ἐφώτιζον πᾶσαν τὴν γῆν iv. 8 (9)—οἱ διαλογισμοί μου vii. 15.

Thirdly, when variations of other kinds occur, the Syriac generally retains the older reading. E.g.

vii. 27.   ܪܡܝܫܐܐ (i.e. ὑψίστου), Chisianus ὑψίστῳ.

xi. 10.   ܢܣ ܠܝܣ (i.e. κατασύρων), Chisianus κατὰ σύρων.

Exceptions are very rare, e.g.

iii. 3.   ÷ καὶ ἔστησαν οἱ προγεγραμμένοι κατέναντι τῆς εἰκόνος —The Syriac adds the gloss in the wrong place,

÷ ܗܢܘܢ ܕܟܬܝܒܝܢ ܡܢ ܠܥܠ . ܥ ܘܩܡܘ ܠܩܘܒܠ ܗ—— ܕܨܠܡܐ —

Lastly, the critical signs introduced by Origen into the text —namely the asterisk ✳ to mark words wanting in the LXX. and supplied from the later versions (chiefly that of Theodotion), the obelus ÷ to mark words wanting in the Hebrew text, and the metobelus ✸ to mark the end of a phrase belonging to one of the two aforesaid categories—have, as a rule, been faithfully reproduced in the Syriac, whereas in the Chisianus they are often misplaced or altogether omitted.

By the comparison of these two Codices it is doubtless possible to recover, at least with tolerable accuracy, the source from which both are derived, that is, the text of Origen. But between Origen and the author, or authors, of the Greek translation there lies a period of some three centuries, and it is but too evident that during this time the text underwent manifold changes.

In order to reduce the Greek text, as far as possible, to its primitive form, we have first to eliminate the stories of Susanna and of Bel and the Dragon, which appear to have circulated independently before they were incorporated with the book of Daniel. But even when these stories have been set aside, there remains a great deal which cannot have belonged to the original Greek text. It is obvious, at a glance, that the interpolations are not evenly distributed throughout the book, but are most numerous and extensive in chapters iii to vi. The other chapters (i, ii and vii to xii) contain, it is true, many small additions and differ from the Masoretic text in innumerable details, but they may still be said to run parallel with it, so that the variations, when they occur, admit of being definitely classified. In chapters iii to vi, on the contrary, the original thread of the narrative is often lost in a chaos of accretions, alterations, and displacements.

That such a text must have had a very complicated history, can hardly be questioned. The existing phenomena are perhaps most satisfactorily explained by supposing that chapters iii to vi were translated, or rather paraphrased, into Greek, before the rest of the book, and that after the text had undergone many changes, a subsequent translator added the remaining chapters at the beginning and end. This hypothesis is further supported by the consideration that, for the Egyptian Jews, some parts of the book of Daniel must have possessed a very much greater interest than others. The narratives in chapters iii to vi turn precisely upon those topics which are most prominent in the literature of Hellenistic Judaism—the folly of idolatry, the impotence of *human* strength and wisdom (represented by Nebuchadnezzar, Belshazzar, the Chaldean sages etc.) as compared with the *divine* wisdom made known to Israel (represented by Daniel and his friends). The visions, on the contrary, with their manifold allusions to special circumstances, must have been to a great extent unintelligible, and the motive for translating and circulating them would consequently not be very strong.

If the above hypothesis be admitted, it is not, of course, necessary to suppose that any great interval elapsed between the first translator and the second, for popular stories, copied upon cheap and perishable materials and passing frequently from hand to hand, are liable to very rapid textual corruption, and that the afore-mentioned chapters (iii to vi) were translated, not for the learned, but for the entertainment and edification of the people is obvious. Only on such an assumption is the extremely free handling of the text conceivable.

That the translation of chapters i, ii and vii—xii is the work of one hand cannot indeed be proved with certainty, but is highly probable, for throughout these eight chapters the mode of rendering is substantially the same. As nearly all the passages in which the Masoretic text appears to be corrupt, occur in these chapters, I shall henceforth confine my remarks to them.

Even when full allowance has been made for alterations of the Greek text, it cannot be denied that the translator was both ignorant and careless, and in many passages, no doubt, the Greek Version was from the beginning mere nonsense.

Our object being to recover, as far as possible, the Hebrew and Aramaic text used by the translator, we must class the variations, here as elsewhere, under three headings, viz.

1. Variations due to corruption of the Greek text.

2. Variations which possibly or probably originated with the translator.

3. Variations due to real differences of reading in the text from which the translation was made.

I will now give classified lists of passages in which the Greek text differs from the Masoretic—not aiming, of course, at completeness, but at exhibiting specimens of as many kinds of variation as possible.

I.

The following are, I think, to be regarded as Greek corruptions—

i. 19. ἦσαν for ἔστησαν, cf. ii. 2.

vii. 19. τοῦ διαφθείροντος πάντα for τοῦ διαφέροντος παρὰ πάντα, cf. verses 3, 23.

viii. 26. ηὑρέθη for ἐρρέθη.

ix. 24. σπανίσαι for σφραγίσαι.

x. 1. πρώτῳ for τρίτῳ.

x. 14. ὥρα for ὅρασις.

xi. 17. πείσεται for στήσεται.

xi. 32. ἐν σκληρῷ λαῷ for ἐν κληροδοσίᾳ, cf. vv. 21, 34.

xii. 1. χώραν for ὥραν—Bugati conjectures (with great im-
probability, it seems to me) that the translator read
אתר for עת.

— ὑψωθήσεται for ἐκσωθήσεται or some other compound
of σωθήσεται.

Under this heading also must be placed those parallel renderings which have been inserted into the text, e.g.

viii. 16. καὶ ἐκάλεσε καὶ εἶπεν, Γαβριήλ, συνέτισον ἐκεῖνον
τὴν ὅρασιν.

xi. 13. ἐπ᾽ αὐτόν.

xii. 2. καὶ αἰσχύνην.

Also words wrongly repeated, as

vii. 8. ἐν τοῖς κέρασιν αὐτοῦ, taken from v. 7.

Finally, some passages, especially viii. 11, 12 and ix. 25—27,
where the text is in great, if not inextricable, confusion.

II.

The variations possibly due to the translator necessarily fall
into many subdivisions. First, there may be cases in which he
intentionally altered the sense, but unhappily we are here on
very uncertain ground, since it may generally be questioned at
what stage in the process of transmission any such alteration
was made. Thus, for instance, there can be little doubt that
the substitution of τὴν πόλιν Σιών for עיר קדשך, in ix. 24, is
intentional, for it seemed inappropriate to speak of the holy
city *of Daniel*. But though the removal of this stumbling-
block is probably due to the translator, it may perhaps have
taken place before or after him.

The same thing applies to glosses and expansions of the
text, which are very numerous, e.g.

i. 21. ἕως τοῦ πρώτου ἔτους [τῆς βασιλείας] Κύρου βασιλέως
[Περσῶν].

vii. 1. τότε [Δανιήλ] τὸ ὅραμα [ὃ εἶδεν] ἔγραψεν.

vii. 24. διοίσει [κακοῖς].

vii. 25. καὶ παραδοθήσεται [πάντα].

viii. 3. κριὸν ἕνα [μέγαν].

viii. 4. [πρὸς ἀνατολὰς καὶ] πρὸς βορρᾶν καὶ πρὸς δυσμὰς καὶ μεσημβρίαν.

viii. 8. τέσσαρα [κέρατα], as also in v. 22.

viii. 27. ἡμέρας [πολλάς].

ix. 7. τῷ [λαῷ] Ἰσραήλ.

ix. 10. ἐνώπιον [Μωσῆ καὶ] ἡμῶν.

ix. 19. ἐπὶ τὴν πόλιν σου [Σιὼν] καὶ ἐπὶ τὸν λαόν σου [Ἰσραήλ].

x. 12. ἐναντίον [κυρίου] τοῦ θεοῦ σου.

x. 20. μετὰ τοῦ στρατηγοῦ [βασιλέως] τῶν Περσῶν.

xi. 15. καὶ οὐκ ἔσται [αὐτῷ] ἰσχὺς εἰς τὸ ἀντιστῆναι [αὐτῷ].

xii. 8. καὶ οὐ διενοήθην [παρ᾽ αὐτὸν τὸν καιρόν].

Omissions are, as might be expected, much less frequent than additions, and they are generally of still more uncertain origin, e.g.

i. 17. ...נתן להם. [האלה ארבעתם] והילדים
καὶ τοῖς νεανίσκοις ἔδωκεν...

vii. 3. חֵיוָן [וְשָׁבְרָן]
θηρία.

viii. 5. על פני [כל]-הארץ
ἐπὶ προσώπου τῆς γῆς.

viii. 27. ונחליתי [נהייתי] ואני דניאל
καὶ ἐγὼ Δανιὴλ ἀσθενήσας...

ix. 18, 19. כי על רחמיך [הרבים] אדני שְׁמָעָה : אדני סְלָחָה
ἀλλὰ διὰ τὸ σὸν ἔλεος κύριε σὺ ἰλάτευσον.

xi. 41. בְּאֶרֶץ [הַצְּבִי]
εἰς τὴν χώραν μου.

xii. 9, 10. רבים [וְיִצָּרְפוּ] יִתְבָּרְרוּ ויתלבנו : עד [עת קֵץ]
ἕως ἂν πειρασθῶσι καὶ ἁγιασθῶσι πολλοί.

Changes in the order of words are rare, e.g.

vii. 8. .... קרן אחרי זעירה סלקת ביניהון
ἄλλο ἓν κέρας ἀνεφύη ἀνὰ μέσον αὐτῶν μικρόν (where ἄλλο and ἓν are perhaps doublets, the latter pointing to a reading חדה cf. viii. 9).

vii. 21.   עֹבְדָא קְרָב
           πόλεμον συνιστάμενον.

vii. 24.   יְקוּם אַחֲרֵיהֶן·
           μετὰ τούτους στήσεται.

viii. 4.   יָמָּה וְצָפוֹנָה
           πρὸς βορρᾶν καὶ πρὸς δυσμάς.

xi. 36.   יְדַבֵּר נִפְלָאוֹת
           ἔξαλλα λαλήσει.

Of free renderings, and passages in which the translator evidently guessed at the sense, almost every other verse supplies examples.   Only a few characteristic instances can be given—

i. 10.   וְחִיַּבְתֶּם אֶת רֹאשִׁי לַמֶּלֶךְ
           καὶ κινδυνεύσω τῷ ἰδίῳ τραχήλῳ.

vii. 28.   רַעְיוֹנַי יְבַהֲלֻנַּי
           ἐκστάσει περιειχόμην.

x. 21.   מִיכָאֵל שַׂרְכֶם
           Μιχαὴλ ὁ ἄγγελος.

xi. 2.   יָעִיר הַכֹּל אֵת מַלְכוּת יָוָן
           ἐπαναστήσεται παντὶ βασιλεῖ Ἑλλήνων.

xi. 5.   מֶלֶךְ הַנֶּגֶב
           βασιλείαν Αἰγύπτου,

           and so, throughout the chapter, נֶגֶב is rendered by
           Αἴγυπτος.

xi. 30.   צִיִּים כִּתִּים
           Ῥωμαῖοι (cf. the Targums on Numb. xxiv. 24).

Sometimes a personal pronoun in the genitive is inserted where there is no suffix in the original, e.g.

viii. 23.   τῶν ἁμαρτιῶν αὐτῶν — הַפֹּשְׁעִים.

ix. 21.   ἐν τῇ προσευχῇ μου — בַּתְּפִלָּה.

xi. 7.   ἐπὶ τὴν δύναμιν αὐτοῦ — אֶל־הַחַיִל.

Sometimes a suffix is ignored, e.g.

vii. 20.   ἐπὶ τῆς κεφαλῆς — בְּרֵאשֵׁהּ.

vii. 26. τὴν ἐξουσίαν — שָׁלְטָנֵהּ.

viii. 18. ἐπὶ πρόσωπον — עַל־פָּנָי.

In the use of the Article a like freedom prevails, e.g.

i. 16. ἀπὸ τῶν ὀσπρίων — זֵרְעֹנִים.

x. 1. τὸ πλῆθος τὸ ἰσχυρόν — צָבָא גָדוֹל.

x. 3. τὰς τρεῖς ἑβδομάδας τῶν ἡμερῶν — שְׁלֹשָׁה שָׁבֻעִים יָמִים.

xii. 4. οἱ πολλοί — רַבִּים.

xii. 11. τὸ βδέλυγμα τῆς ἐρημώσεως — שִׁקּוּץ שֹׁמֵם.

Conversely—

viii. 27. אֶת מְלֶאכֶת הַמֶּלֶךְ — βασιλικά.

xi. 31. הַשִּׁקּוּץ משמם — βδέλυγμα ἐρημώσεως.

xii. 13. לְקֵץ הַיָּמִין — εἰς συντέλειαν ἡμερῶν.

The Singular is sometimes put for the Plural, e.g.

viii. 20. מַלְכֵי מדי ופרס — βασιλεὺς Μήδων καὶ Περσῶν.

xi. 13. לְקֵץ הָעִתִּים שָׁנִים — κατὰ συντέλειαν καιροῦ ἐνιαυτοῦ.

xi. 17. בַּת־הַנָּשִׁים — θυγατέρα ἀνθρώπου.

xi. 24. מבצרים — τὴν πόλιν τὴν ἰσχυράν.

xi. 25. מַחֲשָׁבוֹת — διάνοια (Syro-Hex. ܡܚܫܒܬܐ i.e. δια-
νοίᾳ).

xi. 39. וְהִמְשִׁילָם בָּרַבִּים — καὶ κατακυριεύσει αὐτοῦ ἐπὶ πολύ
(Syro-Hex. ܘܐܫܠܛ ܐܢܘܢ ܥܠ ܣܓܝܐܐ).

xi. 44. שְׁמָעוֹת — ἀκοή.

And sometimes, but more rarely, the Plural for the Singular, e.g.

ix. 12. רָעָה גְדֹלָה — κακὰ μεγάλα.

xi. 8. יָבֹא — ἀποίσουσιν.

xi. 32. יַחֲנִיף — μιανοῦσιν.

Mistakes on the part of the translator are numerous, e.g.

i. 11. אֲשֶׁר מִנָּה שַׂר הסריסים — τῷ ἀναδειχθέντι ἀρχιευνούχῳ (i.e.
pronouncing מִנָּה).

vii. 8. אתעקרו—ἐξηράνθησαν.

viii. 3, 4. .... וְהַגִּבְהָה עָלָה בָּאַחֲרֹנָה : רָאִיתִי — καὶ τὸ ὑψηλότερον
ἀνέβαινε· μετὰ δὲ ταῦτα εἶδον ....

ix. 6. אֶל כָּל־עַם הָאָרֶץ — παντὶ ἔθνει ἐπὶ τῆς γῆς.

xi. 33. יָבִינוּ לָרַבִּים — συνήσουσιν εἰς πολλούς.

xi. 45. הַר צְבִי קֹדֶשׁ — τοῦ ὄρους τῆς θελήσεως τοῦ ἁγίου (connecting צבי with the Aramaic verb צבא).

III.

I now pass on to those cases in which the Greek translation
presupposes a Hebrew or Aramaic reading different from that
in the Masoretic text. Great caution is here necessary, for
after all the proofs we have seen of the carelessness and incom-
petence of the translator, it must appear highly probable that
he sometimes mis-read the text before him. Thus, for example,
in xi. 17 we find τὸ ἔργον αὐτοῦ corresponding to מַלְכוּתוֹ — but
it would be very rash to conclude that מלאכתו actually stood in
the MS. from which the translation was made ; it is much more
likely that the translator erred. Of such cases a long list might
easily be drawn up, but there remain many passages in which
we are obliged to assume a variant in the Hebrew, e.g.

i. 3. אשפנז — Ἀβιεσδρί (Syro-Hex. ܐܒܝܣܕܪܝ), or, according
to some patristic citations, Αβριεσδρι, Αβδιεζδρι.

viii. 8. חזות — ἕτερα (i.e. אחרות).

viii. 9. יתר — καὶ ἐπάταξεν (ותך).

id. הצבי — βοῤῥᾶν (הצפון).

ix. 17. למען אדני — ἕνεκεν τῶν δούλων σου δέσποτα
(למען עבדיך אדני)

x. 17. מעתה — ἠσθένησα (מעדתי cf. Ps. xviii. 37).

xi. 1. עמדי — εἶπεν (אמר).

xii. 3. מצדיקי הרבים — οἱ κατισχύοντες τοὺς λόγους μου
(מחזיקי דברי[ם]).

The intrinsic merits of these readings cannot be here discussed, but most people will be disposed to admit that the above passages point to real variants in the Hebrew.

Since therefore the text which lay before the translator was not identical with the Masoretic, the question necessarily arises, What was the relation between these two texts? Is one to be regarded simply as a corrupt form of the other, or is each an independent witness? Unfortunately the question of the *independence* of the texts has frequently been confounded with the totally different question of their relative *merit*. The fact that in numberless cases the Hebrew reading on which the LXX. is based, is manifestly inferior to the reading in the Masoretic text, has led many people to conclude that all the variants of the LXX. are to be explained as corruptions. That this is not so can be proved by several passages, of which the following is perhaps the most conclusive. In viii. 24, 25 the Masoretic text has —

והשחית עצומים ועם קדשים : ועל שכלו והצליח מרמה בידו ......

a passage quite impossible to translate grammatically. In the LXX. we read— καὶ φθερεῖ δυναστὰς καὶ δῆμον ἁγίων· καὶ ἐπὶ τοὺς ἁγίους τὸ διανόημα αὐτοῦ καὶ εὐωδηθήσεται τὸ ψεῦδος ἐν ταῖς χερσὶν αὐτοῦ.... i.e. reading ועם קדשים ועל קדשים שכלו instead of ועם קדשים . ועל שכלו. It is scarcely possible to doubt that the LXX. reading is here more primitive than the Masoretic, but it does not follow that it is the original. The most probable supposition is that ועם קדשים and ועל קדשים are doublets, the latter being the true reading, for it is necessary to the sense, whereas the omission of ועם קדשים produces no syntactical difficulty.

If once it is admitted that the Hebrew text on which the LXX. is based, is independent of the Masoretic, it must always appear possible that a passage which has been corrupted in the one, may in the other have been preserved in a purer form— that is to say, each case must be decided on its own merits. The very fact that the Greek translator often missed the sense where it is perfectly plain to us, and where his text evidently agreed with the Masoretic, renders it highly improbable that he was capable of making plausible emendations. Where therefore the reading at the basis of the LXX. appears, upon careful examination, to be superior to the Masoretic text, we cannot but conclude that here an older reading has survived.

COMMENTARY.

CHAPTER I.

THIS Chapter not only serves as an introduction to the book, but also teaches several practical lessons. The conduct of Daniel and his friends, given up into the power of the Gentiles but strictly faithful to the religion of Israel, is evidently intended as an example. In dealing with the heathen world the most minute attention to the Divine Law is necessary, and will always meet with a reward. How well this teaching accords with the circumstances of the Maccabean period is at once apparent. It may seem strange that the point on which special stress is here laid is precisely that part of Judaism which moderns consider least essential and least valuable in a religious sense—the law of clean and unclean meats. But under Antiochus Epiphanes this was a vital matter. To the pious Jews of that time the eating of unlawful food seemed a crime as heinous as idolatry itself (I Macc. i. 62, 63). This feeling is of course something altogether different from the asceticism of medieval Christianity. "The king's food" is refused by Daniel, not because it is pleasant, but because it may contain unclean ingredients, whereas "herbs" offer no such danger[1].

The statement in *v.* 1 that Nebuchadnezzar besieged Jerusalem in the third year of Jehoiakim seems to be due to a combination of II Kings xxiv. 1, 2 with II Chron. xxxvi. 6. In Kings the "three years" are not of course the first three years of Jehoiakim's reign, nor is there any mention of a siege. The idea that Jerusalem was captured under Jehoiakim appears first in Chronicles, but no date is given. The author of Daniel

---

[1] Similarly Josephus tells us that certain Jewish priests of his acquaintance, who had been sent to Rome, "did not forget their duty to God, and lived upon figs and nuts" (*Vita Jos.* 3).

follows the account in Chronicles, at the same time assuming
that the "three years" in Kings date from the beginning of
Jehoiakim's reign, and that "the bands of the Chaldeans" were
a regular army commanded by Nebuchadnezzar.

1, 2. "*In the third year of the reign of Jehoiakim king of
Judah, Nebuchadnezzar king of Babylon came to Jerusalem and
besieged it.*" Elsewhere in Daniel the name Nebuchadnezzar
is always written without א; the older form נבוכדראצר (or
נבוכדראצור Jer. xlix. 28 *Kĕthīb*) which is usual in Jeremiah and
Ezekiel and corresponds to the *Nabū-kudurri-uṣur* of the inscriptions and to the Ναβουκοδρόσορος of Abydenus, never
occurs in this book. In *v.* 2, as in Chronicles, it is not clearly
stated whether Jehoiakim was taken to Babylon, for the reference of the suffix in וַיְבִיאֵם is uncertain; Hitzig makes the
suffix apply both to Jehoiakim and to the vessels, and renders
בֵּית אֱלֹהָיו "to the land of his god," citing Hos. ix. 3, 15. According to Von Lengerke the suffix refers to the vessels only.
Ewald supposes some words to have fallen out and wishes to
read, "Jehoiakim king of Judah, *together with the noblest men
of the land*" etc. It must be admitted that the present construction of the sentence is awkward, for, if Hitzig be right, the
word בית is used first in one sense and immediately afterwards
in another, whereas if we adopt the view of Von Lengerke, the
repetition וְאֶת־הַכֵּלִים is altogether superfluous. In any case the
transportation of captives as well as of vessels, is presupposed
in *v.* 3. מִקְצָת is for מִקְצָת, as in Neh. vii. 70. The form קְצָת is
contracted, in Aramaic fashion, from an original *kăṣdăwăt*, as
מְנָת from *mănăyăt*. קְצָת from meaning "limit" (see *v.* 5)
comes to mean "totality"; hence מִקְצָת is "part of the whole,"
i.e. "some," cf. גְּבוּל "frontier," hence "territory" (Exod. x. 14).
The name שִׁנְעָר is an archaism; it occurs nowhere else but Gen.
x. 10; xi. 2; xiv. 1, 9. Josh. vii. 21. Is. xi. 11. Zech. v. 11.
Writers of the exilic period speak of Babylonia as ארץ בבל (Jer.
li. 29), ארץ כשׂדים (Ezek. xii. 13), or כשׂדים simply (Is. xlviii. 20.
Jer. l. 10). It has been supposed that שִׁנְעָר is a corruption
of *Shumēr*, the name given to South Babylonia in the inscriptions (see Schrader, *Cuneiform Inscr.* p. 118).

3—5. Of אשפנז no satisfactory interpretation has hitherto

been given. The LXX. has 'Αβιεσδρί according to the Codex
Chisianus (Syro-Hex. ܐܒܝܣܕܪܝ). Lenormant thinks that these
forms are corruptions of אשבנזר, which he explains as meaning
"the goddess has formed the seed" (*La Divination*, p. 182).
The רב סריסיו must of course be identical with the שׂר הסריסים of
vv. 7—11, since רב is the Aramaic equivalent of שׂר. The
phrase מִבְּנֵי יִשְׂרָאֵל is understood by most commentators as including both the following classes, the members of the royal
family and the nobles. But it is equally permissible to suppose
that the "Israelites" here form a class by themselves, and that
by the royal family and the פרתמים are meant the family of
Nebuchadnezzar and the Babylonian nobility. Verse 6 certainly
implies that some of the youths in question were at least *not*
Judaeans. The word פרתמים which occurs only here and in
Esther, is probably the Persian *fratama* "first[1]." Symmachus
and the Pĕshīṭtā translate "Parthians," a view which might
easily suggest itself at a time when the Parthians were the
dominant race in Iran[2]. For מאום instead of מום cf. Job xxxi.
7. מַשְׂכִּלִים is here "intelligent"— הִשְׂכִּיל and הֵבִין are used in
Daniel both for "understand" and "teach," cf. the French *ap-
prendre*. מַדָּע, found only in Daniel, Chronicles, and Ecclesiastes, is doubtless borrowed from the Aramaic; the corresponding
Hebrew form is מֹדָע, which however has acquired the secondary meaning of "friend" (Prov. vii. 4). כֹּחַ is "capacity"
generally, both physical and mental. וּלְלַמְּדָם depends upon
וַיֹּאמֶר in the preceding verse. סֵפֶר וּלְשׁוֹן כַּשְׂדִּים "*literature and
the tongue of the Chaldeans*," according to the Masoretic accentuation; Hitzig prefers to connect סֵפֶר closely with what follows, so that the whole phrase would be equivalent to סֵפֶר
כַּשְׂדִּים וּלְשׁוֹנָם. By "the Chaldeans" we are to understand the
learned caste (cf. chap. ii. 1, 4), and their "tongue" must therefore be the language of their sacred books. It is, of course,
vain to inquire what particular language the author has in
view, e.g. whether he means to refer to Accadian as distin-

---

[1] The phrase *martiyā fratamā* "fore-
most men" occurs several times in the
Achaemenian inscriptions.

[2] The Targum on Esth. i. 3 (De Lagarde, *Hagiographa Chaldaice*, p. 202,
line 8) renders פרתמים by פרתונאי
which seems to be a corruption of
פרתווָאי "Parthians."

guished from the ordinary Assyrio-Babylonian. The existence
of a learned or priestly language was a feature common to
most, if not every one, of the great oriental monarchies. מִנָּה
"assign," "appoint," is properly a poetical term (Ps. lxi. 8. Job
vii. 3), and, like many such terms, passed into the later prose;
for "appointing" a person to an office it is used in *v.* 11, also in
I Chron. ix. 29 and frequently in the Palestinian Talmud (cf.
the Aramaic מַנִּי Dan. ii. 24, 49; iii. 12). פתבג was evidently
supposed by the Masoretes to be connected with the Heb. פַּת
"morsel," for which reason it is written פַּת־בַּג. But the term
is no doubt Persian, and exists in Syriac in the form *paṭbāghā*.
According to the historian Deinōn, who lived in the middle of
the 4th century, B.C., ποτίβαζις was the name given to a repast
of cakes and wine, such as was prepared for the kings of Persia[1].
The Persian word was probably *patibāga* (Sanscrit, *pratibhāga*)
"portion", and ποτίβαζις seems to represent a pronunciation in
which the *g* sounded like the modern Persian ع (see De
Lagarde, *Gesammelte Abhandlungen*, p. 73). מִשְׁתָּיו is Singular,
cf. מַעֲשָׂיו I Sam. xix. 4. וּלְגַדְּלָם is connected somewhat loosely
with what precedes, "and (it was intended) to rear them" etc.;
compare chap. ii. 16. מִקְצָתָם "at the end of them," lit. "from
the time when they should end." The suffix *ām* here refers to
a feminine noun, שָׁנִים, as is often the case (cf. מֵהֶם chap. viii.
9). For the Imperf. יַעַמְדוּ "they were to stand," see Driver,
Hebrew Tenses, 2nd ed. p. 51.

6, 7. The name Daniel (i.e. God is my judge) is written
דָּנִאֵל in Ezek. xiv. 14, 20; xxviii. 3. In the form דָּנִיֵּאל it appears
as the name of a son of David (I Chron. iii. 1), and as the name
of a contemporary of Ezra (Ezra viii. 2. Neh. x. 7). The names
חֲנַנְיָה, מִישָׁאֵל, and עֲזַרְיָה also appear among the contemporaries of
Ezra (Neh. viii. 4; x. 3, 24), but this is probably accidental,
since all three occur elsewhere, and we therefore have no proof
that the author of Daniel intended to identify Hananiah,
Mishael, and Azariah, with their namesakes in Nehemiah.
מִישָׁאֵל is usually explained as meaning "Who is what God is?",

[1] See Athenaeus, Bk. xi. p. 503:—
Δείνων ἐν τρίτῳ Περσικῶν φησὶν οὕτως·
ἔστι δὲ ποτίβαζις ἄρτος κρίθινος καὶ πύ-
ρινος ὀπτὸς καὶ κυπαρίσσου στέφανος καὶ
οἶνος κεκραμένος ἐν ᾠῷ χρυσῷ οὗ αὐτὸς
βασιλεὺς πίνει.

the שׁ being the relative particle. Hitzig takes it as a contraction of מִישָׁאֵל "Who is equal to God?", the middle element being the verb שָׁוָה, cf. Is. xl. 25. It is true that שָׁוָה (Kal) is never construed as transitive, but in proper names the use of the verbal conjugations is often peculiar, e.g. פְּלַטְיָהוּ, and probably אֱלִישָׁע, יִשַׁעְיָהוּ. The change of name upon entering a new state of life was common in antiquity (Gen. xli. 45. II Kings xxiii. 34; xxiv. 17). For the phrase וַיָּשֶׂם לָהֶם שֵׁמוֹת cf. chap. v. 12. In chap. iv. 5 Daniel is said to have been called בלטשאצר after the name of the god of Nebuchadnezzar, i.e. after בֵּל (Is. xlvi. 1), and the Masoretic vocalization follows this etymology. But in reality בלטשאצר is the Babylonian *Balâṭsu-uṣur* or *Balâtashu-uṣur* (i.e. "protect thou his life"). Through what channel this name reached the author of Daniel it is of course impossible to say. The LXX. uses Βαλτάσαρ both for בלטשאצר and for בלשאצר. שדרך and מישך are of uncertain origin; the former is explained by Friedr. Delitzsch as *Shudur-Aku* (i.e. "command of Aku," the Moon-deity), and Schrader thinks this probable. עֲבֵד־נְגוֹ has long ago been recognized as a corruption of עבד-נבו " servant of Nebo," which is found in a bilingual (Assyrio-Aramaic) inscription (Schrader, *Cuneiform Inscr.* p. 429). Long after the Christian era the name עבדנבו was borne by heathen Syrians (see Cureton's *Ancient Syriac Documents*, p. 14 of the Syriac text, line 5). In the Palmyrene inscriptions also we find such names as נבובד, נבוקוא, נבוזבד, and ברנבו (De Vogüé, N⁰ˢ. 24, 67, 73).

8—16. For the phrase וַיָּשֶׂם דָּנִיֵּאל עַל־לִבּוֹ cf. Is. lvii. 1, 11. The root גאל "defile" occurs in old Hebrew poetry (Zeph. iii. 1. Is. lix. 3, perhaps also Job iii. 5); as a ritual term it appears first in post-exilic writings (e.g. Mal. i. 7, 12)—for the idea of ceremonial uncleanness the Pentateuch and Ezekiel employ טמא. Verse 9 explains the reason of the mild answer that follows. For אֲשֶׁר לָמָה יִרְאֶה (*v.* 10) "*lest he should see,*" cf. דִּי לְמָה לֶהֱוֵא "lest there should be," Ezra vii. 23; *dalmâ* in this sense is common in Syriac. On זֵעֵפִים see p. 31, and on גִּיל and חַיָּב p. 30. These two latter words are borrowed from the Aramaic. In old Hebrew the root חוב is unknown[1]. The ל

---

[1] In Ezek. xviii. 7 חוֹב seems to be either a corruption of שׁוֹב, as Cornill has suggested, or else a mere dittography, the first two letters of חבלתו

in לְמֶלֶךְ does not mean "before," but is connected with the idea of a forfeit or debt (Aram. חוֹב) owed *to* some one; hence we may render, "*and lest ye make my head a forfeit to the king.*" הַמֶּלְצַר (*v.* 11), which occurs nowhere but in this chapter, is very obscure. That it is not a proper name but a title preceded by the definite article, is now generally admitted. The derivation from the Persian, according to which it means "wine-head" (i.e. keeper of the cellar), appears highly improbable, partly because the מלצר is appointed by the chief of the eunuchs to have charge of Daniel, and supplies food as well as wine, partly because the Persian *s* in *sara* "head" could scarcely be represented by צ. Schrader and Friedr. Delitzsch think that the word may possibly be the Assyrian *maṣṣaru* "guardian," from the root נצר. In *v.* 12[1] זֵרֹעִים obviously has the same meaning as זֵרְעֹנִים in *v.* 16; the latter form occurs in the Talmud, whereas זֵרֹעִים is found here only, unless we regard it as merely a phonetic variation of זֵרוּעִים (Lev. xi. 37. Is. lxi. 11). It is of course possible that זֵרֹעִים may be a scribe's mistake for זֵרְעֹנִים, but since in Daniel different grammatical forms are so often used in the same context without distinction of meaning, we have no right to assume a corruption[2]. Perhaps we may compare with זֵרֹעִים and זֵרְעֹנִים the forms קִמּוֹשׁ Is. xxxiv. 13 and קִמְּשֹׂנִים Prov. xxiv. 31 —also a kind of plant. מַרְאֵינוּ in *v.* 13 (see also *v.* 15) must be a Singular. The verb תֵּרָאֶה has the Aramaic vocalization, cf. תֵּעָשֶׂה Gen. xxvi. 29. Josh. vii. 9. II Sam. xiii. 12. In *v.* 15 בְּרִיאֵי בָשָׂר is a *constructio ad sensum,* referring to the suffix in מַרְאֵיהֶם (so Hävernick); for the phrase cf. בְּרִיאוֹת בָּשָׂר Gen. xli. 2, 18. On the construction in *v.* 16 וַיְהִי נֹשֵׂא "*so he was wont to take away,*" see Driver, *Tenses,* p. 199.

---

having been repeated, and a ו inserted afterwards. The Arabic حَوْب or حُوب "sin" (Koran iv. 2) is doubtless a loan-word from the Jewish Aramaic, the genuine Arabic equivalent of the Aramaic root being خَاب "to fail."

[1] I cannot forego the pleasure of quoting Jerome's remark on this verse. *Incredibilis fidei magnitudo non solum sibi corpulentiam polliceri esu vilioris cibi sed et tempus statuere!*

[2] Cf. for example ותתפעם ii. 1 and ותפעם ii. 3, תעמדנה and יעמדנה viii. 22, הרשענו ix. 5 and רשענו ix. 15, זרעות xi. 15 and זרעים xi. 31, חלקלקות xi. 21, 34 and חלקות xi. 32.

17—20. בְּכָל־סֵפֶר "in all kinds of books," בְּכָל־חָזוֹן "in all kinds of visions," cf. כָּל־עֵץ Gen. ii. 9. The mention of visions and dreams has special reference to the following chapter and to the latter half of the book. In v. 18 לְמִקְצָת has precisely the same meaning as מִקְצָת (see v. 5). "So they stood before the king" (v. 19), i.e. they became his personal attendants. With עָשֶׂר יָדוֹת (v. 20) compare חָמֵשׁ יָדוֹת Gen. xliii. 34; for the comparative use of עַל see chap. xi. 5 and Eccles. i. 16. The absence of the conjunction in הַחַרְטֻמִּים הָאַשָּׁפִים is in accordance with chap. v. 15. חַרְטֻמִּים (see p. 31) is probably an Egyptian word, but its etymology is uncertain. It occurs only in the Pentateach, where it always stands in the plural, and in the book of Daniel[1]. אַשָּׁפִים (with the Aramaic forms אָשַׁף, אָשְׁפִין, אָשְׁפַיָּא) is found nowhere in the Old Testament but in Daniel; the word was originally derived from the Assyrian. It may here be remarked that in Daniel the various words used for diviners, magicians, etc., are nowhere distinguished from one another. When such persons appear, as in chaps. ii. 2; iv. 4; v. 7, they appear all together, so that we cannot say whether the author meant each term to stand for a separate class or whether he employed these terms indiscriminately. In ancient Babylon, as among the heathen Semites generally, there were many distinct kinds of divination and of magic. But the later Jews, like the Christians, regarding all such practices as sinful, seldom distinguished them accurately. The attempt of Lenormant to discover in Daniel allusions to the existence of *five* principal kinds of divination and magic, must be pronounced, by an impartial reader, altogether fanciful.

21. This short verse has given rise to much controversy. If וַיְהִי means "he remained alive" (Bertholdt, Nöldeke), this involves a contradiction to chap. x. 1. In order to avoid the difficulty, Hengstenberg explains, "he lived to see the first year of Cyrus," i.e. he did not die till after the Return of the Exiles. But if the author of the book attached such importance to the Restoration in the first year of Cyrus, it must appear somewhat

---

[1] Whether Cornill be right in reading חרטמים for כל־סתום in Ezek. xxviii. 3 cannot here be discussed.

64

strange that he never alludes to the event, except indirectly in ix. 25. Kirmss and Hitzig substitute וַיְהִי for וַיְהִי. Ewald thinks that some words have fallen out, and reads "So Daniel was *at the king's court* until the first year of king Cyrus."

CHAPTER II.

This piece is partly a narrative, partly an apocalypse. The narrative, as has often been observed, bears considerable resemblance to Gen. xli., and in a few places the verbal agreement is so close as to make it quite certain that the author of Daniel had in his mind the story of Joseph. In both stories, a heathen king has a dream which terrifies him; he sends for the magicians, but they are helpless, and at length the true interpretation is given by a foreign captive, who is at once raised to high honours. In matters of detail there are, of course, great differences, but this is merely what might have been expected[1].

The meaning of Nebuchadnezzar's dream is of great importance for the right understanding of the book. That the four Gentile Empires represented by the image are identical with the Four Empires in chap. vii., is acknowledged by almost all interpreters both ancient and modern. But as to which Empires are meant there has been much disagreement.

In ancient times, *two* interpretations were current. The one is represented by Ephraim Syrus, who doubtless derived it, as he derived so much else, from Jewish tradition. According to this view, the Four Empires are (1) the Babylonian, (2) the Median, (3) the Persian, (4) the Greek or Macedonian. But the immense majority of the later Jews and of the Christian

[1] Compare the story related in Ibn Hishām's Life of Mohammed, ed. Wüstenfeld, p. 9 ff., about Rabī'a ibn Naṣr, king of Yemen. It is obviously unhistorical, and appears to have been borrowed in part from Daniel while in other respects it diverges.

Fathers held the Empires to be (1) the Babylonian, (2) the Medo-Persian, (3) the Greek, (4) the Roman[1].

In the Middle Ages the *second* interpretation was usually accepted both by Christians and Jews. But it was not universal, for by this time a *third* interpretation had arisen, according to which the Fourth Empire is not the Roman, but the Mohammedan. Those who adopted this last theory, contrived to retain the number 4 by amalgamating two of the preceding Empires. Thus in the additional chapter which is found in the Coptic version of Daniel, the Four Empires are said to be (1) the Persian, (2) the Roman, (3) the Greek, (4) the Ishmaelite. Here the Babylonian Empire has been completely swallowed up by the Persian, and the Greek and Roman Empires are transposed. Again, Ben-Ezra tells us in his commentary on Daniel that Rabbi Saadia the Gāōn explained the "iron" as the Roman Empire and the "clay" mingled with the iron as the Ishmaelite. But this, Ben Ezra argues, is impossible, for how can the Roman and Ishmaelite Empires be treated as parts of the same Empire? Accordingly he concludes that the Third Empire comprises both the Greek and the Roman, and that the Fourth Empire is the Ishmaelite.

In modern times, the controversy as to the Four Empires has generally turned on the question whether the Fourth Empire is the Greek or the Roman. That it is the Greek has been maintained by almost all those who deny the antiquity of Daniel and by some of the most learned supporters of the traditional date, such as Dr Westcott. But most of the "defenders of Daniel" have thought it necessary to believe that the Fourth Empire is the Roman.

In order to explain the Four Empires rightly, we must be guided by the statements contained in the book of Daniel

---

[1] As a specimen of the ingenious arguments by which the Christian Fathers supported their theory of the Four Empires, it may be mentioned that Jerome regards the "brass" in Dan. ii. as representing the Greek Empire, because brass is the most *resounding* of metals, and thus symbolizes *the eloquence of the Greek language*. The view of Porphyry, according to whom the Third Empire is that of Alexander and the Fourth that of Alexander's successors (see Jerome on Dan. vii. 7), does not seem to rest on any tradition.

itself. That the *First* Empire is the Babylonian appears clearly
from chap. ii. 37, 38, where Daniel, addressing Nebuchadnezzar
as the representative of the Babylonian monarchy, declares,
"Thou art the head of gold[1]". The *Second* Empire is not
named either in chap. ii. or chap. vii. But since we are told
that at the death of Belshazzar the Empire came into the hands
of the Median king Darius (v. 30 ; vi. 1 ; ix. 1), there can be no
doubt that the Second Empire is the Median. In chap. vi. 29
Darius the Mede is followed by Cyrus the Persian ; hence the
Third Empire is the Persian. The *Fourth* Empire can be no
other than that of Alexander and his successors.

    This view is fully confirmed by the visions in chaps. viii.
and xi. The he-goat of chap. viii. is expressly stated to be the
Greek Empire (*v.* 21), and this evidently corresponds to the
Fourth Empire of chaps. ii. and vii.—firstly in that it is a
"divided" empire (compare ii. 41 with viii. 22), secondly in that
it ends with the rise and overthrow of a certain king sym-
bolized by a "little horn" (compare vii. 8, 24 with viii. 9, 23).
That the Greek Empire is to be the *last* of the Gentile Empires
appears from chap. viii. 17, where the vision is said to refer to
"the time of the end". Moreover in the last vision of all
(chaps. x—xii), the rise and progress of the Greek Empire are
related with many details, but nothing whatever is said of any
subsequent Gentile Empire. Thus to introduce the Roman
Empire into the book of Daniel is to set at nought the plainest
rules of exegesis. That most of the later Jews and of the
Christian Fathers believed the Fourth Empire to be the Roman,
proves nothing as to its real meaning, for the belief was the
natural result of their circumstances, and, as we have seen,
when the Mohammedan Empire had to be accounted for, there
were interpreters who declared the Fourth Empire to be the
Mohammedan. In both cases the object in view was to justify
the book of Daniel, not to explain it.

    The objections which have been urged against the above
interpretation are mainly as follows. It is alleged that in

---

[1] Strangely enough, Hitzig concludes from this verse that the First Empire of Dan. ii. is merely the reign of Nebu- chadnezzar, and the Second Empire the reign of Belshazzar.

Daniel the Median Empire is not distinguished from the Persian, since the ram in chap. viii. represents "the kings of Media and Persia". But the two Empires are not hereby identified, they are merely classed together, the difference between them being sufficiently indicated by the fact that one of the ram's horns comes up *after* the other (*v.* 3). It is indeed stated that the he-goat (i.e. the Greek Empire) breaks both the horns of the ram (i.e. Media and Persia), but this does not imply that the Median and Persian Empires terminate together, any more than the breaking up of the whole image at once (ch. ii. 35) implies that all the four Gentile Empires terminate together.

Again it is urged that in chap. vi. 9, 13, 16 we read of "the law of the Medes and Persians", not "the law of the Medes". This objection is based upon a misunderstanding of the term "Empire". In Daniel the existence of a nation is something quite different from its Empire or supremacy (שָׁלְטָן), as may be seen by the fact that in chap. vii. 12, the first three beasts are deprived of their Empire, but are suffered to live. That the Medes and Persians had much in common was well known in antiquity, and it is therefore not surprising that they should be represented in Daniel and in Esther (chap. i. 19) as being governed by the same laws. But this does not by any means prove that the Median supremacy and the Persian supremacy are contemporaneous.

1—3. The events here related are said to have taken place in the second year of Nebuchadnezzar. In order to reconcile this statement with chap. i. 5, 18, various arbitrary hypotheses have been invented. Thus Rashi explains the second year of Nebuchadnezzar to mean "the second year after the destruction of the Temple", while many modern writers (Hengstenberg, Hävernick, Zöckler and others) have taken refuge in the assumption that in chap. i. 1 and Jer. xxv. 1 Nebuchadnezzar is reigning conjointly with his father Nabopalassar and that "the second year" is the second year after Nabopalassar's death. Others, as Ewald and Lenormant, emend the text, and read "the twelfth year". For the use of the plural חֲלֹמוֹת where a Singular is meant, cf. חֶזְוֵי רֵאשִׁי chap. iv. 3 and חֶזְוֵי רֵאשֵׁה vii. 1.

The phrases וַתִּתְפָּעֶם רוּחוֹ (*v.* 1) and וַתִּפָּעֶם רוּחִי (*v.* 3) are evidently suggested by Gen. xli. 8. וּשְׁנָתוֹ נִהְיְתָה עָלָיו is the Hebrew equivalent of וְשִׁנְתֵּהּ נַדַּת עֲלוֹהִי (chap. vi. 19). נִהְיָה has here the secondary sense of being "past" or "over"; with this use of עָלָיו cf. עָלַי chap. x. 8, also Jer. viii. 18. Hos. xi. 8. Jon. ii. 8. That in *v.* 2 the חַרְטֻמִּים stand first in the list is certainly not accidental, but is due to Gen. xli. 8.   The term מְכַשֵּׁף, which was used among the Hebrews from a very early period (cf. Exod. xxii. 17), is commonly supposed to mean a "reciter of charms or incantations". Prof. Robertson Smith argues, in the Cambridge *Journal of Philology*, N°. 27, pp. 125, 126, that the root כשׁף properly means "to cut" and that כְּשָׁפִים are "herbs or other drugs shredded into a magic brew". Hence מְכַשֵּׁף (or כַּשָּׁף Jer. xxvii. 9) would be primarily a preparer of magical drugs.

4—6. On the sudden transition from Hebrew to Aramaic, see p. 26. The word אֲרָמִית "in Aramaic" is probably a gloss intended to warn the reader that what follows is in Aramaic[1]. With the phrase "*O king, live for ever*", compare I Kings i. 31. Neh. ii. 3. In much later times the Sāsānian kings were addressed with the formula *anōshak buwēdh* "be immortal!" (Nöldeke, *Ṭabarī*, p. 366 note). In עבדיך (*Ḳĕrī* עַבְדָךְ) from a form *'ăbădaik*, the *Shĕwā*, which replaces *ă*, is vocal (cf. מַלְכִין *v.* 21 and מַלְכַיָּא *v.* 37). The old termination *aik* or *ayikh* has been changed by the Masoretes into *ākh*, as usual[2]. On כשׂריא (*Ḳĕrī* כַשְׂדָּיֵא) see Kautzsch, *Gramm.* p. 28. The word אַזְדָא (*vv.* 5, 8), for which Baer reads אָזְדָא, was understood by most of the older commentators as another form of אָזְלָא "going"; so Theodotion renders ἀπέστη. But אזדא is no doubt the Persian *azdā* "certain", "sure", as Nöldeke has shewn (see Schrader, *Cuneiform Inscr.* p. 430). Hence we must render, "*The word (which has gone forth) from me is sure*". הַדָּמִין תִּתְעַבְדוּן lit. "ye shall be made into (separate) limbs", i.e. "*ye shall be cut limb from*

[1] This is the view of Lenormant, who points out that a precisely similar gloss occurs in Ezra iv. 7, where we should read, "The writing of the letter was in Aramaic, and accompanied by a translation—[ARAMAIC] *Rehum the chancellor*" etc.

[2] So also איתינא (pron. *ĭthainā*), chap. iii. 18, has been changed into אִיתָנָא; but on the other hand we find עֲלֶינָא (in some editions עֲלֶינָא) Ezra iv. 12, 18 ; v. 17.

limb"; thus the Pĕshîṭtā translates ܡܗܕܡ ܕܗܕܡ ܗܕܡܐ.

הַדָּם is from the Persian; the Zend form is *haṅdāma,* mod. Pers. *andām,* "limb". Instead of תִּתְעַבְדוּן (Hithpeel) less correct editions have תִּתְעַבְּדוּן (Hithpaal). וּבָתֵּיכוֹן נְוָלִי יִתְּשָׂמוּן " *and your houses shall be made a dunghill"*, cf. Ezra vi. 11, where for נְוָלִי we find נְוָלוּ; both forms are abstracts from the verb נַגֵּל " to defile, disgrace", common in later Jewish Aramaic. As to the custom in question, see II Kings x. 27. יִתְּשָׂמוּן (cf. יִתְּשָׂם Ezra iv. 21. מִתְּשָׂם Ezra v. 8) is a Hithpeel. "The doubling of the *t",* says Prof. Wright (*Comparative Grammar,* p. 254), "may be an attempt to compensate for the radical which has disappeared by contraction, and so to give the word something of the outward form of the normal הִתְקְטֵל; or it may be merely imitated from the Ethtaf'al (Ittaf'al)". In *v.* 6 תְּהַחֲוֹן (Haphel) is exactly equivalent in sense to the Pael (cf. *v.* 4). נְבִזְבְּיָתָךְ (cf. נְבִזְבָּה chap. v. 17) is doubtless a foreign word, probably Persian; whether Haug be right in deriving it from a hypothetical form *nibajvā* "gift" is uncertain (see Ewald's *Jahrbücher der bibl. Wissensch.* 1853, p. 160[1]). The particle לָהֵן is here translated "therefore" by most commentators, as also in *v.* 9 and chap. iv. 24; elsewhere לָהֵן means "but", "only", in Biblical Aramaic, and Ewald thinks that here and in the two other passages cited the word has its ordinary sense. He therefore renders "*only declare to me the dream and its interpretation."*

7—11. תִּנְיָנוּת "a second time" is properly an abstract noun formed from תִּנְיָן "second"; substantives and adjectives used as adverbs not unfrequently have the *form* of a construct state, though in reality they stand in the absolute (see Nöldeke, *Mandäische Grammatik,* p. 201). The meaning of *v.* 8 seems to be, "*I know of a surety that ye are gaining time, because ye have seen that certain is the word which I have spoken"*, i.e. perceiving that I will take no direct refusal, ye seek to escape by delay. Instead of מִן־יַצִּיב we also find יַצִּיבָא chap. iii. 24; for this adverbial use of מִן cf. מִן־קְשֹׁט *v.* 47. The phrase זְבַן עִדָּנָא "to buy the time", does not occur elsewhere; it is variously explained as

---

[1] The word appears again in the Palestinian Targum, Deut. xxiii. 24, נבזבית בית מוקדשא "gifts for the Temple", but in Jer. xl. 5 the Targum, as edited by De Lagarde, has מתנן ומזיבן.

meaning " to gain time" (Gesenius, De Wette, Von Lengerke), and " to profit by favourable opportunities" (Hävernick, Hitzig), after the analogy of τὸν καιρὸν ἐξαγοραζόμενοι Eph. v. 16. Col. iv. 5. The former of these interpretations is supported by the Pĕshīṭtā which has ܘܒܢܐ ܗܘ ܐܠܡ ܕܪܒܐ ܐܢܬܘܢ " ye ask for time"; that the Syriac translator read בעין for זבנין, as Graetz supposes, is very improbable. כל־קבל די חזיתון is rendered by Hitzig "although ye have seen" (cf. chap. v. 22), but the ordinary meaning "because" is not inappropriate in this verse[1]. The form קֳבֵל, properly meaning "before" (cf. לְקָבֵל chaps. iii. 3 ; v. 1, 5, 10) seems to be an old diminutive, corresponding to the Arabic kubaila[2]; with suffixes another form is used, לְקָבְלָךְ v. 31 (Syr. lĕkubhlākh, Arab. ḳablaka). In v. 9 חֲדָה הִיא דָתְכוֹן can scarcely mean "*your purpose is one and the same*" (Von Lengerke, Hitzig), but rather "*there is but one sentence* (i.e. punishment) *for you*" (Ewald)—cf. וְדָתָא נֶפְקַת in v. 13. דָּת "judicial sentence" and hence "law", is the Old Persian dāta (so also in Zend), mod. Pers. dād "justice". In Biblical Aramaic דָּת is treated as feminine on account of the final ת. The clause וּמִלָּה כִדְבָה וגו' does not stand in any very close logical connection with what precedes, "*and (moreover) lying words and mischief have ye prepared*" etc. For the Haphel הזמנתון the Kĕrī substitutes the Hithpaal, "ye have prepared yourselves to utter" etc. With אִנְדַּע, for אַדַּע, cf. מַנְדְּעָא v. 21, תִּנְדַּע v. 30, יִנְדְּעוּן chap. iv. 14. This insertion of Nūn as a substitute for the doubling of a consonant is not rare in Biblical Aramaic and occurs sometimes in the later Targums (e.g. ינדע Eccles. viii. 5. ינדעון Ps. ix. 21. מנדעא Ps. xix. 3)—in Syriac it is almost unknown, but is very common in the Mandaitic dialect[3]. In v. 10

---

[1] Cf. לקבל די הו בנה "because he built", in an Aramaic inscription of the Ḥaurān (De Vogüé, N°. 3).

[2] Perhaps Syr. ܬܚܘܬ "under", which is never used with suffixes, may also be a diminutive form, answering to tuḥaita.

[3] It would of course be a mistake to regard the forms with the inserted n as characteristic of any particular period. The probability is that *both* pronunciations long continued in use side by side. Thus we find that several Arabic words borrowed from the Aramaic are written sometimes with n, sometimes with the doubling, e.g. injār or ijjār "roof" (Syr. eggārā), injāna or ijjāna "basin" (Syr. aggānā).

אִתַי (less correctly אִיתַי), with suffixes אִיתֵינָא (*Kĕrī* אִיתָנָא chap. iii. 18), אִיתָךְ (*Kĕrī* אִיתָךְ chap. ii. 26), אִיתֵיכוֹן (chap. iii. 14, 15), אִיתוֹהִי (chap. ii. 11), corresponds to Hebr. יֵשׁ; the original form of the word was probably *yĭthai* (Nöldeke, *Mand. Gram* p. 293) —in אִתַי the initial י has lost its consonantal sound, but the original ending has been retained. On the form יוּכַל see p. 39. "*Seeing that no great and mighty king hath asked*" etc. "Great king" was a title borne by the kings of Assyria (II Kings xviii. 28), and afterwards by the kings of Persia. Whether such forms as מֶלֶךְ (cf. אֶבֶן *v.* 34, צְלֵם chap. iii. 5, חֵלֶם iv. 2, אֶרֶז vii. 8) are to be regarded as Hebraisms, is doubtful, see Kautzsch, *Gramm.* p. 92[1]. With אָחֳרָן "other" (*v.* 11) cf. אוּחְרָן in the Targums (Onk. Num. xxiii. 13, see Merx, *Chrestomathia Targumica*, p. 25 — the pronunciation אוּחְרָן is incorrect), and the Samaritan עורן (= חורן), Lev. xxvii. 20. Num. xxiii. 27 ; the Christian Palestinian seems to weaken the *ā* of the last syllable to *ē*, חורין or חורן, so also the Syriac ܐ݇ܚܪܝܢ (East-Syriac ʼḥrēn, West-Syriac ʼḥrīn). The expression "*gods whose dwelling is not with flesh* (i.e. *with mankind*)" scarcely refers to any distinct class of deities, but is simply a confession of impotence on the part of the Chaldeans—no mortal man, only beings of a higher sphere, can perform the king's request.

12—16. The wise men of Babylon having been condemned to death, Daniel and his friends, who seem not to have been present during the interview with the king, are sought out for slaughter. This shews that the "wise men" form a guild or association of which Daniel and his friends are members, but as to the precise nature of that association nothing is told us. With the phrase הֲתִיב עֵטָא וּטְעֵם "*returned answer with counsel and prudence*," (*v.* 14) cf. מְשִׁיבֵי טָעַם Prov. xxvi. 17. The word עֵטָא (from an older form ʻiṭăt, Arab. عَظَة) is one of the rare instances, in Aramaic, of a verbal noun in which the first radical is dropt ; similar cases are חֲמָא (chap. iii. 13) or חֱמָא (id. *v.* 19) from the root יחם, and שִׁנְתֵּהּ (ch. vi. 19) from יֹשׁן. Why the first

---

[1] In the Christian Palestinian dialect we find מישך (pron. מְשֻׁךְ or מְשַׁךְ) "skin", מילך "counsel". Similarly in the Pĕshīṭṭā *urah* (from primitive *ŭrḥ*), Ezra viii. 21. See Nöldeke in the *Z. D. M. G.* xxii. 475.

vowel has been lengthened in עֲטָא and not in חֲמָא, חֶמָא, it is impossible to say. The chief of the executioners is here named אַרְיוֹךְ which Schrader and Friedr. Delitzsch take to be the Babylonian *Irî-Aku* or *Éri-Aku* (i.e. servant of the Moon-god). The author of Daniel probably borrowed the name from Gen. xiv. 1. *"Why is the decree so harsh on the part of the king?"* (*v.* 15). מְהַחְצְפָה, contracted מַחְצְפָה (chap. iii. 22), is the Haphel participle of חצף, a root which denotes "stiffness", "hardness", or "shamelessness" (i.e. *hardness* of face)[1]. In *v.* 16, זְמַן (for which some editions wrongly have זְמָן), stat. emphat. זִמְנָא (chap. iii. 7), is derived from the Old Persian *zarvan*, cf. the late Hebr. זְמָן (Neh. ii. 6) and Arab. *zaman* or *zamān*; the Syr. *zěbhan* (stat. emphat. *zabhnā*), which occurs also in Palmyrene, comes nearer to the original Persian form. With יִנְתֶּן־לֵהּ cf. תִּנְתֵּן Ezra vii. 20. This verb, like the corresponding Syriac form *nettel*, appears only in the Imperfect and in the Infinitive מִנְתַּן (Syr. *mettal*); in the Targums the *n* is assimilated, יִתֵּן! Inf. מִתַּן. The phrase וּפִשְׁרָא לְהַחֲוָיָה is elliptical, *"and (this was) in order that he might tell"* etc., cf. also *v.* 18 and chap. i. 5.

17—23. "The God of heaven" (*v.* 18), which occurs already in Gen. xxiv. 7, was a favourite expression among the postexilic Jews (Ezra v. 11; vi. 9, 10; vii. 12, 21, 23. Neh. i. 4, 5; ii. 4, 20). רָז "secret" is a Persian word, in common use down to modern times; in Syriac also it is frequently employed, especially for "mystery" in the ecclesiastical sense. In *v.* 19 גְּלִי is not the passive participle, which would be גְּלֵה or גְּלֵא, but an instance of the old Perfect Passive, corresponding to Arab. *juliya*; in *v.* 30 this same word is written גְּלִי, cf. קְרִי Ezra iv. 18, 23 and the plural form רְמִיו Dan. iii. 21; vii. 9 (see Wright, *Comp. Gramm.* p. 225). וּנְהִירָא עִמֵּהּ שְׁרֵא "*and the light dwelleth with Him*" (*v.* 22); for נְהִירָא (Syr. *nahhīrā* "light") the *Kěrī* substitutes נְהוֹרָא, which is the common form in later Jewish Aramaic—in chap. v. 11, 14, we find נַהִירוּ with the abstract ending. שְׁרֵא is not a Perfect, but a Participle, passive in form

---

[1] Hence, in the Targums and Talmud, the Adj. חֲצִיף "shameless". On the other hand the Arab. *ḥaṣîf* is used in a good sense viz. "firm", "solid" in judgment", "prudent". The idea that this root expresses "haste" is due to the loose renderings of some ancient Versions in Dan. iii. 22.

though not in meaning; this use of the passive participle is frequent in Syriac, e.g. *kĕne* "having obtained", "possessed of", as contrasted with *kānē* "obtaining"—similar is Hebr. לָבוּשׁ "having put on", "clothed with", and אָחוּז "having grasped", "holding" (Cant. iii. 8)[1]. In *v.* 23 Baer reads אֲבָהְתִי with Hebraized ending, but אֲבָהָתִי is better attested. With יְהַבְתְּ, shortened from יְהַבְתָּ, compare עֲבַדְתְּ chap. iv. 32 and הַשְׁפֵּלְתְּ v. 22. The longer form is however commoner in Biblical Aramaic, and there can be little doubt that, at the time of the writers, the final *ā* was always pronounced (see חֲזַיְתָה chap. ii. 41 *bis*). Instead of the הוֹדַעְתָּנָא of the ordinary editions, Baer has הוֹדַעְתֶּנָא, which Kautzsch (*Gramm.* p. 60) regards as a pausal form of הוֹדַעְתַּנָא, cf. לְשִׁיזָבוּתָנָא chap. iii. 17 [2].

24—28. In הַעֵלְנִי (so Baer, not הְעֵלְנִי) the suffix is added to the Imperative in the same manner as in the Targums (e.g. בָּרִיכַנִי Onḳ. Gen. xxvii. 34, 38. הוֹדְעַנִי Exod. xxxiii. 13), that is, without the intervening *ai* which here appears in Syriac. On הַנְעֵל (*v.* 25) for הַעֵל see what has been said on אִנְדַּע in *v.* 9. In הִשְׁכַּחַת, "I have found", the tone is thrown back (as in הִתְגְּזֶרֶת *v.* 34, for הִתְגְּזָרַת) and instead of the usual *ē*, the last syllable takes *ă*, owing to the guttural ח [3]. יְהוּד, in the place of the old Hebrew יְהוּדָה is probably, as Hitzig observes, a secondary formation from יְהוּדִי; so, in Arabic, *yahūd* "Jews" is the collective of *yahūdī* "a Jew". כָּהֵל "able" (*v.* 26) is evidently synonymous with יְכֵל (chaps. iii. 17; iv. 34); both roots may be variations of כּוּל, and the formation of כהל would then be according to the analogy of Aram. רהט Hebr. רוּץ, Aram. בהת Hebr. בּוּשׁ. גָּזְרִין (*v.* 27) "prognosticators", properly "those who de-

---

[1] See Nöldeke, *Syr. Gramm.* p. 194, *Mand. Gramm.* p. 380. The frequency of this usage in Syriac may perhaps be due in part to Persian influence, since in Persian the past participle of all active verbs may be used either in an active or in a passive sense, e.g. *karda* "having done" or "done".

[2] In those MSS. of the Targums which have the so-called Babylonian vocalization, the suffix of the 1st pers.

Pl. is always -ănā, never -ānā, both in verbs and nouns (Merx, *Chrest. Targ.* p. 12). It will be remembered that in the Babylonian vocalization no difference is made between *Pathaḥ* and *Sĕgōl*.

[3] Prof. Kautzsch's explanation of הַשְׁכַּח as being a Peal, not a Haphel (*Gramm.* p. 174), is certainly erroneous. See Nöldeke in the *Göttingische gelehrte Anzeigen*, 1884, p. 1019.

termine (what is doubtful)"; גזר is originally "to cut" (see *v.*
34), and in the Semitic languages, as is well known, the ideas
of "cutting" and "determining" are closely allied. In *v.* 28 the
words "*He hath made known to king Nebuchadnezzar what shall
be in the latter days*" (cf. also *vv.* 29, 45) seem to have been suggested by Gen. xli. 25.

29—35. The king, while lying awake, was meditating as
to the future, and the dream was afterwards sent by God for the
purpose of enlightening him. With עַל־דִּבְרַת דִּי (*v.* 30) "in order
that", cf. Eccles. iii. 18; vii. 14; viii. 2. יְהוֹדְעוּן "*they should
make known*", i.e. "that it (the interpretation) should be made
known"; this vague use of the Plural, which is common in
Daniel (e.g. iii. 4; iv. 13, 22, 29; v. 20, 29), is likewise a favourite construction in the Mishnah. For אֲלוּ (*v.* 31) "*behold !*",
which occurs again in chaps. iv. 7, 10; vii. 8, we find also אֲרוּ
chap. vii. 2, 5, 6, 7, 13; both words are probably phonetic variations of the same interjection, but which is the more primitive
is uncertain. That אֲרוּ is for רְאוּ "see !" appears highly improbable. דִּכֵּן, "that", is formed from דֵּךְ by the addition of the
demonstrative *n* (Wright, *Comp. Gramm.* p. 111); cf. the Biblical
Aramaic תַּמָּה "there" (Arab. *thamma*) with the later תַּמָּן (Nöldeke, *Gött. gel. Anz.* 1884, p. 1020). זִיו "brightness", and
hence in the Plural "cheerful appearance" (chap. v. 6, 9) is probably an Assyrio-Babylonian word (see Friedr. Delitzsch, *Pro-
leg. eines neuen Heb. und Aram. Wörterb.* p. 152, and Nöldeke
in the *Z. D. M. G.* XL. p. 732). רֵוֵהּ "*his appearance*", which
occurs again in chap. iii. 25, is the only certain trace in Aramaic
of a root corresponding to Hebr. ראה; the word is found also in
the Targums (e.g. אִתְּתָא שַׁפִּירַת רִיו "a woman of beautiful appearance", Onḳ. Deut. xxi. 11)[1]. That רֵו is not borrowed from
the Hebrew is shewn by its form, which is contracted from ראו
(exactly resembling the synonymous חזו in חֶזְוֵהּ Dan. vii. 20);
the disappearance of the radical א is after the analogy of מְחָא
for מְחָתָא, מְזָא for מְאֲזָא. In *v.* 34 the stone is described as
striking the image "upon its feet", thus implying that the

---

[1] From the Aramaic רו the Persian *rū*, "face", for which there is no
Aryan etymology, seems to be derived.

Gentile powers represented by the image are not contemporaneous but follow one upon another—the destruction of the Fourth Empire involves the complete overthrow of the Gentile supremacy. On מְחָת (so Baer), instead of מְחָת see p. 39. The form דָּקוּ (v. 35) is difficult to explain. Elsewhere in Daniel the verb דקק is used in the Haphel only, and דָּקוּ, if correctly pointed, must be from a root דוק or דיק equivalent to דקק. But whether דקו be meant as transitive, like יְהוֹדְעֻן in v. 30, or as intransitive "they fell to pieces", we cannot say. כַּחֲדָה "all together" is used also in the Targums (e.g. יתחברון כחדא Ps. ii. 2), cf. the Hebr. כְּאֶחָד Ezra ii. 64, and Syr. ܡܚܕܐ (for ܡܢ ܚܕܐ) "at once". אִדְּרֵי is from a Sing. אִדַּר emphat. אִדְּרָא, which is common in later Jewish Aramaic, and appears in Syriac as eddĕrā. In form this word resembles emmĕrā (cf. אִמְּרִין Ezra vi. 9) and ṣeppĕrā (cf. צִפְּרִין Dan. iv. 30), but whether it is originally Aramaic may be doubted[1]. In מְלָאת we have a relic of the old form, מְלָאת, in which the א was a consonant.

36—45. For the general meaning of vv. 36, 37, compare Jer. xxvii. 5, 6. Instead of the older דארין (pron. דָּאֲרִין) the Ķĕrī has דָּיְרִין, which is the ordinary form in Syriac, cf. also קאמין (Ķĕrī קָיְמִין) chap. iii. 3, זאעין (Ķ. זָיְעִין) v. 19, and דאנין (Ķ. דָּיְנִין) Ezra vii. 25; but in the stat. emphat. of the Plural the א is allowed to stand (קָאֲמַיָּא Dan. vii. 16). In v. 39 אָחֳרִי, stat. absol. fem. of אָחֳרָן, corresponds to the אוּחֲרִי of the Targums (Onk. Gen. xxvi. 21, 22), to the Samaritan חורי (Num. xiv. 24), and to the Christian Palestinian חורי (stat. emphat. חוריתא). ארעא מִנָּךְ "lower than thou"—for the stat. emphat. ארעא the Ķĕrī has the absol. אֲרַע (cf. the Targum, I Esth. i. 2, ארע מיניה); both forms are substantival ("the ground", i.e. lowness), though they are used in the place of an adjective, and so the Hebrew מָרוֹם "height" is used for "high" (Ps. x. 5; xcii. 9). That the Median Empire should be described as "lower", i.e. less power-

---

[1] In Arabic we find the forms andar, from Aram. אדר or אנדר with dissimilation, and baidar, from בי דרי (=בֵּית אִדְרַיָּא); see the note by Fleischer in Levy's Wörterb. über die Targumim, I. 417, b. Prof. De Lagarde (Gesammelte Abhandlungen, p. 10) suggests that אִדַּר is an Iranian word, which is of course quite possible, though the Arabic forms prove nothing in favour of the hypothesis.

ful, than the Babylonian, is natural, for of the Median Empire next to nothing was known in the time of the author, whereas the greatness of Babylon was well remembered. Of the Persian Empire we are told that it bears rule "over all the earth". Cf. Ezra i. 2, and the book of Esther *passim*. As in chap. vii., the author dismisses the first three Empires very briefly and hastens on to describe the Fourth, the only one which had a practical interest for himself and his readers. In both chapters great stress is laid upon the conquering power of the Fourth Empire, which is to "crush" all opposition (cf. *v.* 40 with chap. vii. 23). But here much fewer details are given than in chap. vii.; no mention is made of Antiochus, and the last days of Gentile supremacy are depicted only in general terms—the Gentile Empire will be divided, some parts being stronger than others. In *v.* 40 כָּל־קֳבֵל דִּי is rendered "even as" by Gesenius, Von Lengerke, Ewald, and Hitzig, but it seems more natural to take the phrase in its usual sense—the author gives the reason of the foregoing comparison, "*And there shall be a Fourth Empire, strong as iron, forasmuch as iron crusheth and breaketh all*" etc. At the beginning of *vv.* 41 and 43, דִּי is used as in chap. iv. 20, 23[1], i.e. "*(the fact) that thou sawest . . . . . (signifies that) it shall be a divided Empire, and (a portion) of the firmness of the iron shall be in it, forasmuch as thou sawest the iron mixed with the miry clay*". That נִצְבְּתָא is "firmness" (cf. יַצִּיב "sure") seems more probable than that it means "nature", from נצב "to plant". With מִן־קְצָת מַלְכוּתָא (*v.* 42) "part of the Empire", cf. מִקְצָת chap. i. 2. At the beginning of *v.* 43 the *Kĕrī* has וְדִי, for דִּי, which is in accordance with chap. iv. 23. "*They shall be mingling themselves by marriage alliances*"—this, the traditional Jewish interpretation, doubtless gives the real meaning[2]; the reference is to the marriages between the Ptolemies and the Seleucidae (chap. xi. 6, 17); for the expression זְרַע אֲנָשָׁא cf. Jer. xxxi.

---

[1] Compare the Syriac construction—

ܕܠܐ ܡܟܣܝܐ ܐܢܐ
ܡܛܠ ܕܟܣܝܬܐ ܕܡܢܝ
ܐܬܬܪܝܡܬ ܠܗ, "and that I am not veiled (is) because the veil of

corruption is taken away from me" (Wright, *Apocryphal Acts*, p. ܡܚܒ bottom).

[2] So Rashi translates, though he makes a wrong application—מתחתנים יהיו עם שאר האומות.

26. הֵא־כְדִי "like as", exactly corresponds to the Palmyrene
היכדי (De Vogüé, N°. 71—היכדי כתבת "according as I have
written"). In *vv.* 44 and 45 the Divine Kingdom is portrayed.
It is to be set up "in the days of those kings", that is, when
the Greek Empire is in a state of division, and it will last for
ever. Of a personal king nothing is said, but the eternal
sovereignty of Israel is put prominently forward—"the kingdom
shall not be left to another *people*". Instead of יְקִים, which
occurs again in chap. iv. 14, we find also יְהָקִים v. 21; vi. 16. The
first part of *v.* 45 should probably be connected with *v.* 44 (so
Von Lengerke, Ewald), "*it shall crush and destroy all these
kingdoms, but as for it, it shall abide for ever, forasmuch as thou
sawest that from the mountain a stone was cut*" etc. In *v.* 45 the
word חַסְפָּא certainly does not stand where we should have
expected it, but whether Ewald be justified in altering the text
according to the LXX., so as to place חַסְפָּא at the head of the
list, may be doubted[1]. The verse ends with a solemn statement of the truth of the revelation—"*A great God hath made
known to the king what shall be hereafter, and certain is the
dream and sure its interpretation*". מְהֵימַן (Syr. *mĕhaiman*), which
occurs again in chap. vi. 5, is the passive participle of הֵימִן
(chap. vi. 25), a verb which seems to be borrowed from the
Hebr. הֶאֱמִין.

46—49. The interpretation ended, Nebuchadnezzar falls
down before Daniel and honours him as a god. We need not
stop to inquire whether a strict monotheist would suffer himself
to be thus worshipped, for the whole description is evidently
ideal—Nebuchadnezzar at the feet of Daniel represents the
Gentile power humbled before Israel (cf. Is. xlix. 23 ; lx. 14).
The king's homage, though ostensibly paid to Daniel, is in
reality paid to Daniel's God (*v.* 47). Very similar is the fabu-
lous story in Josephus (*Antiq.* XI. 8. 5), where Alexander pros-
trates himself before the Jewish High Priest. In *v.* 46 נִסָּכָה,
which properly means "to pour" drink-offerings (Hebr. נְסֵךְ cf.
נִסְכֵּיהוֹן Ezra vii. 17), seems to be used of oblations generally. In
v. 47 מִן־קְשֹׁט דִּי is elliptical, "(*I know*) *of a truth that*" etc. מָרֵה,

---

[1] Compare the different arrangement of the metals in chap. v. 4 and 23.

for which some MSS. read מָרֵא as in ch. v. 23, has the vocalization of a Participle Peal. The form מראי "my lord" (ch. iv. 16,
21, K̆thīb) shews that in the time of the author the א retained
its consonantal sound[1]. In v. 48 the words וְרַב סִגְנִין depend
upon הַשְׁלְטֵהּ, i.e. "he made him rule over all the province of
Babylon, and (appointed him) chief governor" etc. סִגְנִין (Hebr.
סְגָנִים), which never occurs in the Singular in the Old Testament,
is from the Babylonian shaknu "governor" (shakānu, "to place",
"to appoint", see Schrader, Cuneiform Inscr. p. 411). Daniel,
it would seem, wishing to remain "at the king's court", requests
that his three friends be entrusted with the business (עֲבִידְתָּא)
of the government (v. 49). This verse is obviously written in
view of the following narrative.

CHAPTER III.

(Verses 1—30.)

The general purpose of this Chapter is perfectly clear—
from beginning to end it is a polemic against the heathen worship and in particular against idolatry. The Israelite who has
to choose between idolatry and death, should unhesitatingly
prefer the latter. Even when there appears no hope of deliverance, the God of Israel is able to succour those who persevere
in obedience to Him.

I have already pointed out that the idea of punishment by
burning was probably suggested to the author by Jer. xxix. 22.
Other passages may have contributed something, particularly
Is. xliii. 2, for that sharp distinction which we are accustomed
to draw between the literal and the metaphorical was not
always recognized in antiquity. It has often been asked why in
this chapter there is no mention of Daniel. The reason seems

---

[1] Cf. Arab. al-mar'u "the man"; in the Syriac forms, emphat. māryā or mārā, constr. mārē, with suffixes mārēh, mārhōn etc., the final א sometimes becomes ', sometimes is treated as a mere vowel-sign, and sometimes disappears altogether.

to be that he could not have been introduced without marring the effect. To represent him as being cast with his friends into the furnace would have involved too gross and startling an inconsistency, after the scene at the close of chap. ii. On the other hand, if Daniel had intervened to save his friends, there would have been no opportunity for the display of the divine power, preserving them unhurt amidst the flames of the furnace. On these grounds the non-mention of Daniel is perfectly natural.

1—6. On the form אֲקִימֵהּ see p. 37. אקים צלם " to set up a statue, or idol", is the usual phrase in the heathen inscriptions of Palmyra and the Ḥaurān. The "plain" or "valley" of Dūrā has not been identified with certainty; according to Schrader there were in Babylonia several localities bearing the name of *Dûru* (*Cuneiform Inscr.* p. 430). Very important is the list of officials, in *vv.* 2 and 3, who are summoned by the king to the dedication of the image. It need hardly be said that in these foreign words the Masoretic vocalization is entitled to very little respect and may safely be ignored. אחשדרפניא (cf. Ezra viii. 36. Esth. iii. 12) are "satraps", from the Old Persian *khshatra-pāwan* lit. "warden of the realm". On סגניא see chap. ii. 48. פחותא (Sing. פֶּחָה Ezra v. 14, constr. פַּחַת) "governors", from the Assyrian *pakhatu* (Schrader, *Cuneiform Inscr.* p. 577). The word אדרגזריא has often been explained as a compound of אדר and גזר, but it is probably the Persian *endarzgar* "counsellor", a title which was still in use under the Sāsānians (Nöldeke, *Ṭabarī*, p. 462 note), and the resemblance with גזרין (chap. ii. 27) is therefore accidental. גדבריא is commonly taken to be a variation of גִּזְבָּרַיָּא "treasurers" (Ezra vii. 21), from the Persian *ganjabara*; but the analogy of *v.* 27 and chap. vi. 8 favours the hypothesis of Graetz and others that גדבריא is a mere scribal error for הדבריא. דתבריא "judges" is from the Old Persian *dātabara*, in Pahlawī *dātōbar*, and in mod. Persian *dāwar*. The meaning of תפתיא is altogether obscure; that it signifies "counsellors" and is connected with the Arabic *aftā* "to advise" (of which *Muftī* is the participle) appears very improbable, since the root in question has this meaning in Arabic only, nor would the grammatical form of the word, with prefixed ת, admit of

any easy explanation. Still less likely is Graetz's view that
תפתיא is a mistake for הפתיא, from Greek ὕπατοι. Possibly
the word may be a mutilated form of some Persian title ending
in *pat* "chief", cf. Pahlawī *magupat* "chief priest", *spahpat*
"general", etc. On the form קאמין (*v*. 3) see ch. ii. 38. כָּרוֹזָא
(*v*. 4) "herald", common in Syriac also, is probably not borrowed directly from the Greek κῆρυξ, but is formed, after the
usual Aramaic fashion, from the verbal root כרז, which however
does not appear in the Peal (see chap. v. 29). The Plural עַמְמַיָא
(Syr. ʽamĕmē), from Sing. עַמָא, is a relic of the old plural form
in which the second radical had the vowel *ă* (see Nöldeke, *Syr.
Gramm.* p. 58). The Singular of אֻמַיָא occurs in Biblical Aramaic in the stat. absol. only, אֻמָּה *v*. 29; this word is common to
Hebrew, Aramaic, and Arabic, and of course originally means
"the offspring of one mother", thus presupposing the so-called
matriarchal condition of society. Of the six musical instruments enumerated in *vv*. 5, 7, 10 and 15, two, viz. קַרְנָא "the
horn" and מַשְׁרוֹקִיתָא "the pipe", have Semitic names, and three
are Greek, viz. קיתרס "lute", *Kĕrī* קַתְרֹס (as in the Targums, e.g.
Is. v. 12), Gr. κίθαρις or κιθάρα—פסנתרין "harp" (for which *v*. 7
has פסנטרין), Gr. ψαλτήριον — סומפניה "bag-pipe" (omitted in
v. 7: in *v*. 10 *Kĕthīb* סיפניה, a popular mispronunciation) Gr.
συμφωνία, see p. 41. שַׂבְּכָא, probably a kind of harp, is of
doubtful origin; that it is identical with Gr. σαμβύκη cannot
be questioned, but whether the Greeks borrowed the word from
the Arameans, or the Arameans from the Greeks, or whether
both nations borrowed it from some third language, is uncertain.
That it is from the root שׂבך "to interlace" appears very improbable. The statement in Athenaeus (Bk IV. p. 175) that the
σαμβύκη was invented by the Syrians, does not of course prove
the word to be Aramaic. Besides the above-named instruments
there are others which the author sums up in the phrase
וְכָל־זְנֵי זְמָרָא "and all manner of music". זְנֵי, of which the Singular occurs in Syriac (emphat. zĕnā, constr. zan or zen) and
perhaps in Hebrew (Ps. cxliv. 13), but not in Biblical Aramaic,
seems to be from a Persian word *zan*, the etymological equivalent of Gr. γένος (see De Lagarde, *Reliquiae juris ecclesiastici,
graece*, p. xxviii). The Persian origin of this word is admitted

also by Nöldeke (*Syr. Gramm.* p. 83). The Masoretic vocalization of קָם (*v.* 6), which is the best attested reading (cf. also *vv.* 11, 15 and Ezra v. 3, 9), is certainly erroneous, for not only do we find *măn* in Syriac[1], but also in the Targums with Babylonian vocalization this word has a short vowel (see p. 39). שַׁעֲתָא (for שָׁעֲתָא, Syr. *shā'ĕthā*, cf. stat. abs. שָׁעָה chap. iv. 16) means in Biblical Aramaic an indefinite space of time, as *sā'a* often does in Arabic; hence is derived the signification "hour"[2]. אַתּוּן "furnace" occurs also in Syriac and Arabic; its derivation is unknown.

7—18. כְּדִי "when" (cf. chaps. v. 20; vi. 11, 15) is found likewise in Palmyrene (De Vogüé, Nº. 15). In *vv.* 8—10 the denunciation of the Jews by the Chaldeans bears a great resemblance to the denunciation of Daniel by the other officials in chap. vi. 13, 14. In both cases the object of the author is the same, viz. to encourage those Jews who, for refusing to abandon their religion, were accused by their enemies of "setting the king at nought" (iii. 12; vi. 14). גֻּבְרִין (emphat. גֻּבְרַיָּא *v.* 12) stands for גַּבְרִין, which is the Syriac form; the change of *a* to *u* is due to the following labial, as in the Christian Palestinian שובתא (pron. *shubbĕthā*) "Sabbath", Syr. *shabbĕthā*. The singular phrase אֲכַלוּ קַרְצֵיהוֹן "they ate their pieces", i.e. "they accused them" (cf. chap. vi. 25), is common also in Syriac; as to the precise origin of the metaphor some doubt prevails. The different use of the expression שָׂם טְעֵם in *vv.* 10 and 12 is remarkable. On יַתְּהוֹן (*v.* 12) see p. 38. רְגַז (*v.* 13) is vocalized according to the analogy of such forms as כְּסַף, although the original vowel is not *ă* but *ŭ*, as appears from רוגזא in the Targums —see also כְּתַל chap. v. 5. Instead of חֲמָא we find also חֵמָא (*v.* 19), cf. what has been said on עֲטָא chap. ii. 14. Very peculiar is the form הֵיתָיוּ which seems to have a passive sense, "*they were brought*" (cf. הֵיתַיִת chap. vi. 18 and שִׁיצִיא, *Kĕrī* שֵׁיצִי, Ezra vi. 15), whereas הַיְתִיוּ (chap. v. 3) is "they brought". It has been suggested that these passives are formed after the analogy

[1] The Syriac *mān* is "what?", contracted from *mā den* (Nöldeke, *Syr. Gramm.* p. 44).

[2] The word שָׁעָה in post-Biblical Hebrew seems to be borrowed from the Aramaic, for otherwise it would naturally have *ō* in the first syllable.

of the passive particle מֵיתִי "brought" (see the latest editions of Gesenius' *Handwörterbuch*, s. v. אֵתָה). If this be thought unsatisfactory, there appears no way out of the difficulty but to suppose that הֵיתָיו is wrongly pointed, and that for הֵיתָיִת and שֵׁיצִיא we should read הַיְתִיו and שֵׁיצִיו. The meaning of הַצְדָא (v. 14) is very obscure. It is commonly rendered, "*Is it of set purpose?*" the ה being the interrogative particle, and צדא a noun equivalent to Hebr. צְדִיָה (Num. xxxv. 20, 22). That הַצְדָא is connected with the Targumic אַצְדִי "to mock" (Gesenius' *Handwörterbuch*, 11th ed. s. v. צדא) is very unlikely, since the form would be without analogy. Possibly we should read הַאַזְדָא "*is it certain?*" (cf. chap. ii. 5, 8); the Pĕshīttā has bĕḳushtā "in truth", and Theod. εἰ ἀληθῶς. In *v.* 15 the construction is of course elliptical, the apodosis being omitted in the first part, cf. Exod. xxxii. 32. The verb שֵׁיזִב (Syr. *shauzebh*) is derived from the Assyrio-Babylonian *shuzub* "to rescue", the Causative of *izibu* "to go away" (Hebr. עָזַב, Arab. 'azaba); the Syriac form seems to come nearer to the original. In *v.* 16 the Masoretic punctuation makes נְבוּכַדְנֶצַּר to be a Vocative, but it is more natural to take it as standing in apposition to מַלְכָּא (so Hitzig). "*We have no need to answer thee a word concerning this*", i.e. concerning the question asked by Nebuchadnezzar at the end of *v.* 15. With the construction פִּתְגָם לַהֲתָבוּתָךְ cf. I Kings xii. 6, 9, 16. פִּתְגָם is found also in Ezra, Esther, Ecclesiastes and the Targums; that פִּתְגָם, not פִּתְנַם, is the correct form, appears from the Syr. *pethĕghāmā* with aspirated *g*. The word is derived from the Old Persian *patigāma* (in mod. Persian *paighām* or *paigham*), properly, "motion towards" something, hence "message", "word"[1]. Verse 17, according to the Masoretic punctuation, can mean only, "*If our God, whom we serve, be able to deliver us, He will deliver (us) from the furnace of burning fire and out of thy hand, O king*", i.e. if our God be able to deliver at all, we shall be harmed neither by the fire nor by

[1] The Old Persian form is hypothetical—whether the vowel of the paenultima was long does not appear quite certain. In any case the form *pratigama*, which is sometimes given, is incorrect, as the Sanscrit *prati* occurs nowhere in Old Persian. *Paitigama* (Delitzsch, *Hoheslied und Koheleth*, p. 340) would be Zend.

any other punishment which thou mayest inflict. Von Lengerke unnecessarily alters the punctuation, so as to make the
protasis end with יְקֵדְתָּא ; he is accordingly obliged to render the
ו of וּמִן־יְדַי by "then" (Germ. "so"). Ewald translates הֵן "behold !"—a sense which it never bears in Biblical Aramaic. As
to the vocalization of אֱלָהָנָא and לְשֵׁיזָבוּתַנָא, see what has been
said on הוֹדַעְתֶּנָא chap. ii. 23. With יָכִל (where the primitive ĭ is
retained) compare נָחֵת chap. iv. 10, נְזַק vi. 3, דְּלִק vii. 9. Verse 18,
"And if not, be it known" etc., does not of course imply any real
doubt as to the divine power; the idea simply is that the deci-
sion of the speakers cannot be altered, come what may. The
expression "thy gods" (see also v. 12) is evidently introduced
for the purpose of assimilating the situation of Shadrach,
Meshach, and Abednego to that of the faithful Jews who
refused to worship the "gods" of Antiochus.

19—25. The plural form אשתנו (pron. אִשְׁתַּנּוּ—Kĕrī אִשְׁתַּנִּי,
Singular) agrees with אַנְפּוֹהִי; compare the construction in
II Sam. x. 9. With מֵזֵא from אֲזָא (which occurs in the Targums) cf. מְתָא v. 2. In the form with Suffix, מֵזְיֵהּ, the restoration of the primitive י accords with Syriac usage, cf. מִצְבְּיֵהּ chap.
iv. 32. For a parallel to the phrase חַד שִׁבְעָה "sevenfold", see
the Pĕshīṭtā, Exod. xvi. 5, ܣܒ ܗܕܡ ܟܠ ܕܩܝܡ
ܟܠܝܘܡ "twice as much as they gather every day". חֲזֵה
"fitting", "proper", is common in the later Jewish Aramaic (in
the Targums חֲזִי—so also חֲמִי from the synonymous verb חֲמָא).
The late Hebrew use of רָאוּי in this sense is doubtless an imitation of the Aramaic. For the transition of meaning, compare
Arab. maʿrūf "known", hence "equitable". In v. 20 לְמֵרְמֵא
depends upon the preceding לְכַפָּתָה. As to the passive Perfects
כְּפִיתוּ (v. 21) and רְמִיו, see what has been said on גְּלִי chap. ii. 19.
In v. 21 Theod., Aquila, Symm., and the Pĕshīṭtā[1], render
סַרְבָּלֵיהוֹן by "their trousers"—with which Von Lengerke, Hitzig,
and Ewald agree. De Lagarde (Gesammelte Abhandlungen, p.
206) and Fraenkel (Aramäische Lehnwörter, p. 48) derive the

---

[1] Theod. σὺν τοῖς σαραβάροις αὐτῶν—
Pĕsh. ܣܪܒܠܝܗܘܢ; Jerome
remarks, "Pro braccis, quas Symmachus ἀναξυρίδας interpretatus est, Aquila
et Theodotio saraballa dixerunt, et
non, ut corrupte legitur, sarabara".

word from Gr. σαράβαλλα (σαράβαρα), which is probably Persian (in mod. Persian *shalwār*), like the Syr. *sharbālā* and the Arab. *sirwāl*. Others translate "their tunics", cf. סַרְבְּלָא "tunic" in the Talmud, Arab. *sirbāl*; the origin of this term is unknown —it seems to have no connection with the above-mentioned words for "trousers", in spite of the close phonetic resemblance. פטישיהון (*Kěrī* פַּטְּשֵׁיהוֹן with *Dāghesh dirimens*), in the Pěshīṭṭā ܦܛܝ̈ܫܝܗܘܢ, Theod. τιάραις, is very obscure. The later Jews and Syrians evidently had no certain tradition as to the meaning of this term, which they explained sometimes as "trousers", sometimes as "tunic". The latter view is adopted by Gesenius, Von Lengerke, and Hitzig, but it can scarcely be said to rest on any real evidence. Bertholdt's identification of פטיש with the Greek πέτασος "broad-brimmed hat" is improbable on account of the ש[1]. That כַּרְבְּלָתְהוֹן means "their mantles" may be argued from the phrase מְכָרְבָּל בִּמְעִיל בּוּץ I Chr. xv. 27, but the connection of this word with the root כבל "to fasten" is very doubtful[2]. לְבוּשֵׁיהוֹן "their garments" is added for the purpose of including all their other articles of apparel. In v. 22 the passive participle אָזֵה is for אֲזֵה. On מַחְצְפָה see chap. ii. 15. שְׁבִיבָא (cf. שְׁבִבִין דִּי־נוּר chap. vii. 9 and שְׁבִיב אִשּׁוֹ Job xviii. 5) is not necessarily akin to the Syr. *shābh* "to burn", still less to the Arab. *shabba* (since ش corresponds etymologically to Aram. שׂ, ס), but seems to mean primarily a "streak" or "tongue" (cf. Syr. *shěbhībhā* "cord", Arab. *sabīb* "wisp of hair", and *sabība* "streak of blood"); hence שְׁבִיב requires to be specified by the addition of a word for "fire". In v. 23 תְּלָתֵּיהוֹן (so Baer rightly reads, according to the Masora, not תְּלָתְהוֹן) exactly corresponds to the Syr. *tělātaihōn*, which appears to have been formed on

---

[1] From a passage in the מדרש איכה (cited by Levy in his *Neuheb. u. Chald. Wörterbuch*, s.v. פטיש) it might appear that in Jewish Aramaic פטיש meant something worn on the feet, i.e. a kind of "shoe". But from this passage no conclusion can be drawn, as the reading is uncertain.

[2] The later Jewish Aramaic כרבלתא "comb of a cock" probably has a dif-

ferent origin. But this word gave rise to the Rabbinical notion that in Daniel כרבלתהון signifies "their headcoverings"; hence the English Authorized Version renders "their hats". It may be remembered that George Fox the Quaker deduced from this passage the celebrated doctrine that men ought not to take off their hats to royalty.

the analogy of *tĕraihōn* "they two", though this would still
leave unexplained the hardening of the *t*. In *v.* 24 occurs a
very strange word, הַדָּֽבְרוֹהִי, which is peculiar to Daniel and
always appears in the Plural (*v.* 27; iv. 33; vi. 8). In each
case the context shews that הדבריא is a term referring to the
personal attendants of the king, but the origin of the word is
unknown. The notion, formerly held by Gesenius, that it means
"leaders", "guides", from the Semitic root דבר, and that the
initial ה is the Hebrew article, may be dismissed at once.
Several attempts have been made to explain the word from the
Persian, but none are satisfactory. All that can be said is that
we probably have here some Persian title ending in *bara* (cf.
גזבר, דתבר), and that the beginning of the word may have been
distorted in pronunciation[1]. In *v.* 25, as in chap. iv. 34, we
should certainly expect the Pael מְהַלְּכִין, as some MSS. actually
read, instead of the Haphel מַהְלְכִין (cf. Kautzsch, *Gramm.* p. 58).
The term בַּר אֱלָהִין, as applied to an angel or other heavenly
being, is in accordance with Gen. vi. 2. Job i. 6. It is, of
course, absurd to argue that this expression implies any particular acquaintance with Babylonian mythology.

26—30. Nebuchadnezzar, on seeing the three Jews un-
harmed and accompanied by an angelic figure, draws near to the
door of the furnace. The exact nature of the furnace here mentioned is not clear, but it would seem that there was an opening
above from which the men were thrown (*v.* 20), and at the side
a door through which they could come out. In the phrase
לָא־שְׁלֵט נוּרָא (*v.* 27) the subst. נוּרָא is construed as masc. (cf.
נוּר דָּלִק chap. vii. 9), whereas it is usually fem., as in Syriac[2]. On
the other hand עֲדָת seems to agree in gender with נוּר, according
to the construction in *v.* 19, since רֵיחַ is never fem. For the

---

[1] That הדבר comes from a Persian
word *hamdāwar*, is an unfortunate
speculation of Von Bohlen, which has
been adopted in the recent editions of
Gesenius' *Handwörterbuch*. The Persian *dāwar*, "judge", is a modern contraction (see *vv.* 2 and 3 of this chapter), and *hamdāwar*, if it meant anything, would mean, not "one who

judges conjointly" with somebody else,
but "one who has the same judge"
as somebody else, cf. in Old Persian
hamapitā "born of the same father",
and the numerous modern Persian
words with the prefix *ham*.

[2] Similarly the Arab. *nār* is fem. in
most cases, rarely masc.

plur. נשמיהון, the *Ḳĕrī* unnecessarily substitutes the Singular. Why the "trousers" (assuming this to be the meaning of סַרְבָּלֵיהוֹן) are specially mentioned, is not obvious at first, but probably this article of apparel was made, as in parts of the modern East, of some light and consequently inflammable material. לָא שְׁנוֹ "*had not changed (in colour)*", cf. chap. v. 9. The suffix in בְּהוֹן presumably refers to גֻּבְרַיָּא אִלֵּךְ. In *v.* 29 the decree issued by the king is of a very strange character, inasmuch as he threatens "nations" with a punishment possible only in the case of individuals (cf. chap. ii. 5. Ezra vi. 11); the word בַּיְתֵהּ, "his house", shews that the author is here using a current phrase. שלה is taken by the Masoretes and by most modern commentators as a scribal error for שָׁלוּ "carelessness" (chap. vi. 5. Ezra iv. 22; vi. 9), hence "*any thing amiss*". But probably Hitzig is right in reading שָׁלָה "*word*" (for שְׁאָלָה, cf. chap. iv. 14. I Sam. i. 17). With יֻכַּל (and תֻּכַּל chap. v. 16) compare the יִכּוֹל of the Targums; in the Christian Palestinian dialect also, verbs פ״י often take *o* in the second syllable of the Imperfect (*Z. D. M. G.* XXII. 500). כִּדְנָה "thus", cf. Ezra v. 7; much less natural is the rendering of Von Lengerke and Hitzig "like this (God)".

CHAPTER IV.

(III. 31—IV. 34.)

The last three verses of Chapter iii. evidently belong to what follows, and in the modern versions they accordingly are joined to Chapter iv. This piece is a narrative in the form of an epistle—purporting to be addressed by king Nebuchadnezzar to "all the peoples, nations, and languages that dwell in all the earth". But that this epistle is really by the same author who wrote the preceding and the following chapters must be admitted by everybody, or there is an end of all argument based on internal evidence. One peculiarity which cannot fail to strike the reader, is that in the middle of the narrative (chap. iv. 25—30) the author, forgetting for the moment that he is writing in the name of Nebuchadnezzar, speaks of the king in the third person, but afterwards returns to the first (*vv.* 31 —34).

The purpose of this piece is different from that of the preceding. It is not a warning against the Gentile religion, but a demonstration of the real helplessness of the Gentile power in the presence of the True God. To the Jewish subjects of Antiochus Epiphanes the king's power might well seem irresistible; accordingly the author here teaches, for the encouragement of his despairing brethren, that the mightiest of men has no more strength against God than the meanest, that by the divine decree a great king may in a moment be degraded not merely to the level of a beggar but to that of a brute. In order to heighten the effect of this moral lesson, Nebuchadnezzar himself, the subject of the story, is introduced as the narrator.

The question whether the narrative is based upon any historical event or tradition, has often been discussed. The Christian Fathers, who defended its truth against Porphyry, evidently knew of no external testimony that confirmed it, nor have the discoveries of modern Assyriologists thrown the smallest light upon the subject. Hengstenberg and others have appealed with great confidence to a fragment of Berossus, where it is said that Nebuchadnezzar "fell ill and died" ($\dot{\epsilon}\mu\pi\epsilon\sigma\dot{\omega}\nu$ $\epsilon\dot{\iota}\varsigma$ $\dot{a}\rho\rho\omega\sigma\tau\dot{\iota}a\nu$ $\mu\epsilon\tau\eta\lambda\lambda\dot{a}\xi a\tau o$ $\tau\dot{o}\nu$ $\beta\dot{\iota}o\nu$, see Josephus, *Contra Ap.* I. 20). But to argue from this that Nebuchadnezzar's illness must have been of a very extraordinary nature, is absurd, for Berossus uses almost the same words in speaking of the death of Nebuchadnezzar's father (*ibid.* I. 19).

Very much more worthy of notice is a fragment of the historian Abydenus, which Eusebius has preserved (*Praep. Evang.* IX. 41). The passage is as follows: "This also have I found concerning Nebuchadnezzar in the book of Abydenus *On the Assyrians.* Megasthenes relates that Nebuchadrezzar became mightier than Herakles and made war upon Libya and Iberia; having conquered these countries he transported some of their

inhabitants to the eastern shore of the Sea. Afterwards, as the
Chaldean story goes, when he had ascended the roof of his
palace, he was inspired by some god or other, and cried aloud,
' O men of Babylon, lo I Nebuchadrezzar announce to you the
future calamity, which neither Bel my ancestor nor our queen
Beltis can persuade the Fates to avert. There shall come a
Persian, a mule, who shall have your own gods as his allies, and
he shall make you slaves. Moreover he who shall help to bring
this about shall be [the son] of a Median woman, the boast of
the Assyrians[1]. Would that, before his countrymen perish[2],
some whirlpool or flood might seize him and destroy him
utterly! or else would that he might betake himself to some
other place, and might be driven through the desert, where is
no city nor track of men, where wild beasts seek their food and
birds fly hither and thither, would that among rocks and mountain clefts he might wander alone! And as for me, may I,
before he imagines this, meet with some happier end!' When
he had thus prophesied, he suddenly vanished"[3].

Obscure as this passage is in some of its details, one fact
may be regarded as certain, viz. that we have here a popular
legend of Babylonian origin, coloured, of course, by the Greek
medium through which it has passed. The prophecy put into
the mouth of Nebuchadnezzar evidently refers to the overthrow
of the Babylonian Empire by Cyrus, "the mule". The "son of
a Median woman" (assuming this to be the original reading) is
the last Babylonian king, Nabūnāid, who is represented as
having a share in the ruin of his country[4].

---

[1] Instead of οὗ δὴ συναίτιος ἔσται Μήδης, τὸ Ἀσσύριον αὔχημα Von Gutschmid
proposes to read οὗ δὴ συναίτιος υἱὸς
ἔσται Μήδης, τὸ Ἀσσυρίων αὔχημα.

[2] Instead of δοῦναι Toup proposes
δῦναι.

[3] For a minute discussion of this
passage see Prof. Schrader's essay in
the *Jahrbücher für Protestantische
Theologie* for the year 1881.

[4] It would appear that the popular
Babylonian legend made the last Babylonian king a son of Nebuchadnezzar,

who had a Median wife (Berossus, ap.
Jos. *Contra Ap.* I. 19). Hence arose
the notion, which we find in Herodotus (Bk I. 188), that the last Babylonian king, Labynetus II. (i.e. Nabūnāid) was a son of Labynetus I. (i.e.
Nebuchadnezzar). In Daniel likewise,
Nebuchadnezzar's son (Belshazzar) is
the last Babylonian king. Thus Daniel agrees with the Babylonian legend
and with Herodotus in a point where
both are opposed to historical truth.
Abydenus who relates the legend was,

The resemblances between the narrative in Daniel and the Babylonian legend in Abydenus can scarcely be accidental. But to suppose that either story has been directly borrowed from the other is impossible. It would appear that of the two stories that in Abydenus is on the whole the more primitive. Its local character is strongly marked, and it shews no signs of having been deliberately altered to serve a didactic purpose. In Daniel, on the other hand, we find a narrative which contains scarcely anything specifically Babylonian, but which is obviously intended to teach a moral lesson. It is therefore probable that some Babylonian legend on the subject of Nebuchadnezzar had, perhaps in a very distorted form, reached the ears of the author of Daniel, who modified the story in order to make it a vehicle of religious instruction. That this may have been the case will hardly be denied by any one who considers that, in the second century before Christ, many thousands of Jews were settled in Babylonia and kept up constant communication with their co-religionists in Palestine.

Chap. iii. 31—33. The Prologue of the Epistle. On the form דָּאֲרִין see chap. ii. 38. Instead of the formula יִשְׂגֵּא שְׁלָמְכוֹן (cf. chap. vi. 26) we find also, at the beginning of epistles, שְׁלָמָא כֹלָּא (Ezra v. 7), and in Syriac usually the simple *shĕlām*. For the temporal sense of עַם in עַם־דָּר וְדָר (*v.* 33) cf. עַם לֵילְיָא chap. vii. 2, the Hebrew עַם שֶׁמֶשׁ Ps. lxxii. 5, and the Arabic *ma'a d-dahr* "with time", i.e. "as long as time lasts"[1].

Chap. iv. 1—6. The narrative now begins. שְׁלֵה "restful", "secure", and hence "prosperous", is an adj. of the same form as נְקֵא chap. vii. 9. רַעֲנַן, probably borrowed from the Hebrew, does not occur elsewhere in Aramaic; for the metaphor see Ps. xcii. 15. הֵיכַל is usually supposed to be identical with the Assyrio-Babylonian *ikallu* "palace"; in any case this word, whatever its origin, must have been very widely diffused, since it is found already in Amos viii. 3 and many centuries later was employed both in the Aramaic dialects and in Arabic. For the use of the Imperfect in *v.* 2, see p. 37. Instead of הַנְעָלָה (*v.* 3)

like Berossus, perfectly aware that in reality there reigned several kings between Nebuchadnezzar and Nabūnāid, and that the former was not the father of the latter.

[1] See Elfachri, ed. Ahlwardt, p. 117.

we also find הֶעָלָה chap. v. 7. In *v.* 4 עללין (*Kĕrī* עָלִּין, which agrees with the Syriac form) is from a Singular עָלֵל or עֲלָל (not עָאֵל as in Syriac), used in the Targums, in Christian Palestinian, and in Palmyrene (see *Z. D. M. G.* XXXVII. 566)—cf. also chap. v. 8. וְעַד אחרין (*v.* 5) is usually taken to mean "*and (so it was) till at last*" etc. Gesenius believed אחרין (*Kĕrī* אָחֳרָן, not אָחֳרֵן as most editions read) to be an adj. in the Singular, used adverbially. According to Hitzig it refers to Daniel, "*and (so they came) till, as last man, Daniel entered*" etc.; Hävernick and Von Lengerke explain it as a plural form. But nowhere else does אחרין or אחרן mean "last" or "at last", and it is therefore probable that we should read וְעַד אָחֳרָן "*and yet another entered*" etc., as J. D. Michaelis renders. The *Kĕthīb* אחרין represents another pronunciation of אָחֳרָן, the *ā* being weakened to *ē*, cf. the Christian Palestinian חורין "another". In שֻׁם (cf. Ezra v. 1, in the Targums שׁוּם), the primitive *ĭ* has been changed to *u* through the influence of the following labial; see what has been said on גֻּבְרִין chap. iii. 8. As to the name בלטשאצר cf. chap. i. 7. The phrase דִּי רוּחַ־אֱלָהִין קַדִּישִׁין בֵּהּ seems to be imitated from Gen. xli. 38 אִישׁ אֲשֶׁר רוּחַ אֱלֹהִים בּוֹ. "The holy gods" was, in all probability, an expression commonly used by the heathens of Syria, since it occurs in Phoenician inscriptions (האלנם הקרשם, in the Inscription of Eshmun-ʿazar). In *v.* 6 Daniel is described as "*chief of the magicians*", referring to chap. ii. 48. אֲנֵס is apparently "*reduces to straits*"; in Esth. i. 8 (the only other passage in the Old Testament where this verb occurs) it means "to compel", as it does in the Talmud.

7—15. The imagery in the dream which Nebuchadnezzar now relates is obviously borrowed in great part from Ezek. xxxi. 3—14. "*And as for the visions of my head upon my bed, I looked and behold*" etc. The king first perceives a great tree, and afterwards, in *v.* 8, sees it become yet greater and stronger; for the sequence of the tenses in *v.* 8, cf. *vv.* 2, 31. חֲזוֹתֵהּ "*the sight thereof*", is, if correctly pointed, from a form similar to Syr. ṣĕlōthā "prayer", mĕḥōthā "blow", but perhaps we should pronounce חָזוּתֵהּ (cf. chap. viii. 5, and Kautzsch, *Gramm.* p. 115). Theodotion has τὸ κύτος αὐτοῦ "its expanse", which is probably a mere guess. In any case we have no right to assume, with

Hitzig and Ewald, that חזות means "breadth", and to connect
it with the Arab. *ḥauza* or the Hebr. חָזֶה "breast". With עָפְיֵהּ
(*v.* 9) "the foliage thereof", cf. עֲפָאִים (for עֲפָיִים) Ps. civ. 12. On
אִנְבֵּהּ for אִבְּהּ, see what has been said on אַנְדַּע chap. ii. 9. מָזוֹן,
like the corresponding Syr. *māzōnā*, has a long vowel in the
first syllable. Nöldeke is inclined to regard this *mā* as a very
ancient form of the prefix (*Mand. Gramm.* p. 130). In תִּמְלַל
(as contrasted with תְּדֻק chap. ii. 40, 44) we have one of the very
rare instances, in Aramaic, of a geminate verb uncontracted in
the Haphel, cf. Hebr. הַרְנִינוּ, אַרְנֵן, תַּרְנִין. For ידרון (i.e. יֵדְרוּן) the
Ḳĕrī substitutes the fem. form יְדֻרָן (cf. *v.* 18); in the Targums
the substantive צְפַר or צִיפַּר (of which the Sing. does not happen
to occur in Biblical Aramaic) is, like the Hebr. צִפּוֹר, usually
feminine. In *v.* 10 the angel who descends from heaven is
described as "*a watcher and a holy one*". Here for the first
time in Jewish literature we find this peculiar use of עִיר
"watcher"; in the Book of Enoch the term is extremely common, as also in the Syriac Fathers. There is no reason to
suppose that in Daniel the word "watcher" refers, as it does in
some patristic writings, to a particular class of angels; in Enoch
it is used, sometimes at least, for angels generally (see Dill-
mann, *Das Buch Henoch übersetzt und erklärt*, pp. 104, 105).
With קַדִּישׁ, as applied to an angel, cf. Hebr. קְדֹשִׁים in Zech. xiv.
5. Ps. lxxxix. 6. Job xv. 15; the last passage clearly shews
that when angels are called "holy", this conveys no idea of
moral purity or goodness, but expresses the awfulness and mys-
teriousness of their nature[1]. It is therefore quite fanciful to
assume, with Von Lengerke and others, that this angel is designated as "holy" in order to distinguish him from the fallen
angels; עִיר וְקַדִּישׁ is merely a collocation after the fashion of
גֵּר וְתוֹשָׁב Gen. xxiii. 4 etc. On the vocalization of נְחַת, see יְכֻל
chap. iii. 17. To whom the angel is speaking in *vv.* 11 and 12
we are not told. Possibly this vagueness is intentional, indicating that the judgment upon the king is to be brought about
by wholly inscrutable means. "*Nevertheless leave ye the stump*

---

[1] On the phrase "a watcher and a
holy one" the Christian Father Polychronius remarks, ἅγιον καλεῖ οἷον ἐξαί-
ρετόν τινα παρὰ πάντας τοὺς ἀνθρώπους
κεκτημένον τὴν φύσιν.

of its roots in the earth" (*v.* 12) evidently means that the punishment does not involve total destruction—a hope of restoration still remains (Job xiv. 7—9). But the following words, "*and with a band of iron and brass in the grass of the field*", are certainly obscure. It is very far-fetched to refer this to "the chains with which madmen are bound" (Jerome), or to "the bands of iron put round a tree to prevent it from cracking" (Von Lengerke). Hitzig and Ewald take the phrase as metaphorical, though neither makes it quite clear. Perhaps the most natural supposition is that since "iron" and "brass" are familiar types of firmness and unflinching severity (Deut. xxviii. 48. Jer. i. 18. Micah iv. 13), "the band of iron and brass" is a figure of speech for the stern and crushing sentence under which the king is to lie (see *v.* 14). עִקַּר is, of course, for עְקַר, the second vowel being primitively long, as in חִוָּר "white" (chap. vii. 9); see Kautzsch, *Gramm.* p. 109. The last clause of *v.* 12 is rendered by Von Lengerke "*and with the beasts let him share the herbs of the ground*"—according to which interpretation the author here drops the metaphor of a tree and speaks of Nebuchadnezzar in literal terms (cf. *v.* 30). That such is the case in *v.* 13 is obvious—"*Let his heart be changed from man's*"; אנושא (*Kĕrī* אֲנָשָׁא) is scarcely a Hebraism, since אנוש occurs in Nabatean (Euting, *Nab. Inschr.* N°. 9). מִן־אנושא is equivalent to מִן־לְבַב אנושא (cf. chap. i. 10), and the use of מִן is like that in I Sam. xv. 23. I Kings xv. 13. Less probable is the view of Von Lengerke, who translates "*away from men*", i.e. the king's heart is to be changed so that he will be driven from human society (*vv.* 22, 30). Here the "heart" is, as usual, the intelligence. By "*seven times*" are meant, it would seem, seven years (see chap. vii. 25); so at least the phrase is interpreted by Josephus (*Antiq.* x. 10. 6), by Rashi, by Ben-Ezra, and by most modern commentators. With בִּגְזֵרַת עִירִין "*by the decree of the watchers*" (*v.* 14) compare what has been said on גְּזֵרִין chap. ii. 27. שְׁאֵלְתָּא, properly "the petition", is here a synonym of פִּתְגָמָא "the word", cf. Arab. *ḥāja*, properly "want", hence sometimes "affair", "business"—see also chap. iii. 29. That in this passage the "watchers" are identical with the "holy ones" is shewn by *v.* 10. The use of עִירִין and קַדִּישִׁין instead of עִירַיָּא and

קַדִּישַׁיָּא is in imitation of the poetical style (cf. מְקֻדָּשִׁים Job v. 1). עַד־דִּבְרַת is perhaps a mistake for עַל־דִּבְרַת (chap. ii. 30). With שְׁפַל אֲנָשִׁים "*the meanest of men*", compare כְּסִיל אָדָם Prov. xv. 20. אנשים, אלפים (chap. vii. 10, *Kethîb*), and מַלְכִים (Ezra iv. 13) are the only examples, in Biblical Aramaic, of the plural in *îm*; Kautzsch regards the two first as scribal errors (*Gramm.* p. 85). In *v.* 15 the *Kěrî* unnecessarily substitutes פִּשְׁרֵהּ for פִּשְׁרָא, cf. also *v.* 16.

16—24. On hearing the vision Daniel "*was astonied as it were for a moment*". אֶשְׁתּוֹמַם is a hybrid form, based upon the Hebr. הִשְׁתּוֹמֵם (cf. וָאֶשְׁתּוֹמֵם chap. viii. 27), with change of the ה to א after the analogy of the later Jewish Aramaic (see p. 37); here only do we find *Segôl* in the prefix. Hitzig renders כְּשָׁעָה חֲדָה "*about an hour's time*" (wohl eine Stunde lang). But the כ does not necessarily imply that what follows is a fixed measure (cf. כְּמֶעַט רֶגַע Is. xxvi. 20), and חֲדָה corresponds merely to our indefinite article (cf. אֶחָד chap. viii. 13). In יְבַהֲלָךְ the suffix is added to the simple form of the Imperfect (i.e. without the usual insertion of *in*, as in יְשֵׁיזְבִנָּךְ chap. vi. 17), after the fashion of the East-Aramaic dialects. It is possible that we should read יְבַהֲלָךְ (Jussive, as in the parallel passage, chap. v. 10), since the syntax here admits either of a singular or a plural verb. As to the form מראי (*Kěrî* מָרִי) see what has been said on מָרֵה chap. ii. 47. Before interpreting the dream Daniel repeats it, with some variations. This repetition greatly increases the rhetorical effect of the announcement אנתה הוא מלכא "*it is thou, O king*" (*v.* 19). Instead of the *Kěthîb* רבית (i.e. רְבַיְתָ "thou hast grown") the Masoretes, for no apparent reason, read רְבַת, which would be 3rd pers. fem. The form רְבוּתָךְ (with *Shěwā* in the first syllable, cf. also רְבוּ *v.* 33 and רְבוּתָא *v.* 18; vii. 24[1]) is very peculiar, for the analogy of Syriac would lead us to expect רַבּוּתָךְ "thy greatness", the abstract noun from רַב, רַבָּא "great". Perhaps the following verb רְבָת may have suggested to the Masoretes that the clause meant "thy growth has grown", which would lead to the pronunciation רְבוּתָךְ, and this passage may have influenced the others. For the construction of *v.* 20 see chap.

[1] So also in the Targums with Babylonian vocalization, see Merx, *Chrestom. Targ.* Glossary.

ii. 41, 43. In *v.* 21 that which before has been termed "the decree of the watchers" (*v.* 14) is called "the decree of the Most High". The *Kĕthīb* מטית (*Kĕrī* מְטָת), instead of which most editions have מְטָת, is either a mere blunder, as Kautzsch supposes (*Gramm.* p. 79), or else may have arisen out of another reading מטיה (participle). Verse 23, "*And that they commanded* (i.e. it was commanded) *to leave the stump of the roots of the tree (signifieth that) thy kingdom (shall be) secure to thee from the time when thou shalt recognize that the heavens rule*". Very remarkable is the use of שְׁמַיָּא, "the heavens", for "God". This is without analogy in the Old Testament, but exactly agrees with the use of שָׁמַיִם in the Mishnah (cf. ἡ βασιλεία τῶν οὐρανῶν in the New Testament). On the meaning of לְהֵן (*v.* 24) see chap. ii. 6. חטיך (*Kĕrī* חַטָאָךְ with א for the consonantal י, as in עִלָּאָה for עִלָּיָא) is probably for חטייך, i.e. a Plural of חֲטִי, Syr. ḥĕṭāhā (so Hitzig). Kautzsch regards the word as a Singular (*Gramm.* p. 104). That צִדְקָה (stat. absol. fem., without the change of צ into ט which this root exhibits in Syriac) is not a Hebraism but genuine Aramaic, appears from the occurrence of צדקתא "the due" in the Inscription of Taimā[1]. This proves also that long before the book of Daniel was written the word had acquired the special sense of a "payment for religious purposes", so that Theodotion is possibly right in rendering בְּצִדְקָה ἐν ἐλεημοσύναις "by alms-giving"; צְדָקָה often has this meaning in the Talmud, and quite similar is the Syr. zedhkĕthā. Von Lengerke, Ewald and others, prefer to translate "*by righteousness*". פְּרֻק (Theod. λύτρωσαι, Vulg. redime) is rendered "redeem" by Hitzig and Ewald. But though פרק, both in Hebrew (Ps. cxxxvi. 24) and Syriac, may mean to "redeem" persons, it never signifies to "expiate" offences, for ܦܢܘܩ, which the Pĕshīṭṭā here employs, proves nothing as to native Syriac usage. More probably we should translate, with Von Lengerke, "break off," "cast away"; the metaphor is taken from the breaking of a yoke (cf. וּפָרַקְתָּ עֻלּוֹ מֵעַל צַוָּארֶךָ Gen. xxvii. 40, as also in the Mishnah כל הפורק ממנו עול תורה "every man who casts off the yoke of the Law", *Ābōth* III. 9). עֲוָיָתָךְ (in the less

---

[1] See Nöldeke's article, "Altara-　　　　*Sitzungsberichte der königl. preuss.* mäische Inschriften aus Teimâ," in the　　*Akademie der Wissenschaften*, 1884.

correct editions עֲוָיָתָךְ) presupposes a singular עֲוָיְתָא stat. absol.
עֲוָיָא (see the Targum, Ps. li. 4, 7); to derive it from a Singular
עֲוָתָא (Kautzsch, *Gramm.* p. 102) is contrary to analogy, since
the Plural would then be עֲוָנְתָא. With בְּמְחַן עֲנִין cf. מָחוֹגֵן עניים
(*Kĕrī*, 'מ עֲנָוִים) Prov. xiv. 21. עֲנִין (not עֲנָיִן, as most editions
have) is for עֲנָיִין, from עֲנִי which may have been formed, after a
false analogy, in imitation of Hebr. עָנִי. " *If haply there may be
a lengthening of thy prosperity*"—for הֵן in this sense cf. Ezra v.
17; Von Lengerke points out the similarity of this clause to
Acts viii. 22, "repent......if haply (εἰ ἄρα) the thought of thy
heart may be forgiven thee". Hitzig renders, " *If thy prosperity
is to be lasting*", taking הֵן as simply conditional.   אַרְכָה (pointed
as if from a primitive form *arakat*) has the same meaning here
as in chap. vii. 12 (cf. Ezek. xii. 22), and שְׁלֵוְתָךְ seems to be an
abstract noun corresponding to the adj. שְׁלֵה in *v.* 1.   The
Pĕshīttā renders this clause " until He removes *thy sins* far
from thee", pronouncing שְׁלִוּתָךְ or שְׁלְוָתָךְ, instead of שְׁלֵוְתָךְ.   So
also Ewald interprets, and, substituting אַרְכָה " healing" (Is. lvii.
8) for אַרְכָה, he translates " *If haply thy folly may be healed*".

25—34. In כֹּלָּא, " *all this*", the emphatic termination has
the force of a demonstrative.   עַל הֵיכַל מַלְכוּתָא דִּי בָבֶל (*v.* 26) " *on
(the roof of) the royal palace at Babylon*", cf. II Sam. xi. 2.   In
v. 27 בְּנַיְתַהּ is far better attested than בְּנֵיתַהּ, but is altogether
anomalous.   In the Old Testament " to build a city" often
means nothing more than to fortify it or erect buildings within
it (II Chron. xi. 5, 6).   לְבֵית מַלְכוּ " *for a royal residence*", cf.
בֵּית מַמְלָכָה Amos vii. 13.   Instead of בִּתְקַף we should rather
expect בִּתְקֹף (as some editions read, though on insufficient authority), or else בִּתְקַף, after the analogy of רְנַז, כְּתַל.   Perhaps the
vocalization בִּתְקַף may have arisen from an attempt to assimilate this word to the following לִיקָר.   In *v.* 30 the effect of
the sentence upon Nebuchadnezzar is described — since " the
heart of a brute" (*v.* 13) has been given him, he becomes gradually changed in outward appearance.   The last part of the
verse is of course elliptical—כְּנִשְׁרִין " *like (the feathers of) eagles,
כְּצִפְּרִין like (the claws of) birds*", cf. מִן־אֲנוּשָׁא in *v.* 13.   The comparing of hair to plumage is not unnatural, as Meinhold sup-
poses, nor is there any reason to doubt the accuracy of the text;

the special mention of "eagles" is due to the length of their feathers (Ezek. xvii. 3). The Aramaic טפר (Syr. *ṭephru*), like its Arabic equivalent ظٌفُر, applies equally to the nails of human beings, the claws of birds, and the hoofs of quadrupeds (cf. chap. vii. 19). In *v*. 31 "the days" are the seven years before mentioned (*vv*. 13, 22, 29). That Nebuchadnezzar recovers his reason on looking heavenwards offers a curious parallel with Euripides, *Bacchae* 1265 ff., where the same thing happens to the frenzied Agauē. The resemblance is the more remarkable because the Bacchants, like Nebuchadnezzar, are in some sort assimilated to animals—they not only wear the skins of beasts but also suckle young fawns and wolves (*Bacchae*, 699). Both in Daniel and in Euripides the looking heavenwards indicates a return to humanity. This conception is perhaps based upon some popular superstition. With חַי עָלְמָא cf. חֵי הָעוֹלָם chap. xii. 7. The latter part of *v*. 31 and the whole of *v*. 32 form a parenthesis; in *v*. 33 the author takes up the narrative again by repeating the statement in *v*. 31 that Nebuchadnezzar recovered his reason, and the effects of the change are then described. It is quite unnecessary to suppose, with Hitzig, that *v*. 31 and *v*. 33 refer to separate events. Verse 32 is in part suggested by Is. xl. 17. כְּלָה חֲשִׁיבִין is usually rendered "*are counted as nought*" (Theod. ὡς οὐδὲν ἐλογίσθησαν—so also the Pĕshīttā). According to this interpretation לָה (elsewhere written לָא) is here used as a substantive, "nothingness". But for this there is no analogy either in Aramaic or Hebrew, for from Job vi. 21 no safe conclusion can be drawn. The Talmud, *Yōmā* 20ᵇ, explains that לה here means חרגא "mote"—which is, of course, a mere fancy. Perhaps we should take לה חשיבין as a single conception, "*persons of no account*", cf. in Hebrew לוֹא לֶחֶם "that which is not bread", Is. lv. 2, and the Targum, Is. liii. 3, בסירין ולא חשיבין "despised and not respected". חֵיל שְׁמַיָּא "*the host of heaven*", is a phrase used both of the angels and of the stars, for the latter, as is well known, were often regarded as living beings[1]. "*There is none who can reprove Him, and say to Him,*

---

[1] Such passages as Is. xl. 26 and Job xxxviii. 7 admit of being taken as mere poetical metaphors, but more than this must be meant in the Book

What hast Thou done?" cf. Job ix. 12. Eccles. viii. 4. The phrase " to strike on the hand", i.e. to reprove, interfere with, is found in the Hebrew of the Mishnah (*Pĕsāḥīm* IV. 8, מיחו בידם " they reproved them") and elsewhere in later Jewish literature. In *v.* 33 the words וְלִיקָר מַלְכוּתִי הַדְרִי וְזִיוִי יְתוּב עֲלַי are omitted in the Pĕshīttā—but this is a mere blunder, due to the homoioteleuton יתוב עלי. Von Lengerke renders, *"And moreover to the renown of my kingdom, of my majesty, and of my splendour, it* (i.e. מַנְדְּעִי " my reason") *returned to me"*. Hitzig and others take ל as introducing the subject of the clause, *"and also the glory of my kingdom, my majesty and my splendour returned to me"*—but the passages cited by Hitzig in support of this are not conclusive. Rosenmüller takes הדרי וזיוי alone as the subject, *" And to the glory of my kingdom my majesty and my splendour returned to me"*, and explains ליקר מלכותי as meaning " ut gubernatio mea et regni administratio debito gauderet aestimio civibusque proficua esset". Instead of יְבְעוֹן (so Baer, in most editions יְבָעוֹן) we should expect יְבְעוֹן, since the Pael of this verb is not employed elsewhere. For הָתְקְנַת " *I was established*" most MSS. have הָתְקְנַת which, if intended for the 1st pers., is quite anomalous. On the use of the Hophal in Biblical Aramaic, see p. 37, and compare, besides הוּסְפַת in this verse, chaps. v. 13, 15, 20; vi. 24; vii. 4, 11. The verb תקן " to be straight" occurs in Biblical Hebrew in the Ḳal and Piel only (Eccles. i. 15; vii. 13; xii. 9), but in the Targums, as in Syriac, the Aphel אתקן is found[1]. In *v.* 34, מרומם is, of course, borrowed from the Hebrew; the verb רומם " to exalt" occurs again in the Targums and in Christian Palestinian, which shews that it had really passed into common use. On מַהְלְכִין see chap. iii. 25. In this last verse the author sums up the teaching which the chapter is intended to convey.

of Enoch (xviii. 14—16), where we read of a prison " for the stars of heaven and the host of heaven". These stars, we are told, are fallen angels. See also Rev. ix. 1.

[1] The root תקן probably has no con-

nection with the Arabic *yaḳina* "to be sure", since this latter is derived, through the Aramaic, from Gr. εἰκών; see Fraenkel, *Aramäische Fremdwörter*, p. 273.

98

CHAPTER V.

(V. 1—VI. 1.)

The Fifth Chapter of Daniel relates events which are said
to have taken place at the end of the reign of the Chaldean
king Belshazzar (*v.* 30), son of Nebuchadnezzar (*vv.* 2, 11, 13,
18, 22). The question whether king Belshazzar ever existed,
has already been discussed (p. 18). We have seen that Nabūnāid, the last Babylonian king, really had a son named Bīl-
shar-uṣur. As to the end of this prince nothing is known, for
Prof. Schrader's suggestion that he may have been slain in
battle at the time of the fall of Babylon (*Cuneif. Inscr.* p. 435),
seems to be a mere hypothesis. That the name Belshazzar is
of Babylonian origin cannot be doubted, but what legends connected with the name may have reached the author of Daniel,
it is impossible to say.

The general teaching of this chapter has considerable
affinity with that of the preceding one. In both we see the
representative of the heathen power exalting himself in utter
forgetfulness of the True God, and smitten forthwith by a sudden and mysterious judgment. But in this chapter the author
makes far more obvious allusions to the circumstances of his
own time than in chap. iv. The offence of Nebuchadnezzar is
simply pride, whereas Belshazzar commits the more heinous
crime of profaning the vessels taken from the Temple at Jerusalem and of bestowing upon idols the worship due to the True
God only (*v.* 23). So far Belshazzar answers exactly to Antiochus Epiphanes. But here, as elsewhere, the author of Daniel
introduces into the narrative elements which are purely ideal.
Thus the honour which Belshazzar pays to Daniel cannot have
been suggested by anything in the conduct of Antiochus, but
serves to shew how the Gentile power must in the end be
brought to reverence the representatives of the God of Israel.

1—5. בלשאצר, less correctly בלאשצר (*v.* 30; vii. 1; viii. 1),

is, as we have seen, a corruption of *Bīl-shar-uṣur*, i.e. "Bel,
preserve thou the king!" With עֲבַד לְחֶם "he made a feast" cf.
the corresponding Hebrew phrase עֹשִׂים לֶחֶם Eccles. x. 19. The
words *"and in the presence of the thousand he was drinking wine"*
are added for a special reason, since in the ancient East kings
usually feasted in an apartment by themselves or with a few
persons only (Athenaeus, Bk IV. p. 145). בְּטְעֵם חַמְרָא (*v.* 2) *"as
they tasted the wine"*, i.e. in the midst of the revel; here only in
Biblical Aramaic is טְעֵם used in its literal sense—the Hebr. טַעַם
also may be either literal (Num. xi. 8) or metaphorical (Prov.
xi. 22). The mention of the vessels which Nebuchadnezzar
brought from the Temple at Jerusalem evidently refers back to
chap. i. 2, מָאנַיָּא being exactly equivalent in meaning to the
Hebr. כְּלִים. מָאן (which happens not to occur in the Singular in
Bibl. Aram.) can, of course, have no connection with מָן "what?"
(as is suggested in the 11th ed. of Gesenius' *Handwörterbuch*,
s.v. מָאן), but is a noun with prefixed מ, akin to the Hebr. אֳנִיָּה
"ship" and the Arabic *inā* "vessel" (see Nöldeke, *Mand. Gramm.*
p. 129). וְיִשְׁתּוֹן *"that they might drink"*, cf. וְאִנְדַּע *"that I may
know"*, chap. ii. 9. The women who attend the feast are distinguished as the "wives" and the "concubines" of the king.
The term שֵׁגָל was applied by the Jews, and perhaps by the
Arameans also, to the wife of the Persian king (Neh. ii. 6).
Whether the title was restricted to one wife we cannot say—
among the old Hebrews a royal court might include many מְלָכוֹת
(Cant. vi. 8, 9), so that there is nothing surprising in the use of
the plural שֵׁגְלָתֵהּ. The word לחנתא "concubine", which the
Targums employ both in the Sing. and the Pl., is peculiar to
West-Aramaic, the corresponding Syriac term being *dĕrūkhtā*.
The primary meaning of לחנתא is unknown; Fleischer supposes
it to have been originally a term of abuse, akin to Arab.
lakhnā'u. With נפקו (*Ḳĕrī* נְפָקָה), in *v.* 5, compare אתעקרו chap.
vii. 8 and נפלו id. 20. In all these cases the *Kĕthīb* is probably
the original reading, and the *Ḳĕrī* a correction for the purpose
of making the verb agree with the feminine subject (see
Kautzsch, *Gramm.* p. 46). The use of נפקו etc. for both genders
alike is not necessarily a Hebraism but may be due merely
to grammatical laxity, for the same phenomenon appears

7—2

in Nabatean (Euting, *Nab. Inschr.* N⁰ˢ· 3, 8) and modern
Arabic[1]. נֶבְרַשְׁתָּא "lamp", in Syriac *nabhreshtā*, is a foreign
word of unknown origin. גִּירָא "chalk" (cf. גִּר Is. xxvii. 9) is not
found in Syriac, but is common in later Jewish Aramaic and
appears also in Arabic. With כְתַל (Pl. emphat. כְתְלַיָּא Ezra v. 8)
cf. רְנַו chap. iii. 13. "*And the king saw the hollow of the hand
which wrote*"—we must suppose the hand to have appeared
above the place where the king was reclining. פַּס (stat. emphat.
פַּסָּא *v.* 24) answers to the Rabbinical Hebrew פַּס, sometimes in
the fem. form פִּסָּה, and to the Syriac *passĕthā*, which, like Hebr.
כַּף, may mean both the "palm" of the hand and the "sole" of
the foot[2].

6—12. On זִיוֹהִי see chap. ii. 31. שְׁנוֹהִי is usually explained
as meaning "was changed *for him*", but this use of the suffix is
very doubtful. We should probably read either שְׁנַיִן עֲלוֹהִי (acc.
to *v.* 9), as Kautzsch proposes (*Gramm.* p. 156), or else simply
שְׁנוֹ. קִטְרֵי חַרְצֵהּ "*the joints* (lit. fastenings) *of his loins*"; for the
phrase, cf. Ps. lxix. 24. חַרְצָא, prop. "the lower part of the
back", is the common form in later Jewish Aramaic; in Syriac
we find *ḥaṣṣā*, with assimilation, but in Mandaitic הֽאלצא (pron.
halṣā), agreeing with Hebr. חֲלָצַיִם. The Arab. *khaṣr* sides
with Jewish Aramaic in having *r*, but transposes the last two
consonants; whether the primitive Semitic form had *r* or *l* is

---

[1] The old fem. plur. of the Perfect,
with the ending *ā*, is common in the
Targums; in Christian Palestinian the
ā seems to have been weakened to *ē*
(e.g. אֲזֵלि "they went", זֲבֵנִ "they
bought", אֲשֽכַחִ "they found", in the
Lectionary, p. 33). This final ִ is not
to be confounded with the final ـ
which appears in the corresponding
Syriac forms, according to the so-
called Western orthography, since in
the latter case, the ـ is a mere con-
ventional sign introduced by scribes in
order to distinguish the fem. pl. from
the masc. sing.

[2] The Targums use פִּסְתָּא for
"palm", but for "sole" פַּרְסְתָא,

which is of course identical with Syr.
parsĕthā and Hebr. פַּרְסָה "hoof".
[In II Kings ix. 35 the Targum, as
edited by De Lagarde, has פרסת ידיא,
but the Bomberg editions read פיסת
ידה]. Since the existence of a root
פסס is very doubtful, the idea naturally suggests itself that פַּס may have
been formed from פַּרס, with assimilation of the ר; but the objection to this
hypothesis is that the forms with ר
still continued to be used, though with
a difference of meaning. The Phoenician פס "tablet" is probably metaphorical, from the resemblance of the
object to the "flat" of the hand.

therefore uncertain. Instead of מִשְׁתָּרַיִן (Hithpaal) we should
expect rather מִשְׁתְּרַיִן (Hithpeel), since in Bibl. Aram., as in
Syriac, the Pael שְׁרִי (Ezra v. 2) means "to begin", not "to
loosen"—for from מְשָׁרֵא (v. 12) no conclusion can be drawn. The
Targum however uses מַשְׁרֵי (which, if the text be correct, must
be a participle Pael) for "looseneth", in Job xii. 18. אַרְכֻבָּתֵהּ
(so Baer, in accordance with the best MSS.) "his knees", is
a form with prosthetic א, and occurs also in the Targums
(Eccles. xii. 3), side by side with the more primitive רְכוּבַיָּא,
רְכוּבְתָּא (cf. Arab. rukba). The doubling of the ב in the Biblical
form is probably a late change (Kautzsch, Gramm. p. 31).
The promise made by Belshazzar in v. 7 seems to be in part
suggested by Gen. xli. 42, where Pharaoh arrays Joseph in fine
linen and places a chain of gold about his neck. הֶעֱלָה stands
for ha‘ālā (or, with dissimilation, הַנְעָלָה chap. iv. 3), according
to the rule in Hebrew that when a guttural has Ḳāmeṣ, a
Paṭhaḥ immediately preceding becomes Sĕgōl or Ḳāmeṣ.
אַרְגְּוָנָא, "purple", is here spelt with ו, as in the other Aramaic
dialects; from the Aramaic is derived the Arabic urjuwān and
probably also the Persian arghawān. The Assyrian form is
given as argamannu (Schrader, Cuneif. Inscr. p. 155), but whether it was really pronounced with m, like the Hebr. אַרְגָּמָן, or
with w, is uncertain, since m and w are not distinguished in the
cuneiform character. ארגונא and ארגמן are commonly supposed
to be of Indian origin; to this, however, there are two objections, firstly that the red purple dye was produced, not in India,
but on the Mediterranean coasts, secondly that ארגמן occurs
already in Judges viii. 26. המינכא (Ḳĕrī הַמְנִיכָא—the forms
המונכא, המונכא are erroneous), "necklace", appears in later Jewish
Aramaic as מְנִיכָא, in Syriac as hamnīkhā or hemnīkhā, and in
Greek as μανιάκης. That the word is originally neither Aramaic nor Greek appears certain. Possibly it may be from the
Persian himyān, "girdle" (which has passed both into Syriac
and Arabic) with the diminutive ending ak; this hypothesis
would account for the Kĕthîb המינכא, but the change of meaning
involves some difficulty. תַּלְתִּי (in vv. 16, 29, תַּלְתָּא) is ordinarily
translated "third" (Theod. τρίτος), i.e. "as third ruler". In
this case, however, the grammatical form remains wholly inex-

plicable, for the ordinal is תְּלִיתָי (chap. ii. 39), never תְּלְתִּי. Gesenius regarded תְּלְתָּא as stat. emphat. of a form תְּלַת "third rank", while Kautzsch takes it to be an "abnormal" stat. emphat. of תְּלְתִּי (*Gramm.* p. 121). Such a form as תְּלַת, תְּלְתָּא, "third rank", is not only unknown in Aramaic but is wholly unsupported by the analogy of the other Semitic dialects—not to mention the difficulty of supposing that in *v.* 16 תְּלְתָּא is equivalent to שַׁלִּיט תְּלְתָּא in *v.* 29. Still more improbable is the explanation of Kautzsch, for it involves *two* irregularities, the use of תְּלְתִּי instead of תְּלִיתִי, and the disappearance of the long *ī* in the emphatic state. The LXX., the Pĕshīttā, and Josephus (*Antiq.* x. 11. 2) translate "a third part", which in the Targums is תּוּלְתָּא. This interpretation might perhaps suit *v.* 29, but in *vv.* 7 and 16 it is inadmissible, since the verb שְׁלֵט never governs a direct object. That תְּלְתִּי and תְּלְתָּא are mere mistakes for תְּלִיתִי is scarcely probable, for why should so well-known a word as the latter have been thus strangely distorted, and that three times over in the same chapter? In view of these difficulties I would suggest, as a possible solution, that תְּלְתָּא may be the Aramaic equivalent of the Arabic *ath-thilth* (with which it almost exactly agrees in form) "every third day", i.e. "every other day" (cf. לִשְׁלֹשֶׁת יָמִים? Amos iv. 4). In this case תלתי in *v.* 7 would be a mistake due to a scribe who, not understanding תלתא, read the word as תְּלְתִי "third". The proclamation that the interpreter of the writing on the wall should reign over the kingdom on alternate days with the king himself, may seem extravagant, but it is certainly less extravagant than the decree of Darius in chap. vi. 8—10. On עללין, in *v.* 8, see chap. iv. 4. It is somewhat strange that *v.* 8 should describe the wise men as "entering", since in the latter half of *v.* 7 they are already present. Whether their inability to read the inscription was due to its being written in a strange character or, as the medieval Rabbins imagined, to some peculiar arrangement of the letters, we are not told. מִשְׁתַּבְּשִׁין (*v.* 9) is not merely "were perplexed", but "*were thrown into confusion*" (Hitzig). The queen who appears in *v.* 10 is regarded by almost all modern commentators as the mother of Belshazzar, not as his wife. This view is based partly on the fact that she is distinguished from the

king's wives (*v.* 3), partly on the manner in which she speaks
of what had taken place in the days of Nebuchadnezzar (*v.* 11).
Many writers have maintained that the queen here mentioned
is a daughter of Nebuchadnezzar, but there is nothing in the
text to favour this assumption, and the phrase "thy father"
which she·uses in addressing her son (*v.* 11) certainly appears
to indicate that she is speaking rather of her husband than of
her father. לָקֳבֵל מִלֵּי מַלְכָּא is rendered either "*because of that
which had happened to the king*" (Bertholdt, Von Lengerke), according to the use of מִלַּת in chap. ii. 23, or else "*because of the
words of the king*" (Hitzig, Ewald), which agrees better with
the context. The *Kĕthīb* עללת (i.e. עֲלֶלֶת, *Kĕrī* עַלַּת, according to
the later usage) is analogous to עללין in *v.* 8. Instead of the
forms יְבַהֲלוּךְ and יְשַׁתַּנּוֹ we might have expected יְבַהֲלֻנֵּךְ and
יְשַׁתַּנּוּן¹, but the accuracy of the Masoretic text is here confirmed
by the Aramaic inscription of Taimā, in which we find ינסחוהי
"may they expel him!" Hence it follows that יבהלוך and ישתנו
are relics of the old Jussive form of the Imperfect—a form
which in classical Arabic is clearly distinguished from the ordinary Imperfect (the so-called Indicative). Verse 12, as it stands
in the Masoretic text, is quite contrary to syntax, for to take
שָׂכְלְתָנוּ as a stat. constr., with Rosenmüller and Von Lengerke, is
manifestly inadmissible. Accordingly there is little doubt that
we should read מְפַשַּׁר for מְפַשֵּׁר and מִשָׁרֵא for מְשָׁרֵא, according to
the Vulgate and most recent interpreters (see Kautzsch, *Gramm.*
p. 65, note)—i.e. "*Because an excellent spirit and knowledge and
understanding, the interpreting of dreams and the explaining
of riddles and the loosing of spells* (lit. knots), *were found in
Daniel, whose name the king changed to Belteshazzar—now let
Daniel be called, and he will declare the interpretation*". אַחֲוָיַת
is stat. constr. of the Infinitive of אַחֲוִי (= הַחֲוִי), cf. הַנְזָקַת Ezra
iv. 22. אַחֲוִי אֲחִידָה would be the exact equivalent of the Hebr.
הִגִּיד חִידָה (cf. Judg. xiv. 12—14). אֲחִידָה, Syr. *uḥdĕthā* or *uḥa-
dĕthā*, is properly "a thing closed in, concealed", from the verb
אחד (Hebr. אחז). De Lagarde very plausibly suggests that the

---

¹ The only other cases of the absence   Imperfect are the doubtful forms יַחִיטוּ
of the final *n* in the 3rd pers. pl. of the   Ezra iv. 12 and יְאבֵדוּ Jer. x. 11.

Hebr. חִידָה is borrowed from the Aramaic (*Anmerkungen zur griechischen Uebersetzung der Proverbien*, p. 73), in which case the verb חוּד (Judg. xiv. 12) would be merely a denominative. קִטְרִין, "knots", is usually explained to mean "*difficult questions*", but it is much more probable that there is here a reference to the well-known superstitions about magic knots which it required special skill to untie[1]. The verb הִשְׁתְּכַחַת agrees in gender and number with שָׂכְלְתָנוּ (cf. *v.* 14), the intervening words being an explanatory parenthesis.

13—vi. 1. Daniel, on entering, appears to be personally unknown to Belshazzar, although, according to chap. viii. 27, he had been employed in the king's service. In *v.* 15 the words וּפִשְׁרֵהּ לְהוֹדָעָתַנִי are, of course, a continuation of the preceding clause, לְהוֹדָעָתַנִי being equivalent to יְהוֹדְעַנִּי. On the form תוּכַל (*Kěrī* תִּכּוּל), in *v.* 16, see chaps. ii. 10; iii. 29. The general term פִּשְׁרִין is here substituted for the more special חֶלְמִין in the parallel passage, *v.* 12. Instead of נְבִזְבְּיָתָךְ (so Baer), in *v.* 17, some editions have נְבִזְבְּיָתָךְ; the formation of the Plural, with an additional י, is anomalous—on נְבִזְבָּה see chap. ii. 6. In *v.* 18, אנתה is a *Nominativus pendens*, and is taken up by the suffix in אֲבוּךְ (cf. the somewhat less bold construction in chap. ii. 29); the general sense therefore is "Thou, O king, art the son of that Nebuchadnezzar to whom" etc. For מְחָא (*v.* 19), partic. Haphel of חֲיָה, some MSS. and editions wrongly read מָחֵא "striking" (Theod. ἔτυπτεν). In *v.* 20, רם can hardly be taken as a passive partic., but is rather a Perfect with intransitive vocalization, exactly similar to Syr. *mīth* (Hebr. מֵת). כָּרְסְאָ, stat. constr. of כָּרְסְיָא (see chap. vii. 9), is from an older form *kursai* (cf. Syr. *kursěyā*, stat. constr. *kursai*). It is commonly supposed that here the ר is inserted to compensate for the loss of the doubling which appears in Hebr. כִּסֵּא, Assyr. *kussû*; but

---

[1] Among the Syrians the *ḳāṭrai ḳeṭrē*, "tiers of knots", were a species of enchanters (see *Sancti Ephraem Syri Hymni et Sermones*, ed. Lamy, II. p. 419, and Kayser, *Die Canones Jacob's von Edessa*, p. 130). It is related that a Jew cast a spell upon Mohammed by tying knots in a cord and hiding it in a well. The prophet, at the suggestion of the angel Gabriel, sent for the cord and recited over it verses of the Koran; at each verse a knot came undone, whereupon the spell was dissolved (Al-Baidāwī on the Koran, CXIII. 4).

possibly the form with ר may be the more primitive, since in Phoenician also we find כרסים " thrones" (where the י is necessarily *consonantal*, as in the Aramaic forms)—the Arab. *kursī*, " chair", of course proves nothing either way, since it is borrowed from the Aramaic. This word can scarcely be connected with כסה "to cover", or with כֵּסֶא "full moon", but is very probably of non-Semitic origin[1]. Instead of וִיקְרֵה we should perhaps read וִיקְרֵהּ (according to the Pĕshīttā) with Rosenmüller and Hitzig. With הֶעְדִּיו, for הַעְדִּיו cf. הֶחֱסִינוּ chap. vii. 22. In *v.* 21 we find בְּנֵי אֲנָשָׁא substituted for the simple אֲנָשָׁא of chap. iv. 22, 29, 30. The *Kĕthīb* שׁוִּי can be explained only as another form of שְׁוָא "it was equal", a verb common in the Targums and in Syriac (cf. Syr. ܚܕܝ or ܚܕܝ "to rejoice", ܪܘܝ or ܪܘܝ "to be intoxicated"), but the *Kĕrī* שַׁוִּיו " they placed" is preferable, the omission of the ו being due to the ו following; the Syr. *shĕwe* "equal" would of course be שְׁוֵה or שְׁוָא in Bibl. Aramaic, not שְׁוִי. Accordingly וְלִבְבֵהּ עִם־חֵיוָתָא שַׁוִּיו is " *and his heart* (i.e. mind) *they placed* (*on a level*) *with* (*the heart of*) *the wild beasts*". The ellipse עִם חֵיוָתָא, for עִם־לְבַב חֵיוָתָא is exactly similar to that in chap. iv. 13. " The wild asses", עֲרָדַיָּא, are here mentioned as a type of savagery (cf. Job xxxix. 5—8). On כָּל־קֳבֵל דִּי (*v.* 22) see chap. ii. 8, and on the Hebrew form הִתְרֹומַמְתָּ (*v.* 23) see מְרֹומֵם chap. iv. 34. With אָרְחָתָךְ " *thy ways*", i.e. "thy destinies" cf. Jer. x. 23. In *v.* 25 the inscription on the wall is read, in *vv.* 26—28 it is explained, but the divergence between the reading and the explanation has always perplexed commentators[2]. In *v.* 25 Daniel reads מְנֵא מְנֵא תְקֵל וּפַרְסִין; in the explanation no account is taken of the repetition of מְנֵא, and פְּרֵס is substituted for וּפַרְסִין. If the vocalization be correct, תְּקֵל and פְּרֵס cannot signify " weighed" and "divided", as the interpretation in *vv.* 27, 28 seems to require; the form וּפַרְסִין

---

[1] That the Hebr. כֵּסֶא may be from כָּרְסֵא is the view of Olshausen (*Lehrb. der hebr. Sprache*, p. 347). The form of כֵּסֶא would in itself suggest a foreign origin, since this nominal form is found only in adjectives (עִוֵּר, חֵרֵשׁ etc.) and in a few abstract verbal nouns

(e.g. חֵלֶק Lev. xiv. 43, שָׁלֵם Deut. xxxii. 35). According to Schrader (*Cuneiform Inscr.* p. 383) the word is Akkadian.

[2] The ancient Versions, with the exception of the Pĕshīttā, avoid the difficulty by altering the text of *v.* 25.

likewise has no apparent sense. We may therefore assume that the phrase מנא מנא תקל ופרסין was not arbitrarily invented by the author, but was borrowed from some other source, the interpretation in *vv.* 26—28 being an attempt to extract from the words, in spite of grammar, a meaning suitable to the occasion. An examination of the passage was published in the *Journal Asiatique* for 1886 by M. Clermont-Ganneau, who points out that the mysterious inscription consists in reality of *names of weights* (see also Nöldeke in the *Zeitschrift für Assyriologie*, Vol. I. pp. 414—418). מְנָא (stat. absol.) is the exact Aramaic equivalent of the Hebr. מָנֶה (Ezek. xlv. 12; Ezra ii. 69 and in the Mishnah), which the Greeks, borrowing from the Phoenicians, made into μνᾶ, Lat. *mina*. In Syriac the word seems not to occur in the stat. absol. of the Singular; the stat. emphat. is *manyā*. תְּקֵל is stat. absol. of תיקלא (Targum Onk., Exod. xxxviii. 26), Hebr. שֶׁקֶל. פַּרְסִין might be taken as a plural of פְּרַס in *v.* 28 (according to the analogy of לְחֵם stat. emphat. לַחְמָא), but whether the vocalization is here correct may be doubted. In the Mishnah and other Jewish writings the half-mina is called פְּרָס (lit. "division" of the mina), and an Assyrian weight in the British Museum bears the inscription פרש (in the Aramaic character), which Nöldeke explains as being probably equivalent to פרס, since the Assyrians appear to have interchanged שׁ and ס in pronunciation. In Daniel therefore we must either regard פְּרָס and פַּרְסִין as mistakes for פְּרָס and פַּרְסִין, or else suppose that the forms פְּרָס and פְּרָס were synonymous. Thus the inscription is—A MINA, A MINA, A SHEKEL, AND HALF-MINAS. Why these words are here introduced, whether they have any special reference to the situation of Belshazzar or to the times of the author of Daniel, remains altogether obscure. Verses 26—28 are plays upon the words of the inscription; in *v.* 28 the play is a double one. "MINA—*God hath* NUMBERED *thy kingdom and finished it.* SHEKEL—*thou hast been* WEIGHED *in the balance and hast been found wanting.* HALF-MINA—*thy kingdom hath been* DIVIDED *and given to the Medes and* PERSIANS". Instead of the מֹאזַנְיָא (*v.* 27) of the ordinary editions, Norzi and Baer have the doubtful singular form מֹאזְנְיָא. Kautzsch suggests that this form may be due to the pedantry of the scribes, who reflected that the object weighed must be in *one* scale of the balance (*Gramm.* p. 85). וְהַכְרִזוּ עֲלוֹהִי (*v.* 29) "*and they proclaimed concerning him ......*". הַכְרִזוּ, Syr. *akhrez*, is probably taken from some form of the Greek κηρύσσειν, cf. כָּרוֹזָא "herald" chap. iii. 4[1]. The story closes with the summary mention of the murder of Belshazzar—by whom he was slain we are not told—and of the accession of Darius the Mede. That chap. vi. 1 properly belongs to what precedes and refers to what took place immediately upon Belshazzar's death, is obvious. As to Darius the Mede, and as to the meaning of the phrase "*he received the kingdom*", see p. 20 and the introduction to the next chapter. The statement that Darius was about 62 years old when he came to the throne, is probably based upon some chronological calculation of the author, but what data he had before him we have no means of knowing.

CHAPTER VI.

(Verses 2—29.)

This chapter, which closes the first half of the book, is occupied with the history of Daniel during the reign of Darius the Mede, and describes in particular how Daniel, in consequence of his strict adherence to the usages of the Jewish religion, was sentenced to death, but miraculously delivered. The general

---

[1] Kautzsch - supposes (*Gramm.* pp. 58, 119) that from κηρύσσειν the Arameans coined a verb כְּרַז, whence כָּרוֹזָא would be regularly derived, and that the Haphel הַכְרֵז is merely a denominative from כָּרוֹזָא. But of the existence of a Peal כְּרַז there is no proof—for in the Pĕshîṭtā Acts xv. 36 the true reading is ܢܒ̈ܐ — and that כָּרוֹזָא may be formed from

הַכְרֵז is shewn by the Syr. *pĕyāsā* "persuasion", which is formed as if from a Peal, though the verb is *apis*, Gr. πεῖσαι. De Vogüé has argued from the inscription לכרוז on a seal of uncertain date (though from the writing it would appear to be very ancient) that the Aramaic root כרז has no connection with Greek (see the *Corpus Inscr. Sem.* Pt. 2, N°· 86).

aim of the chapter is therefore much the same as that of chapter iii., and in a few places the verbal resemblance between the two narratives must strike every reader (iii. 12 ; vi. 14—iii. 25 ; vi. 24—iii. 28 ; vi. 23). The main difference is that chapter iii. insists upon the negative duty of abstention from idolatry, while chapter vi. dwells upon the positive side of Judaism. This difference naturally affects the form of both stories. Since the author purposes, in chapter vi., to represent an Israelite condemned to death for refusing to abandon the practices of his religion, and since during the Exile the religion of Israel consisted merely in acts of private devotion, it was necessary that Daniel should be placed in a situation which made even the private worship of God a capital offence. The task was not an easy one, and this amply accounts for the startling means which the author here adopts. The story taken in itself is of the strangest character, but on examination it will be seen that the features which most astonish us are essential for the attainment of the didactic purpose. It would therefore be a waste of time to inquire how any ruler not completely insane could issue an edict forbidding his subjects to ask petitions of god or man, himself excepted, for the space of thirty days—why Darius adopts the singular proposal made to him without first consulting Daniel, who is his chief minister—why the enemies of Daniel are at one time represented as coercing the king, and at last are condemned to death *en masse*, together with their wives and children. Nothing can be more unfortunate than the attempts of apologists to make these things appear probable. Thus Hengstenberg and very many others have maintained that the edict of Darius was merely a claim to divine honours such as were paid to the ancient kings of Persia—as if under the kings of Persia it had ever been forbidden, on pain of death, to ask petitions of god or man ! But when we consider the account of the edict in question as a literary device whereby the faithfulness of Daniel is conspicuously shewn forth, for the edification of Israelites persecuted on account of their religion, the difficulties are at once removed.

That this narrative is based on a historical tradition cannot be argued with any show of reason, for, as we have seen (p. 19),

Darius the Mede is unknown to history. It has often been
supposed that the Darius of Daniel is a confused reminiscence
of the historical Darius Hystaspis, but this is scarcely probable.
The author of Daniel knew of four Persian kings (chap. xi. 2),
of whom the first is Cyrus and the last doubtless Xerxes. The
other two are presumably Darius and Artaxerxes. But the
name Xerxes (אחשורש) appears in Daniel as the name of the
father of Darius the Mede (chap. ix. 1). Thus it would seem
that the author, knowing that there had existed a Median
Empire before the Persian supremacy began, but not knowing
any real Median names, gave Persian names to his Median
kings. If it be asked why a Median king, not Cyrus the Persian, is represented as taking possession of the Chaldean Empire,
the answer is found in the Old Testament itself. For in several
passages written during the Exile (Is. xiii. 17; Jer. li. 11, 28)
it is predicted that the Medes will conquer Babylon. This the
author of Daniel, who knew something of the prophetical books,
supposes actually to have taken place.

2—10. For the word אחשדרפניא see chap. iii. 2. In this
chapter the 120 "satraps" are evidently not satraps in the real
sense of the word, for in the time of Darius Hystaspis the whole
Persian Empire contained only 20 satrapies (Herod. III. 89)[1].
Perhaps the 120 satrapies may be merely a variation of the 127
provinces into which, according to Esth. i. 1, the Persian Empire
was divided. עֵלָּא מִן (v. 3) "higher than", "above", does not
occur again in Biblical Aramaic; its opposite is אֲרַעָא מִן (chap.
ii. 39, Kĕthîb). סָרְכִין, which is found also in the Targums,
seems to be from a Persian word sarak "chief" (formed from
sar "head"), cf. Syr. ܣܪܟܐ from ܪܫܐ. In v. 4 עֲשִׁית
is usually taken as a Perfect, with scriptio plena, for עֲשֵׂת or עֲשֵׂת,
but according to Nöldeke it is a participle, passive in form
though in meaning merely intransitive, i.e. "the king (was)
minded" etc. (see the Götting. gel. Anzeigen, 1884, p. 1019).
After the verb הַשְׁכַּחְנָא (v. 6) we must of course understand עִלָּה;
for the use of the Perfect referring to the future after לְהֵן

[1] Similarly the title marzbān, which under the Sāsānian dynasty corresponded in meaning to the older "satrap", is sometimes used by later Arabic writers for Persian officials generally.

"except", cf. the Hebr. construction לֹא אֲשַׁלֵּחֲךָ כִּי אִם־בֵּרַכְתָּנִי Gen.
xxxii. 27. הִרְגִּשׁוּ (v. 7) properly "made a tumult", hence "*came
tumultuously*", cf. the Targum, Ruth i. 19, where וַתֵּהֹם כָּל־הָעִיר
עֲלֵיהֶן is rendered וארגישו כל יתבי קרתא עיליהון. In v. 8 the Masoretic accentuation separates קְיָם from מַלְכָּא, so that the sense
would be "*that the king should establish a statute*", cf. in Hebrew
לָנֶס שָׂפָה הָרֹצֵחַ Numb. xxxv. 6. This rendering is adopted by
Rosenmüller and Hitzig, whereas Von Lengerke, Ewald, and
most moderns, discarding the accents, make קְיָם a construct
state, "*to establish a royal statute*" (Theod. τοῦ στῆσαι στάσει
βασιλικῇ), which view is favoured by אֱסָר מַלְכָּא v. 13; the
objection of Hitzig that the statute must be established not by
the ministers but by the king, is inconclusive, for לְקַיָּמָה, though
grammatically active, may be virtually equivalent to a passive
"that a statute should be established"—so also the Infinitive is
used in v. 9 (דִּי לָא לְהַשְׁנָיָה), and in Biblical Hebrew (לִמְבוֹח Jer.
xxv. 34, לְהָשִׁיב Esth. viii. 8). וּלְתַקָּפָה אֱסָר "*and to make a strong
interdict*"; the Aramaic root תקף (Arab. ثَقَف) according to
Gesenius means originally "to strike", "come upon", but perhaps the more primitive sense is "to be straight, upright",
whence we may derive that of "being strong", "prevailing
over", "seizing" (Koran II. 187). The Hebr. verb תקף (Job xiv.
20; xv. 24) is probably borrowed from the Aramaic. אֱסָר "interdict" corresponds to the Biblical Hebr. אִסָּר (Num. xxx. 3)
and to the post-Biblical Hebr. אִסּוּר. בָּעוּ is not necessarily a
"prayer", but any "petition", as is shewn by the common
Syriac phrase *bĕbhāʿū mennākh* "I entreat thee". גֻּב, in v. 13
written גוּב, stat. emphat. גֻּבָּא v. 17, is properly a "pit", cf. Arab.
jubb "well". אַרְיָוָתָא, pl. of אַרְיֵה (chap. vii. 4), formed like פָּרְסָן
(chap. vii. 9) from כָּרְסָא, exactly agrees with the Syriac form as
vocalized by the East-Syrians (Nestorians); the West-Syrians
pronounce *aryawāthā* with short *a* in the second syllable. This
verse refers to the custom, which existed already among the
Assyrians and from them was passed on to the Persians, of
keeping lions for the chase. According to v. 18, the "pit"
must have had a narrow mouth which could be closed with a
stone; that lions were really confined in pits of this description

appears at least improbable. With *v.* 9 compare Esth. i. 19.
"*The writing and the interdict*", in *v.* 10, means, of course, the
writing which contained the interdict (cf. אֶת־הַמְּגִלָּה וְאֶת־הַדְּבָרִים
Jer. xxxvi. 27).

11—18. The clause וְכַוִּין פְּתִיחָן וגו' is parenthetical, "*now he
had in his upper chamber windows opened toward Jerusalem*".
כַּוִּין would be in the Sing. כַּוָּה, stat. emphat. כַּוְּתָא, which is the
Syriac form. הֲוָא בָרֵךְ (so Baer) "*he was wont to kneel*", for
which most editions have הוּא בָרֵךְ. The practice of praying
three times in the day appears also in Ps. lv. 18, unless we
understand that verse as a mere poetical figure; the turning
towards Jerusalem in prayer is a custom which seems to have
originated among the Jews during the Babylonian Exile (see
I Kings viii. 38, 48, a passage probably composed at that
period), and which continued for many centuries afterwards[1].
The last words of *v.* 11 are usually translated "*as he had been
wont to do aforetime*", see chap. ii. 40; but perhaps here also
כָּל־קֳבֵל דִּי may be taken in its ordinary sense, i.e. "*forasmuch as
he had been wont to do (it) aforetime*". With מִן קַדְמַת דְּנָה cf.
מִקַּדְמַת דְּנָה Ezra v. 11. In *v.* 13 יְבָעֵא is used absolutely, i.e.
without the addition of בָּעוּ as in *v.* 8. בָּל "mind", "thought"
(*v.* 15) does not seem to occur elsewhere in Jewish Aramaic, but
is common both in Syriac and Arabic; its original sense is altogether obscure[2]. Instead of מֵעָלִי (as Baer reads, following the
Masora) some MSS. have מֵעֲלִי and others מְעָלִי, which last is no
doubt the correct pronunciation (see Nöldeke, *Gött. gel. Anz.*
1884, p. 1020); מְעָלִי, from the root עלל, is for מַעֲלִי, like הֵעָלָה
chap. v. 7 for הַעֲלָה, and corresponds to the Syr. *ma"ālai* (in the
phrase ܡܥ̈ܠܝ ܫܡܫܐ II Kings xi. 5 Pĕsh.). Thus מְעָלִי שִׁמְשָׁא
is equivalent to the Hebr. מְבוֹא הַשֶּׁמֶשׁ "the entering in, i.e. the
setting, of the sun". הֲוָה מִשְׁתַּדַּר "*he was bestirring himself*";
this verb appears as אִשְׁתַּדַּל in later Jewish Aramaic, and as

---

[1] As is well known, Mohammed at
first commanded his disciples to follow
the Jewish custom of praying towards
Jerusalem, but afterwards, when he
broke with the Jews, altered the ḳibla
(i.e. facing-point) to Mecca,

[2] The Arabic phrase *lā ubāli*, "I do
not care", of course throws no light
upon the meaning of *bāl*, for if *ubāli*
be connected with *bāl*, as the Arabic
grammarians suppose, it is merely a
denominative verb.

הִשְׁתַּדַּל in the Mishnah (*Ābōth* II. 5 ; IV. 18). The original meaning of the root שדר or שדל seems to be that of "setting in
motion", hence אֶשְׁתַּדּוּר "commotion", "rebellion", Ezra iv. 15,
Syr. *shaddar* "to send", Jewish Aram. שַׁדֵּל "to persuade", prop.
"to incite", "urge on", and Arab. *sadara* or *sadala* "to let
loose", applied to hair, garments, etc.[1] בִּתְדִירָא "*continually*"
(*v.* 17) is in the Targums usually תְּדִירָא ; the word is derived by
Gesenius, no doubt correctly, from דור "to revolve"—that it can
have anything to do with שדר (Kautzsch, *Gramm.* p. 112) is
impossible. On הֵיתָיִת (*v.* 18) see chap. iii. 13. The form שֻׂמַת
"*was placed*" is very peculiar, since the analogy both of Biblical
Aramaic and of Arabic would lead us to expect שִׂימַת, שֻׂמַת, as
Kautzsch proposes to read (*Gramm.* p. 74). Instead of the
חַתְמָה of the ordinary editions, Baer has חַתְמָה ; for וּבְעֶזְקָת he
reads וּבְעִזְקָת (plur. constr.), following the best MSS. "*That
nothing might be changed concerning Daniel*", i.e. that nothing
might be done to rescue him. צְבוּ prop. "purpose", "inten-
tion", is here used, as in Syriac, in a perfectly vague sense.

19—29. טְוָת "*in a state of fasting*" (from *ṭăwăyăt*) is properly a fem. substantive in the absolute state, used adverbially
(cf. Hebr. מְהֵרָה "quickly"). The meaning of דַּחֲוָן is unknown.
Theodotion and the Pĕshīṭtā render it by "*food*", the medieval
Jewish commentators by "*instruments of music*", while most
moderns take it as "*concubines*", in accordance with a signification which the Arabic verb *dahā* sometimes conveys; in Aramaic and Hebrew, however, the root דחא, דחה, always means
"to thrust away", "overthrow"—it is only in Arabic that it has
acquired the sense of "spreading out" like a carpet (Koran
LXXIX. 30), whence its metaphorical application is derived. Rosenmüller compares the Arab. *dukhān* "smoke", and explains
דַּחֲוָן as "*incense*", "*odours*". With the clause וְשִׁנְתֵּהּ נַדַּת עֲלוֹהִי cf.
chap. ii. 1. שִׁנְתֵּהּ is written with *Dāghesh forte*, according to the
analogy of such words as מִלְּתָא, although the root is not שנן but
ישׁן (cf. Syr. *shennĕthā*, constr. *shennath*). "*Then the king rose at
dawn, as soon as it was light*" (*v.* 20)—שְׁפַרְפָּרָא, which is used in

---

[1] See Nöldeke in the *Z. D. M. G.* XL. p. 735—צבו is there, of course, a
misprint for צבון.

the Targums also, has almost exactly the same sense as נִנְהָא;
in Syriac and Arabic we find the simple forms, *shaphrā* and
safar respectively. The phrase בְּקָל עֲצִיב "*with a lamentable
voice*" (*v.* 21) occurs again in the Palestinian Targum, Exod. xii.
31. עֲצִיב is from עצב "to bind", a root common to Syriac and
Arabic, the ideas of "tightness" and "pain" being closely connected in the Semitic languages[1]. In *v.* 22 the verb מַלִּל "*he
spake*" is construed with עִם, as often happens in Syriac even
when the meaning is simply "to speak *to*", not "to hold a con-
versation *with*"[2]. In *v.* 24 the Perfect טְאֵב (Syr. *ṭĕ'ebh*) seems
to have been formed on the analogy of בְּאֵשׁ (see *v.* 15), since in
the former word the א does not properly belong to the root, as
the Hebrew and Arabic forms shew. With הַנְסָקָה for הַסָּקָה cf.
הַנְעָלָה chap. iv. 3; on הֵימָן see chap. ii. 45. אַרְעִית (*v.* 25) is
formed from אֲרַע (chap. ii. 39) as in Hebrew תַּחְתִּית "the lowest
part" (Exod. xix. 17) from תַּחַת. The decree of Darius in *vv.* 26
—28 is mostly composed of phrases used in chaps. ii. 44; iii.
31—33; v. 19. Before דִּי־לָא תִתְחַבַּל (*v.* 27) we must, of course,
understand מַלְכוּ. Verse 29, as contrasted with the corresponding passage, chap. iii. 30, uses הַצְלַח in the intransitive sense.

CHAPTER VII.

We now enter upon the second part of the book, describing
four visions seen by Daniel. These pieces purport to have
been written by Daniel himself, for in chap. vii. 1 we are told
that he "wrote the dream", and from that point to the end of
the book he speaks in the first person, the sole exception being
the heading of chap. x. Though Daniel is never actually designated as a prophet, the literary form of the visions is, to a large

[1] Cf. in Arabic يَوْم عَصِيب "a
painful day" (Koran xi. 79); Al-Baidāwī explains the word عَصِيب as
شَدِيد مِن عَصْبِه اذا شَدَّه. In

Hebrew this root is used only in the
derived sense (I Kings i. 6. Is. lxiii.
10); עָצַב "to fashion" (Job x. 8) is
quite different and probably corresponds to Arab. عَضَب "to cut".

[2] Exactly similar is the modern Persian use of *bā* with *guftan*.

extent, borrowed from the prophetical writings. Thus, in chaps. vii. and viii., Daniel, like Zechariah, is shewn visible objects of which the symbolical meaning is forthwith explained to him by angels. Other details were doubtless suggested by the book of Ezekiel. The author of Daniel likewise follows the prophets in prefixing dates to the visions. This custom was, among the ancient prophets, a perfectly reasonable one, for as their visions referred primarily to the circumstances of the moment, it was desirable, for the right understanding of the piece, that the reader should be informed of its date. But in the visions of Daniel the real subject is always "the time of the end", not the time in which Daniel lived, so that the prefixing of a date is unessential.

The vision in chap. vii. differs from the rest in that it takes the form of a *dream*, based upon the same idea as the dream of Nebuchadnezzar in chap. ii. In both chapters we read of Four Gentile Empires, in both the Fourth Empire is dwelt upon at much greater length than the first three, and in both it is predicted that the Fourth Empire will be overthrown by a divine interposition, in order that an everlasting kingdom may be set up. Here the resemblance between the two visions ceases. In chap. ii. 41—43 much stress is laid upon the *divisions* of the Fourth Empire, but chap. vii. passes them over in silence. Moreover in chap. ii. 34, 35, 44, all the Four Empires perish alike, whereas in chap. vii. 11, 12 the Fourth Beast only is destroyed, the other Beasts being suffered to live, though they are deprived of their dominion. But what especially distinguishes chap. vii. is the prominence which it gives to the last king of the Fourth Empire, who is represented by "a little horn", and who "wages war against the Saints".

To argue from these divergences that the Four Empires of chap. ii. are not the same as those of chap. vii., or that the two chapters are the work of different authors, is altogether unreasonable. We have no right to expect in an apocalyptic writing that strict consistency which we naturally demand of a historian. We must also make allowance for the different frame-work of the two chapters. Chap. ii. describes a revelation sent to Nebuchadnezzar (see *vv.* 29, 30, 45), whereas chap.

vii. is a revelation sent to Daniel, the representative of the true Israel. Hence it is only in the second case that the sufferings of the Saints in the last days can be appropriately mentioned[1].

We may therefore assume, with the great majority of modern interpreters, that the Empires in chap. vii., as in chap. ii., are (1) the Babylonian, (2) the Median, (3) the Persian, (4) the Greek or Macedonian. It is also clear that the "little horn" is Antiochus Epiphanes. This was distinctly recognized by Porphyry, and must also have been known to the Jews of the 4th century after Christ, since it is the interpretation given by Ephraim Syrus, who was quite incapable of inventing it. At the present day it is so generally admitted as not to require demonstration. But there are two questions which deserve to be more particularly examined, namely (1) What are the "ten horns" of the Fourth Beast? and (2) What is meant by the One like a son of man who comes with the clouds of heaven?

As to the former question, there can at least be no doubt that the "ten horns" represent ten individual kings (see v. 24), not ten kingdoms, as is the case with the "four horns" of chap. viii. 8. This appears from the fact that in chap. vii. 8 the "little horn" rises *among* the ten horns, which is explained, in v. 24, to mean that *after* ten kings have arisen, another king will arise. In chap. viii. 9, on the contrary, the "little horn" rises *out of* one of the four horns. If therefore the Fourth Beast of chap. vii. is the Greek Empire and the little horn is Antiochus, it follows that the ten horns must be ten *predecessors* of Antiochus. So far most interpreters are agreed, but as to the identification of these ten predecessors there is great difference of opinion. According to Bertholdt and Von Lengerke, the ten kings are (1) Seleucus Nicator, (2) Antiochus Soter, (3) Antiochus Theos, (4) Seleucus Callinicus, (5) Seleucus Cerau-

[1] This obvious consideration is overlooked by Meinhold, who says, in discussing chap. ii., "Was c. 7. 8. 11 besonders betont ist, dass in der Endzeit Israel hart bedrückt sein, aber aus der äussersten Not von Gott befreit werde, fehlt hier gerade" (*Kurzgefasster Commentar*, 8te Abt. p. 274), and hence argues that the author of chap. ii. cannot have written the latter part of the book. I may here mention that De Lagarde, in the *Gött. gel. Anzeigen* for 1891, pp. 497—520, has endeavoured to prove that Dan. vii. was composed in the year 69 after Christ.

nus, (6) Antiochus the Great, (7) Seleucus Philopator, (8) Heliodorus, (9) Ptolemy Philometor, (10) Demetrius Soter. Others, as Hitzig, Cornill, and Kuenen, begin with Alexander the Great. This is decidedly more natural, for if the Fourth Beast represents the Greek supremacy, why should Alexander be omitted ? It is true that in chap. viii. a distinction is made between "the great horn" (Alexander) and the horn out of which "the little horn" rises, but this is because the "four horns" of chap. viii. are contemporaneous kingdoms, not a series of successive kings. In chap. vii. nothing is said about the divisions of the Macedonian Empire—we have only a series of kings ; hence Alexander must head the list. We have also to consider that the ten kings are mentioned, not on their own account, but because they lead up to the eleventh (Antiochus Epiphanes), i.e. the number 10 is introduced only in order that the readers may the more clearly recognize who is meant by the "little horn". Accordingly Hitzig and Cornill believe the ten kings to be (1) Alexander the Great, (2) Seleucus Nicator, (3) Antiochus Soter, (4) Antiochus Theos, (5) Seleucus Callinicus, (6) Seleucus Ceraunus, (7) Antiochus the Great, (8) Seleucus Philopator, (9) Heliodorus, (10) Demetrius Soter.

Of the ten horns, we are told in *v.* 8, three are "plucked up" on the appearance of the eleventh horn—which signifies that the last king will "humble" three of the former kings (*v.* 24). Porphyry made these three kings to be (1) Ptolemy Philometor, (2) Ptolemy Euergetes II., his brother, and (3) Artaxias, king of Armenia, whom Antiochus Epiphanes defeated and took prisoner. In order to refute this interpretation Jerome strangely asserts that Ptolemy Philometor and Ptolemy Euergetes "died long before the birth of Antiochus"[1]. In reality they both

---

[1] "Frustra Porphyrius cornu parvulum quod post decem cornua ortum est, Epiphanem Antiochum suspicatur, et de decem cornibus tria evulsa cornua, sextum Ptolemaeum cognomento Philometorem, septimum Ptolemaeum Euergetem, et Artaxiam regem Armeniae, quorum priores multo antequam Antiochus nasceretur, mortui sunt. Contra Artaxiam vero dimicasse quidem Antiochum novimus : sed illum in regno pristino permansisse". Jerome, *Comm. in Dan.* VII. 8. Appian says of Antiochus Epiphanes—Ἐστράτευσε δὲ καὶ ἐπὶ Ἀρταξίαν τὸν Ἀρμενίων βασιλέα, καὶ αὐτὸν ἑλὼν ἐτελεύτησεν κ.τ.λ. (*Syr.* 45).

survived him. But we may rightly urge against Porphyry's theory that these three kings were in no sense *predecessors* of Antiochus Epiphanes. That Ptolemy Philometor attempted to seize the throne of Syria on the death of Seleucus Philopator is a notion which rests on the sole authority of Porphyry himself (see Jerome on Dan. xi. 21), and it is highly probable that here, as in some other cases, Porphyry's statements are not derived from an independent historical source but are simply deductions drawn from Daniel. According to Von Lengerke, the three kings are (1) Heliodorus, (2) Ptolemy Philometor, and (3) Demetrius Soter. This interpretation is in part open to the same objections as the former one. It appears therefore much more reasonable to explain the three kings, with Hitzig and Cornill, as (1) Seleucus Philopator, (2) Heliodorus, and (3) Demetrius Soter. Seleucus Philopator, son of Antiochus the Great, died in 175 B.C. According to some historians he was murdered by his minister Heliodorus. In any case Heliodorus placed himself at the head of the state, but was very soon dispossessed by the brother of Seleucus Philopator, Antiochus Epiphanes, who had secured the help of Eumenes king of Pergamum. Meanwhile Demetrius Soter, son of Seleucus Philopator and rightful heir to the throne, was living as a hostage at Rome, whither he had been sent shortly before his father's death[1]. It would seem, from this chapter of Daniel, that some persons at least attributed the death of Seleucus Philopator to the instigation of Antiochus Epiphanes—that the pious Jews should have believed their persecutor to be capable of any crime, was quite natural. Hence there is no difficulty in regarding Seleu-

---

[1] "῾Ὧδε μὲν Ῥωμαῖοι διέθεντο τὰ δορίκτητα, Ἀντιόχου δ᾽ ὕστερον τοῦ μεγάλου βασιλέως τελευτήσαντος γίγνεται Σέλευκος ὁ υἱὸς διάδοχος. καὶ τὸν ἀδελφὸν ὅδε Ἀντίοχον ἐξέλυσε τῆς ὑπὸ Ῥωμαίοις ὁμηρείας, ἀντιδοὺς τὸν ἑαυτοῦ παῖδα Δημήτριον. Ἀντιόχου δ᾽ ἐπανιόντος ἐκ τῆς ὁμηρείας καὶ ὄντος ἔτι περὶ Ἀθήνας, ὁ μὲν Σέλευκος ἐξ ἐπιβουλῆς Ἡλιοδώρου τινὸς τῶν περὶ τὴν αὐλὴν ἀποθνήσκει, τὸν δ᾽ Ἡλιόδωρον Εὐμένης καὶ Ἄτταλος ἐς τὴν ἀρχὴν βιαζόμενον ἐκβάλλουσι, καὶ τὸν Ἀντίοχον ἐς αὐτὴν κατάγουσιν, ἑταιριζόμενοι τὸν ἄνδρα· ἀπὸ γὰρ τινῶν προσκρουμάτων ἤδη καὶ οἵδε Ῥωμαίους ὑπεβλέποντο. οὕτω μὲν Ἀντίοχος ὁ Ἀντιόχου τοῦ μεγάλου Συρίας ἐπεκράτησεν· ὅτῳ παρὰ τῶν Σύρων ἐπώνυμον ἦν ἐπιφανής, ὅτι τῆς ἀρχῆς ἁρπαζομένης ὑπὸ ἀλλοτρίων βασιλεὺς οἰκεῖος ὤφθη". Appian, *Syr.* 45. See also Livy XLI. 19.

cus Philopator and Heliodorus as two of the horns "plucked
up" before Antiochus. But whether the last of the three horns
is Demetrius Soter, appears more doubtful. The latter was not
actually king, but merely heir to the kingdom. Could he therefore be considered as one of the three kings whom Antiochus
"humbled"? The thing in itself is not unlikely. Von Gutschmid, however, has suggested (*Kleine Schriften*, Vol. II. pp.
175—179) that by the last of the three horns is meant, not
Demetrius, but a brother of his, who, according to a fragment
of John of Antioch, was put to death by Antiochus (see Müller,
Fragm. hist. graec. IV. p. 558). This view Kuenen is inclined
to adopt.

Much more important is the question as to the One like
a son of man (*vv.* 13, 14). On this subject two opposite interpretations have existed from a very early period down to the
present day. According to some, the One like a son of man
represents the coming king, i.e. the Messiah; according to
others he represents the kingdom of the Saints. The former
view cannot be proved to have been known in pre-Christian
times, for chaps. xlv—lvii of the Book of Enoch are of uncertain
date, nor is it even settled whether they are the work of a Jew
or of a Christian. But in the New Testament this view is constantly assumed, nor can there be any doubt that the term "the
Son of man", so frequent in the Gospels, contains an allusion to
Dan. vii. 13. The Messianic interpretation seems to have been
almost universal in the early Christian Church (see especially
Justin's *Dialogue with Trypho*, chap. XXXI), and is found likewise in the Babylonian Talmud (*Sanh.* 98ᵃ). In the Middle
Ages it was maintained by Rashi and by most Jewish commentators. In modern times it has been defended by critics so
impartial as Von Lengerke, Bleek, and Ewald.

Yet this view, popular as it has been, presents insuperable
difficulties. In the first place the interpretation contained in
this chapter of Daniel says not a word about a personal Messiah,
but states expressly that the kingdom is to be given to the
people of the Saints (*vv.* 18, 22, 27). If the Being who comes
in the clouds represents a person, that person must surely be of
immense importance. Why therefore does the angelic inter-

preter pass him over in complete silence, and speak of "the Saints" instead? Nor is it legitimate to argue that the description of this Being, in *vv.* 13 and 14, so clearly proves him to be personal as to render a special explanation unnecessary. The One like a son of man, that is, One in human form, obviously stands in contrast with the Four Beasts. Since the Four Beasts represent Four Empires, not four individual kings, it is reasonable to suppose that the One like a son of man also represents an Empire. The human form, as opposed to the bestial, teaches that the last kingdom will not be, like the Gentile kingdoms, a supremacy of brute force, but a supremacy essentially spiritual. As the Gentile Empires rise out of the sea (*v.* 3), so the last Empire comes with the clouds of heaven. The former statement is manifestly figurative, why therefore should the latter be taken literally? The rising out of the sea expresses the fact that the Gentile Empires are of this world (see *v.* 17); the coming with the clouds shews that the last Empire will be ushered in by the power of God. Thus in the chapter itself there is nothing which suggests the idea of a personal Messiah, and it is particularly important to observe that the rest of the book bears out this conclusion, for wherever the author speaks of the future kingdom he maintains the same significant silence as to a future king (chaps. ii. 44; xii. 3). Everything therefore tends to shew that the Being introduced in chap. vii. 13 represents the kingdom of the Israelite Saints. This interpretation was evidently known to Ephraim Syrus, and is accepted by Ben-Ezra. Such is also the view of Hitzig, Nöldeke, Schürer (*Gesch. d. jüd. Volkes*, II. p. 426), and most recent writers.

It has sometimes been objected that the idea of a future kingdom necessarily implied a personal king. But this is by no means borne out by facts. It is notorious that in several of the post-Biblical Jewish writings the future kingdom is conceived simply as a reign of Israel over the Gentiles, without any reference to a personal Messiah[1]. This is the case, for example, in the Assumptio Mosis and in the Book of Jubilees, both of which probably date from about the beginning of the Christian era.

---

[1] On the whole of this question see Prof. Stanton's work, "*The Jewish and* *the Christian Messiah*" (1886), especially pp. 109—118.

1—6. In dating this vision from the first year of Belshazzar, whose death has been already related (chap. v. 30), the
author purposely abandons the chronological order which he has
hitherto followed, that is to say, the visions are not a continuation of the narratives but form a series by themselves. The
words וְחֶזְוֵי רֵאשֵׁהּ עַל־מִשְׁכְּבֵהּ are added as a further specification of
חֵלֶם, cf. כְּתָבָא וְאֶסָרָא chap. vi. 10. "*Then he wrote the dream*";
at the beginning of this new portion of the book it was important to state that Daniel, like other seers, put his revelation
in writing; in the case of the remaining visions this is not
actually said but is everywhere assumed (see chap. xii. 4).
רֵאשׁ מִלִּין "*the sum of the matters*", that is, the essential import
of the revelation, cf. רֹאשׁ דְּבָרְךָ Ps. cxix. 160. On the interjection
אֲרוּ (*v.* 2), see chap. ii. 31. מְגִיחָן is usually taken as intransitive,
"*breaking forth upon the great sea*", according to Judg. xx. 33;
but in this case we should expect עַל־יַמָּא or בְּיַמָּא. It therefore
appears more natural to translate, with Levy (*Chald. Wörterb.*
s.v. גִּיחַ), "*stirring up the great sea*"; the phrase אֲגִיחַ קְרָבָא "to
go to war", lit. "to cause war to burst forth", is extremely
common in the Targums. "The great sea" is usually the Mediterranean (Josh. ix. 1). Here the sea represents the nations of
the earth (cf. Is. xvii. 12), and accordingly, in *v.* 17, it is explained by אַרְעָא "the earth"[1]. In *v.* 3 the Four Beasts are
described as "different one from the other", because they sym-
bolize different Empires. The first (*v.* 4) is the Babylonian. It
appears as a lion with eagle's wings; since it is the earliest of
the great Empires, it is here compared to the noblest of beasts
and the noblest of birds, just as in chap. ii. it is represented by
the most precious of metals. גַּפִּין "*wings*" is, as Nöldeke has
shewn in the *Gött. gel. Anz.* for 1884, p. 1019, from the root גרף,
cf. Arab. *jadafa*, "to fly", "to row". In Syriac also we find

---

[1] Prof. Robertson Smith suggests
that the imagery in Dan. vii. 2 is borrowed from the ideas of cosmogony
which were current in the ancient
East. According to Philo of Byblus
(quoted by Eusebius, *Praep. Evang.* I.
chap. 10), the Phoenicians believed the
world (Αἰών), personified as a man, to
have been born ἐκ τοῦ Κολπία ἀνέμου
καὶ γυναικὸς αὐτοῦ Βάαυ (i.e. Hebr. בֹּהוּ).
Here the wind Kolpia seems to be
רוּחַ כָּל־פֵּאָה "the wind from every
quarter". For other explanations see
Von Baudissin's *Studien zur semitischen Religionsgeschichte*, 1876, I. p.
13.

geppā "wing", but in the Targums the more primitive form גַּדְפָּא occurs. "*I looked until its wings were stript off, and it was lifted up from the earth and made to stand on two feet as a man, and a man's heart was given to it*". Von Lengerke explains these words as referring to the *decline* of the Babylonian Empire—the wings, the symbols of swiftness, are taken away, and it is reduced to the condition of an ordinary human being. But on this hypothesis the last clause would be meaningless, for "a man's heart" evidently implies superior intelligence, not loss of power. Accordingly Hitzig and Ewald see here an allusion to the experiences of Nebuchadnezzar in chap. iv. As in chap. ii. 38, Nebuchadnezzar and his Empire are treated as identical. The Babylonian Empire, on its first appearance, has a purely animal, i.e. heathen, character, but after a while the animal attributes disappear, the Empire is, as it were, humanized in the person of its representative. The passive Perfect הֳקִימַת clearly shews, by its second vowel, that it is not a Hebraism; the form exactly corresponds to the Arab. *uḳīmat*, excepting that the initial ה has been retained. Verse 5 introduces the Median Empire, in the form of a bear. It is "*raised up on one side*", i.e. half crouching, cf. chap. ii. 39 where the Median Empire is described as "lower" than the Babylonian. שְׂטַר "side" is in the Targums סְטַר stat. emphat. סִטְרָא; some editions wrongly read וְלִשְׂטַר־חַד. The vocalization הֲקֵמַת, in some editions הֲקִמַת, assumes that the verb is transitive, "*it raised one side*", but probably we should read הֳקְמַת or הֳקִימַת, as in *v.* 4. The meaning of the "*three ribs in its mouth between its teeth*" is very obscure. Most commentators refer this to three countries (Ewald), or three cities (Hitzig), which were conquered by the Medes. According to Von Lengerke, the author intends merely to represent the Median Empire as a ravenous beast devouring the remains of some slain enemy, the "three" being a round number. At all events the following words, "*And thus they spake to it, Arise, devour much flesh*", seem to shew that the Medes are here regarded as a power whose chief characteristic is destruction—an idea suggested by those passages of the prophets in which the Medes are summoned to ravage Babylon (Is. xiii. 17. Jer. li. 11, 28). The leopard (*v.* 6), representing the Persian Empire, has four wings (i.e. its power extends in all directions, towards the four quarters of the earth), and four heads, by which are meant the four Persian kings (see chap. xi. 2). על־גביה (*Ḳĕrī* עַל־גַּבַּהּ) is usually translated "*on its back*", but the plural form favours the rendering "*on its sides*" (cf. Syr. *gabbā* "side", from the root גנב). The clause, "*and dominion was given to it*", is added in order to emphasize the vastness of the Persian Empire, cf. chap. ii. 39 where this Empire is described as "ruling over all the earth".

7, 8. The Fourth Beast, i.e. the Greek Empire, is too fearful to be likened to any known creature; both in strength and fierceness it far surpasses its predecessors. We are so accustomed to consider the Graeco-Macedonian power as a civilizing agency that this description seems at first singularly inappropriate. We should however remember that the work of Alexander must have appeared to Orientals in a light very different from that in which we usually regard it. The former Empires had generally involved nothing more than conquest, and had left local customs untouched; the Macedonian Empire was, in the fullest sense, "different from all Empires" (*v.* 23), since it produced a radical transformation of the old oriental world. Moreover the atrocious massacres, at Tyre and elsewhere, by which Alexander endeavoured to strike terror into the conquered races, were not easily forgotten, and amply suffice to explain the image here employed—that of a monster "devouring, crushing, and stamping the residue under foot". אֵימְתָנִי "*terrible*" is the fem. stat. absol. of אֵימְתָן, which occurs in the Targums; in Syriac, adjectives in -*thān* form their fem. stat. absol. in -*thānyā*, not -*thānī*. The reading אֵמְתָּנִי, found in some editions, is erroneous. Besides the "iron teeth", *v.* 19 mentions "claws of brass", but Ewald is scarcely justified in inserting these words into *v.* 7, in order to assimilate the two passages; it would be equally reasonable to insert *v.* 21 after *v.* 8. On the "ten horns", see the Introduction to the chapter. With *v.* 8 compare the parallel passage, chap. viii. 9. Antiochus Epiphanes is represented by a "little horn" because he at first appeared feeble and seized the throne by "treachery" (chap. xi. 21). זְעֵיר is doubtless an old diminutive form, from *zu'air*. Instead of the normal סְלִקַת, the Masora prescribes סִלְקַת. On אתעקרו (Kĕrī אִתְעֲקַרָה) see נפקו chap. v. 5. The "eyes like the eyes of a man" are the symbol of intelligence, cf. viii. 23 where Antiochus is designated as מֵבִין חִידוֹת. The "mouth speaking great things" is an allusion to his pride and especially to his blasphemies against the God of Israel (chap. xi. 36).

9—14. The Divine judgment upon the Gentile power is now executed. The scene described is obviously intended to be figurative, since those who are judged are primarily Empires, not individuals; cf. Joel iv. 1, 2, a passage which the author of Daniel may have had in his mind. The forensic imagery is here consistently carried out. Thrones for the heavenly powers are set up, God Himself appears in the likeness of an aged man seated among flames, which, according to the well-known conception of the ancient Hebrews, are the accompaniment of the Deity (Ps. xviii. 9), and the books, recording the crimes of the Gentile potentates, are opened[1]. On the form כָּרְסָוָן see chaps. v. 20; vi. 8. With רְמִיו "were placed" compare the Syriac use of rĕme "thrown" for "lying", and the Hebr. יָרִיתִי Gen. xxxi. 51. Here, as in chap. iv. 14, the heavenly powers are associated with God Himself in judgment. With עַתִּיק יוֹמִין "one ancient of days" cf. the Hebr. בָּא בַּיָּמִים Gen. xxiv. 1 etc. "His raiment was like pure snow and the hair of His head like spotless wool"; most commentators, discarding the Masoretic accentuation, render, "His raiment was white like snow". On שִׂבְבִין see chap. iii. 22. That the throne has "wheels" is in accordance with Ezek. i. and x. In v. 10 נְגֵד וְנָפֵק seems to mean "was advancing and coming forth", נגד being used in its primitive sense (cf. Hebr. נֶגֶד "in front"). For the imagery, cf. אֵשׁ לְפָנָיו תּאֹכֵל Ps. l. 3. On אלפים (Kĕrī אַלְפִין), see אנשים chap. iv. 14. For the genuine Aramaic רבון (pron. רִבֽוָן) the Kĕrī substitutes the Hebraized form רְבְבָן, as if from a Sing. רְבָבָה corresponding to Hebr. רְבָבָה. דִּינָא יְתִב "the judgment sate"—דִּינָא here means

---

[1] The same metaphor is used by the "heathen" Arabic poet Zuhair, "Hide not from God that which ye devise, hoping that it will be concealed, for whatever men seek to hide from God that He knoweth; *it is reserved, laid up in writing, and kept in store against the day of reckoning,* or else requited speedily." (xvi. 26, 27 Ahlw.)

"those who judge", compare the use of סוֹד "deliberation" for
"persons who deliberate" (Jer. xxiii. 18. Ps. lxxxix. 8). In
v. 11 the Greek Empire is finally destroyed on account of the
blasphemies of Antiochus Epiphanes, the idea being that in
him the guilt of the Empire reached its height (cf. כְּהָתֵם הַפֹּשְׁעִים
chap. viii. 23). The other Beasts (v. 12) are humbled, though
not destroyed, i.e. Gentile kingdoms are still to exist for a while,
but they are to acknowledge the supremacy of the Saints (cf.
vv. 14, 27. Is. lx. 10, 12). It may seem illogical that the
Beasts, who represent Empires, should be said to lose their
Empire; what the author means is that the *nations* once dominant are to survive the loss of their dominion. On אַרְכָה, see
chap. iv. 24. In v. 14 the eternal sovereignty of the Saints is
described in terms applied elsewhere to the sovereignty of God
Himself (chaps. iii. 33; iv. 31; vi. 27).

15—28. In vv. 15 ff. the narration of the dream continues.
The author, in order the more clearly to explain his meaning,
represents Daniel as being troubled by what he had seen and
as questioning "one of those that stood by", i.e. one of the
attendant angels mentioned in v. 10. The angel first gives
a brief and general answer (vv. 17, 18), and afterwards, when
Daniel desires more special information as to the Fourth Beast,
supplies further details (vv. 23—27). אִתְכְּרִיַּת (instead of the
more primitive *ithkaryath*, which would correspond to the
Syriac form) is, if correctly pointed, taken from the masc. אֶתְכְּרִי
(cf. הִתְמְלִי chap. iii. 19), with doubling of the י in order to preserve
the preceding vowel (cf. Hebr. פֻּרְיָה from primitive *pāriyat*). For
the idea, cf. וַתִּפָּעֶם רוּחוֹ ch. ii. 1. The construction רוּחִי אֲנָה דָנִיֵּאל
is the same as מִנִּי אֲנָה אַרְתַּחְשַׁסְתָּא Ezra vii. 21. Instead of נִדְנֶה
(so Baer) most editions have נִדְנֶה. The word occurs again in
I Chr. xxi. 27 (נְדָנָהּ "its sheath"), and appears in the Targums
both as נדנא and לדנא; it is no doubt derived from the Persian
nidāna (in Sanscrit *nidhāna*) "vessel", "receptacle". In Daniel
therefore the correct pronunciation is probably נִדְנַהּ "*its sheath*"
(see Nöldeke in the *Gött. gel. Anz.* for 1884, p. 1022—גּוּנַהּ, in
the note, is of course a misprint). The "sheath" of the soul is
the body; for the image cf. Job xxvii. 8. In v. 17 the *Ķĕrī* substitutes the fem. אִנִּי (Syr. *ennēn*) for אִנּוּן (Syr. *ennōn*), which is

properly masc. (cf. chap. vi. 25). אַרְבְּעָה מַלְכִין "*four kings*", i.e four heathen Empires. יְקַבְּלוּן מַלְכוּתָא (*v.* 18) "*they shall receive the kingdom*", i.e. they shall come into possession of supreme power (cf. chap. vi. 1). The Israelite Saints, who are also called simply קַדִּישִׁין (*vv.* 21, 22) are here, as in *vv.* 22, 25, 27, described as קַדִּישֵׁי עֶלְיוֹנִין (LXX. and Theod. ἅγιοι ὑψίστου, Pĕsh. ܩܕ̈ܝܫܐ ܕܡܪܝܡܐ). Since קַדִּישׁ is used especially of angels (see chap. iv. 10), there can be no doubt that the author has selected the phrase קַדִּישֵׁי עֶלְיוֹנִין in order to express the *heavenly* character of Israel as contrasted with the nations of the earth. עֶלְיוֹן "the Most High", as a name of God, is the Hebrew equivalent of עִלָּאָה, עֶלְאָה (Dan. iv. 14, 21); the use of the Plur. עֶלְיוֹנִין is probably to be explained, with Hitzig, as due to the Plural preceding—so also we find בָּתֵּי כְלָאִים used as the Plural of בֵּית כֶּלֶא (Is. xlii. 7, 22). Others take עֶלְיוֹנִין as a Plural of majesty, but in the case of an Adjective this hypothesis is precarious. צְבִית לְיַצָּבָא (*v.* 19) "*I desired to have certain knowledge*"; the verb יַצֵּב bears somewhat the same relation to the Adj. יַצִּיב (see *v.* 16) that the Arab. aikana "to be sure" bears to yakīn "sure". Verse 20 is mainly a repetition from *vv.* 7 and 8, but it adds, respecting the eleventh horn, the words וְחֶזְוַהּ רַב מִן־חַבְרָתַהּ "*and its appearance was greater than (that of) the rest*". This in no wise contradicts the expression "a little horn" (*v.* 8), as is shewn by chap. viii. 9, where the "little horn" rapidly *grows* to a portentous size. Verses 21 and 22 are a parenthesis, in which Daniel recapitulates what he has witnessed, at the same time adding fresh details; that the horn in question waged war against the Saints had not been mentioned previously, and indeed it is difficult to imagine how Daniel could "see" such a war taking place. דִּינָא יְהִב (*v.* 22) is usually explained as "*justice was done*", i.e. the judicial sentence was pronounced in favour of the Saints. But perhaps Ewald may be right in reading וְדִינָא [יְתִב וְשָׁלְטָנָא] יְהִב "*and the judgment sate and the sovereignty was given*" etc., cf. *vv.* 14, 26, 27. וְזִמְנָא מְטָא "*and the time came*", i.e. the time fixed by God as the limit of the heathen domination. When the angel states, in *v.* 23, that the Fourth Empire is to "*devour the whole earth*", this must, of course, be taken in a rhetorical sense; similarly in chap. ii. 39 the Third Empire, i.e. the Persian, "bears rule over all the earth". In *v.* 25, לְצַד "*against*" has much the same meaning as לְנֶגֶד in chap. x. 13; the parallel passage, chap. xi. 36, uses עַל. יְבַלֵּא seems to mean "*he shall afflict*", cf. I Chr. xvii. 9 where לְבַלֹּתוֹ is substituted for the לְעַנּוֹתוֹ of II Sam. vii. 10; elsewhere the Hebr. בִּלָּה takes an impersonal object (Is. lxv. 22. Job xxi. 13. Lam. iii. 4—from the corrupt passage Ps. xlix. 15 no conclusion can be drawn). "*And he shall think to change seasons and law, and they shall be given into his hand for a time and times and half a time*". The primary reference is to the attempt of Antiochus to suppress the Jewish religion; perhaps other acts of the king may also be alluded to, for according to I Macc. i. 41, 42, which can scarcely be a pure fiction, he appears to have interfered even with heathen cults (see chap. xi. 37). By זִמְנִין are meant, not only the great religious feasts, but all religious observances which take place at fixed times (cf. Numb. xxviii. 2). דָּת is used, as in chap. vi. 6, for "the code of religious precepts" (Hebr. תּוֹרָה); in Rabbinical Hebrew דָּת often means "religion" generally. With עִדָּן cf. chap. עִדָּן וְעִדָּנִין וּפְלַג עִדָּן xii. 7. Almost all commentators recognize that "a time" is "a year" and that עִדָּנִין has a Dual sense (cf. עִנְיָן *v.* 8)[1]. Thus the Jewish cult is to be "given into the hand" of Antiochus, i.e. abolished by him, for three years and a half (see the Introduction to chap. viii). In *v.* 26 יִתִּב is, of course, the ordinary Imperfect Peal of יְתִב and corresponds to Syr. *nettebh*; Baer absurdly takes it to be a contraction of יִתְיְתִב. The object of שָׁלְטָנֵהּ is לְהַשְׁמָדָה וּלְהוֹבָדָא understood. עַד־סוֹפָא "*finally*", i.e. for ever (cf. chap. vi. 27). In מַלְכְוָת תְּחוֹת כָּל־שְׁמַיָּא (*v.* 27) the words תְּחוֹת כָּל־שְׁמַיָּא are treated as a substantive, i.e. "the majesty of the kingdoms of (the regions) under the whole heaven"; so in Syriac ܒܝܬ ܥܝܢܐ "between the eyes" is used for "forehead" (Pĕsh. Ezek. iii. 7, 8). יְהִיבַת "*shall have been given*"—for this use of the Perfect to express certainty cf. נֶעֶשְׂתָה chap. xi. 36. The suffixes in מַלְכוּתֵהּ and לֵהּ refer to עַם (cf. עַם יֹדְעֵי אֱלֹהָיו chap.

---

[1] In Syriac, as is well known, the old Dual termination *ain*, *ayin*, almost always becomes *in* and is thus indistinguishable from the Plural.

xi. 32). In *v.* 28 Daniel closes the account of the vision—"*So far is the end* (i.e. limit) *of the matter*". מִלְּתָא includes the whole revelation, both the things seen by Daniel and the things spoken by the angel, cf. הַדָּבָר chap. x. 1.

CHAPTER VIII.

As to the general sense of this chapter there has been comparatively little difference of opinion. In *vv.* 20—25 the author gives so clear an explanation of the vision that even the Christian Fathers could not wholly fail to grasp its meaning. Some details, however, still remain obscure, which is probably due in part to corruptions of the text.

The vision is dated from the third year of Belshazzar but it contains no reference to the Babylonian Empire. Its main subject is the rise and the conclusion of the Greek Empire, which, as we have seen, is the Fourth Empire of chaps. ii. and vii. The author therefore passes as rapidly as possible over the pre-Greek period, and after mentioning the conquests of Alexander hastens on to relate the history of Antiochus Epiphanes, who is represented, as in chap. vii., by a "little horn". Jerome and nearly all modern apologists, while denying that Antiochus Epiphanes is the "little horn" of chap. vii., fully admit that he is the "little horn" of chap. viii., and many fanciful attempts have been made to shew that the two descriptions cannot possibly refer to the same person. But to an impartial reader no real contradiction will appear to exist.

The principal difficulty in this chapter is the statement that the suspension of the daily sacrifice, in the reign of Antiochus Epiphanes, will last 2300 evenings and mornings (*v.* 14), i.e. 1150 days. How is this to be reconciled with chaps. vii. 25; ix. 27; xii. 7, 11, 12? The question is confessedly obscure, and any explanation should be offered with diffidence. It must first be remarked that these five passages agree at least in making the final distress last during three years and a fraction—the only difference lies in the magnitude of the fraction. Chaps.

vii. 25 ; ix. 27 ; xii. 7 offer comparatively little difficulty, for it
might be supposed that the "times, time and half a time", and
the "half of the week", are mere rough computations.   But
where the days are counted, no such vagueness can be admitted.
The question therefore is, Do the 1150 days begin at the same
moment as the 1290 days of chap. xii. 11 ?   The mention of the
abolition of the daily sacrifice in both passages certainly appears
to indicate that this is the case.   Accordingly a period of 140
days must elapse between the end of the 1150 days and that of
the 1290 days.   Perhaps the most probable hypothesis is that
the author of Daniel, like most of the later Jews, regarded the
future redemption of Israel, not as a single momentary act, but
rather as a series of events, which might be separated by inter-
vals of some months.   After 1150 days from the abolition of
the daily sacrifice (i.e. near the beginning of the year 164 B.C.[1])
the Jewish worship in the Temple was to be restored, but the
time of affliction was to last for 140 days longer, and after 45
more days the period of complete rest was to set in (chap. xii.
11, 12).   It is noteworthy that the author of Zechariah xii—xiv.
represents the final deliverance of Israel as about to take place
at a time when Jerusalem is being besieged by the heathen (Zech.
xiv. 2—4).   If, as is in itself highly probable, the author of
Daniel shared this belief, we can understand why the cleansing
of the sanctuary precedes, by some months, the final consummation, for in order that the nations may be "gathered against
Jerusalem to battle", it is necessary that the city should first
have been restored to Israel.   By what means the restoration of
the city is to be brought about, we are not told.

Cornill, who believes the book of Daniel to have been
written soon after the Purification of the Temple (which took
place near the end of the year 165 B.C.), supposes that this
event forms the conclusion of the 1150 days ; since the desecration of the Temple lasted only three years, he is obliged to make
the 1150 days begin, not with the cessation of the daily sacri-

[1] I here follow Schürer in supposing that the desecration of the Temple took place near the end of the year 168 B.C. (*Gesch. d. jüd. Volkes*, I. 155). But some scholars, e.g. Kuenen (*Historisch-critisch Onderzoek*, 2nd ed. II. 455), place it a year later.

fice, but with the publication of the edict against Judaism (I Macc. i. 41 ff.), which he places at the end of October 168 B.C. This theory involves a considerable straining of the text, for why should the daily sacrifice be mentioned in Dan. viii. 13, if in reality the starting-point of the 1150 days has no connection with it? Moreover it is hardly credible that chaps. ix, xi and xii were composed *after* the Purification of the Temple, for in chap. ix. 17 the sanctuary is still "desolate", and the last vision recorded, which distinctly mentions the cessation of the daily sacrifice (xi. 31; xii. 11), says nothing about its restoration. Thus we are forced to conclude that when the book was finished, the restoration of the daily sacrifice was still future.

1—4. For the construction אֵלַי אֲנִי דָנִיֵּאל cf. chap. vii. 15, and for the vocalization of הַנִּרְאָה, where the article is taken by the Masoretes as equivalent to the relative, cf. I Kings xi. 9. Is. lvi. 3. בַּתְּחִלָּה is not "in the beginning" but *previously*", and refers of course to chap. vii. (cf. chap. ix. 21. Gen. xliii. 18, 20). In *v.* 2 the seer finds himself carried in a vision to Shushan, as Ezekiel was carried to Jerusalem (Ezek. xl. 1—3). Shushan (Susa), the capital of Susiana, was one of the principal residences of the Achaemenid kings (Neh. i. 1), and appears from the book of Esther to have been regarded by the later Jews as the seat of the Persian Empire[1]. Hence it is chosen to be the scene of this vision which describes the overthrow of the Medes and Persians by Alexander. בִּירָה "fortress", "citadel", seems to be the Assyrio-Babylonian *bîrtu* (Friedr. Delitzsch, *Assyr. Gramm.*, Glossary), and occurs first in Nehemiah[2]. The fortress of Susa was celebrated in antiquity (Herod. v. 49. Polyb. v. 48). The author speaks of Susa as being "*in the province Elam*" (i.e. Elymaïs). Elam is here used in its wider sense and includes Susiana, from which it is distinguished in Ezra iv. 9. אוּבָל "stream", which occurs here only, seems to be a mere phonetic variation of יוּבָל (Jer. xvii. 8). Ulai has long ago been identified with the Eulaeus, the river on which, according to Pliny and Arrian, Susa was situated. Herodotus, on the other

---

[1] In much later times the tomb of the prophet Daniel was shewn at Susa or, as it was called by the Persians,

Shûsh (Nöldeke, *Ṭabarî*, p. 58).

[2] Ezra vi. 2 is probably of later date.

hand, places Susa on the Choaspes, and it is not clear whether both names belonged to the same river or whether different rivers are meant[1]. The Eulaeus seems to be identical with the modern Kārūn. In *v.* 3 the empires of the Medes and Persians (see *v.* 20) appear to Daniel in the form of a ram—a well-known symbol of power and dominion (Ezek. xxxix. 18)[2]. That a single animal represents both the Median and the Persian Empires is due to the fact that the two nations are regarded as being akin to one another; but in order to shew that the period of Median supremacy and the period of Persian supremacy are distinct, the author tells us that the higher horn of the ram rose last. לִפְנֵי הָאֻבָל "*opposite the stream*", cf. לָקֳבֵל נֶבְרַשְׁתָּא chap. v. 5. קְרָנַיִם and קְרָנָיו (*v.* 7) are Duals, but, for some reason which it is impossible to guess, the first part of the word is vocalized according to the analogy of Plurals; similar cases are דְּרָכַיִם Prov. xxviii. 6, 18 and דְּלָתַיִם, if this be from דֶּלֶת. הָאַחַת is here used for הָרִאשֹׁנָה, in opposition to הַשֵּׁנִית, cf. Gen. i. 5, 8; ii. 11, 13. The ram pushes westward, northward, and southward, but not eastward, for the eastern conquests of the Achaemenidae, which extended as far as India, are of no interest from the point of view of the Jews. In *v.* 4 הִגְדִּיל, as in *v.* 8, does not mean "became great", but "*did great things*" (Ewald).

5—8. מֵבִין "*observing*", cf. Is. lvii. 1. צָפִיר עִזִּים or צָפִיר occurs also in Ezra viii. 35. II Chron. xxix. 21; in Biblical Aramaic likewise we find צְפִירֵי עִזִּין Ezra vi. 17, in Syriac ṣephrāyā. Perhaps the word may have been borrowed from the Aramaic—in older Hebrew a he-goat is usually שָׂעִיר or שְׂעִיר עִזִּים. The original meaning of צפיר is obscure; that it is connected with the Arab. ضَفَرَ "to leap" is improbable, since the cases in which Arab. ض seems to correspond to Aramaic צ are extremely few (see Wright, *Comp. Gramm.* pp. 62, 63), and perhaps not one of them is certain. With the phrase עַל־פְּנֵי כָל־הָאָרֶץ "*over the face of all the earth*" Von Lengerke rightly compares I Macc. i. 3, where it is said of Alexander διῆλθεν ἕως ἄκρων τῆς γῆς. That the he-goat moves without touching the earth signifies

---

[1] On this question see Nöldeke's article *Ulai* in Schenkel's *Bibel-Lexikon*.

[2] So also in Arabic *kabsh* "ram" often means "a chief", "a warrior".

the incredible rapidity of the Greek conquests — the invaders seemed rather to fly than to march. וְאֵין נוֹגֵעַ בָּאָרֶץ should probably be taken as equivalent to וְאֵינֶנּוּ נוֹגֵעַ בָּאָרֶץ, the suffix being understood as in *v.* 27. קֶרֶן חָזוּת "*a conspicuous horn*", called in *vv.* 8 and 21 "the great horn". בַּחֲמַת כֹּחוֹ (*v.* 6) "*in the fury of his might*"; חֵמָה is originally "heat", and may express the "impetuosity" of an onset, just as elsewhere it expresses the "virulence" of a poison (Deut. xxxii. 24. Ps. lviii. 5). In *v.* 7 אֵצֶל must be taken as indicating closer proximity than עַד in *v.* 6. For וַיִּתְמַרְמַר אֵלָיו "*and he was angered against him*", see p. 30; אֶל is here used for עַל. חָזוּת אַרְבַּע (*v.* 8) is usually rendered "*four conspicuous horns*" (Von Lengerke, Hitzig), or, "*as it were four horns*" (Ewald). Both interpretations, however, are extremely forced, and there can be little doubt that Graetz is right in reading אֲחֵרוֹת for חָזוּת, according to the LXX. καὶ ἀνέβη ἕτερα τέσσαρα (Cod. Chis. τέσσασα) κέρατα κ.τ.λ., cf. also the parallel passage in chap. xi. 4. The corruption is easily explained from *v.* 5. The sense of *v.* 8 therefore is—"*And the he-goat did exceeding great things, and when he had become strong the great horn was broken, and there arose others, (even) four, in its place, toward the four winds of heaven*".

9—12. With יָצָא before a feminine subject, cf. I Sam. xxv. 27. I Kings xxii. 36. מִצְּעִירָה is generally supposed to mean "from smallness" or "out of smallness", hence "small" (Von Lengerke). Hitzig considers the מִן "redundant", but none of the passages which he quotes in support of this (II Sam. xiv. 11. Ps. xlix. 15. Ruth ii. 20) is conclusive. Ewald wishes to read מַצְעִירָה "shewing smallness" i.e. "appearing small". Graetz emends the passage by simply striking out the מ, but it is perhaps more probable that we should read קֶרֶן אַחֶרֶת צְעִירָה in accordance with chap. vii. 8 קֶרֶן אָחֳרִי זְעֵירָה. The corruption may be due to the הָאַחַת מֵהֶם almost immediately preceding. For יֶתֶר the LXX. has καὶ ἐπάταξεν (i.e. וַתַּךְ), which at first sight might seem preferable, but the Masoretic reading is confirmed by Is. lvi. 12; hence the ordinary translation "*exceedingly*" must be retained, cf. יַתִּירָה chap. vii. 7, 19 and Syr. *yattīr*. The little horn waxes great "*towards the South, and towards the East, and towards the Glory*". By "the South" is meant Egypt (see chap. xi. 25), by "the East" Media and Persia, and by הצבי, "the Glory", Jerusalem and the Temple, cf. ארץ הצבי chap. xi. 16, 41, הר צבי קדש xi. 45, and also Ezek. xx. 6. Instead of הצבי the LXX. has הצפון, which Graetz adopts, but it has all the appearance of a corruption, since the preceding words might easily lead a scribe to substitute הצפון for הצבי, whereas the contrary process would be inexplicable. This verse refers not merely to the foreign *conquests* of Antiochus, but to the extension of his influence and to the success of his intrigues, cf. chap. xi. 22—24. In *v.* 10 the relation of Antiochus to the Jews is more clearly defined. Here, as in chap. vii., the *heavenly* character of Israel, as distinguished from the nations of the earth, is specially emphasized. The "*host of heaven*" represents the people of God; but the term צבא is here used in a double sense and contains an allusion to the "service" in the Jewish Temple (Numb. iv. 23), as appears from *v.* 13. The "*stars*" are not distinguished from "the host of heaven"; the ו in וּמִן־הַכּוֹכָבִים is explicative, as in Zech. ix. 9 (Hitzig). By the casting down of some of the stars are meant the cruelties perpetrated at Jerusalem by Antiochus and his agents (I Macc. i. 24, 30), and perhaps there may be a special reference to the deposition and subsequent murder of the high-priest Onias III. (see chap. xi. 22). Verses 11 and 12 are among the most difficult in the whole book, as is shewn by the great disagreement between the commentators. That the text is here very corrupt can scarcely be doubted. The transition from the feminine gender to the masculine (הִגְדִּיל *v.* 11) would not in itself present any great difficulty, for it might be supposed that the author here drops the metaphor of a horn and speaks of Antiochus in direct terms, but in the second half of *v.* 12 the feminine gender reappears, although the horn has not again been mentioned— so that the above hypothesis must be abandoned. The idea naturally suggests itself that *v.* 11 and the first half of *v.* 12 may be an interpolation, but this notion is contradicted by *v.* 13. Nor can any help be derived from the LXX., which is here hopelessly confused. Even after we have struck out the obviously interpolated words καὶ ἐρρίφη χαμαὶ ἡ δικαιοσύνη καὶ ἐποίησε καὶ εὐωδώθη, we cannot recover with any degree of certainty the original text of the translation, still less the Hebrew text which lay before the translator. The following are the principal modern interpretations of the passage. Von Lengerke renders—"*Even unto the Prince of the host it exalted itself and took away from him the continual offering, and the place of his sanctuary was given up to destruction, and an host is delivered over together with the continual offering on account of iniquity, and it casteth the truth to the ground and will undertake and carry out with success*". It is scarcely necessary to point out the difficulties of this translation—the construing of צָבָא as feminine[1], the rendering of עַל "together with", etc. Hitzig agrees with Von Lengerke as to *v.* 11, excepting that he reads וְהַשְׁלֵךְ (historic Infinitive) instead of וְהִשְׁלַךְ. In *v.* 12 he substitutes וַתֵּשֶׁלֶךְ for וְתֵשְׁלֵךְ, and translates, "*And a warfare was undertaken against the daily sacrifice with iniquity* (Und zu Felde gezogen ward wider das tägliche Opfer mit Frevel), *and the truth was cast down to the ground, and it* (i.e. the horn) *accomplished this, and made it to prosper*". Ewald in *v.* 11 follows the Ḳĕrī, i.e. "*from him the daily sacrifice was taken away*". In *v.* 12 he has, "*And armed force is imposed upon the daily sacrifice through iniquity* (Und Heerzwang wird auf das Tagtägliche durch Frevel gelegt)" etc. It will be observed that Hitzig and Ewald agree in attributing to צבא in *v.* 12 a sense altogether different from that which it bears in *v.* 11. Thus it appears that the passage, in its present form does not admit of a satisfactory rendering, and since no plausible emendation has, so far as I am aware, been suggested, we can conclude only, from what follows, that *vv.* 11 and 12 contained some allusion to the cessation of the daily sacrifice and to the pollution of the Temple with heathen rites. Beyond this all is mere conjecture.

13, 14. The vision properly so called is followed by a dialogue between two angels. Daniel has already seen that the daily sacrifice is to be suspended, and he naturally desires to

---

[1] Isaiah xl. 2 proves nothing as to the gender of צָבָא, for מלאה צבאה probably means "she hath finished her warfare" (i.e. מָלְאָה, cf. Gen. xxix. 27, 28). The Masoretes, who pronounced מְלָאָה, evidently understood the words as "she is filled with her host"— the Targum has ארי עתידא דתיתמלי מעם גלוותהא.

know how long the period of desolation will last. The question however is not uttered by Daniel himself but by an angel—an idea which was possibly suggested to the author by Zech. i. 12. With וָאֶשְׁמְעָה (in some MSS. וָאֶשְׁמָעָה) cf. אֶשֶׁקָה I Kings xix. 20 and אֶפְשָׂעָה Is. xxvii. 4; Olshausen regards these forms as scribal errors, for in each case the original vowel of the second syllable must have been ă (*Lehrbuch der hebräischen Sprache*, p. 122). On the phrase אֶחָד קָדוֹשׁ see p. 30, and for the repetition of אֶחָד in the sense of "one" and "other" see Exod. xvii. 12. Jer. xxiv. 2. The LXX. presupposes אַחֵר both in the former and the latter clause—but this is no doubt an error. פַּלְמוֹנִי is absolutely unknown elsewhere, and is taken by all moderns as a contraction of פְּלֹנִי אַלְמֹנִי. So Symmachus has τινί ποτε, whereas the LXX., Theodotion and the Pĕshīṭtā, not understanding the word, simply transcribe it, as though it were a proper name. The intentionally vague phrase "some one or other who spake" seems to be used in order to indicate that the angel was invisible to Daniel. What the first speaker said is not told us; the second asks a question which in the Masoretic text presents great difficulties. Von Lengerke translates, "*For how long is the vision—the continual offering and the desolating iniquity—the treading down both of the sanctuary and the host?*" Not to mention the wholly unparalleled construction תת וקדש וצבא מרמס[1] (which, as the accents shew, was intended by the Masoretes), Von Lengerke's rendering is open to the objection that, if the question refers, as doubtless it does, to the *suspension* of the daily sacrifice, the speaker is here made to express himself in as awkward and obscure a manner as can be imagined. Hitzig prefers to connect תֵּת with what precedes, and translates "*For how long is the vision of the daily sacrifice—to leave unchecked the horrible iniquity and to trample down sanctuary and host?* (Bis wie lange das Gesicht vom täglichen Opfer? den entsetzlichen Frevel gewähren zu lassen, und Heiligthum und Heer zertreten?)" Whether this interpretation removes the difficulty may well be doubted, for not only is the placing of תֵּת after its object without analogy, but the meaning "gewähren lassen" is

[1] Hävernick endeavours to defend this by citing Ps. lxxvi. 7 and Jer. xxxii. 20, but neither passage is conclusive.

altogether unproved. Under these circumstances it is impossible to believe the text to be correct. On the whole, the least improbable solution may perhaps be as follows. The LXX. has, "Ἕως τίνος τὸ ὅραμα στήσεται καὶ ἡ θυσία ἡ ἀρθεῖσα καὶ ἡ ἁμαρτία ἐρημώσεως ἡ δοθεῖσα, καὶ τὰ ἅγια ἐρημωθήσεται εἰς καταπάτημα; here στήσεται was probably added as a gloss by the translator or by a later copyist, but the words ἡ ἀρθεῖσα, as Graetz observes, cannot be so explained and imply some additional word in the Hebrew. Graetz suggests הוּרַם; it is however more natural to postulate מוּרָם, for the presence of a participle after הַתָּמִיד would account for the rendering of תֵּת by ἡ δοθεῖσα. To the article in ἡ ἀρθεῖσα and ἡ δοθεῖσα no importance can be attached, for it has been already shewn that the translator added the article in a perfectly arbitrary fashion (p. 51). For וצבא he appears to have read יצבא, as also in *v.* 12 [11]—but this is no doubt an error. The Hebrew basis of the LXX. may therefore have been—

עדמתיהחזוונהתמידמורדמורהמוהפשעעשממתתוקדרשוצבאאמרמס

which may be read—

עַד מָתַי הֶחָזוֹן הַתָּמִיד מוּרָם וְהַפֶּשַׁע שֹׁם מִתִּתּוֹ קֹדֶשׁ וּצָבָא מִרְמָס:

i.e. "*For how long is the vision to be, while the daily sacrifice is taken away, and the Iniquity set up—from the time when he shall tread down the sanctuary and the service?*" In this case התמיר מורם והפשע שֹם is a circumstantial clause descriptive of the period which begins with the treading down of the sanctuary. The angel asks how long this period will continue. The "iniquity" which stands in opposition to the daily sacrifice must be identical with the "abomination" of chaps. xi. 31; xii. 11. For the Passive Participle שִׁים, see Num. xxiv. 21. Obad. 4. The verb שֹׁם is the very word used of the setting up of heathen altars in Jer. xi. 13, cf. also Jer. vii. 30; xxxii. 34. In chaps. xi. 31; xii. 11 the author of Daniel uses the verb נתן in this connection, but שֹׁם and נתן are often employed interchangeably by Old Testament writers, even in the same context (Deut. vii. 15. Is. xli. 19; xliii. 16, 19. Jer. vi. 8; ix. 10. Ezek. xxv. 13; xxxv. 4). That in these passages of Daniel the verb should vary, would be no more astonishing than that we find פֶּשַׁע in one passage

and שִׁקּוּץ in the two others. In this verse both the Masoretes
and the LXX. translator have been guided by the desire of
assimilating the expression to that used in chaps. xi. 31; xii. 11,
but in *both* cases the assimilation has involved a syntactical
anomaly. Verse 14 contains the answer to the angel's question,
and אֵלַי is therefore altogether inappropriate. The LXX., Theodotion, and the Pĕshīttā all read אֵלָיו, which Ewald, Hitzig, and
most modern commentators accept as correct. The phrase
עֶרֶב בֹּקֶר must be explained according to *v.* 26. Consequently it
is not, as Von Lengerke and others have supposed, a period of
24 hours (Gr. νυχθήμερον), but is equivalent to ערב ובקר "successive evenings and mornings" (so Ewald, Hitzig, Kuenen, and
Cornill), cf. Gen. viii. 22. Since it is a question of the suspension of the daily sacrifice, the verse alludes, no doubt, to the
evening oblation (chap. ix. 21) and the morning oblation (Exod.
xxix. 41). וְנִצְדַּק קֹדֶשׁ "*and then the sanctuary shall be justified*";
the Niphal נִצְדַּק, which is used nowhere else, seems to mean
properly "to prove oneself just" and hence "to be manifested as
just", cf. נִקְדַּשׁ "to shew oneself as holy" (Lev. xxii. 32. Ezek.
xx. 41). The justification of the sanctuary is the vindication of
its cause, for as long as it is polluted it lies under condemna-
tion. The vagueness of the words וְנִצְדַּק קֹדֶשׁ certainly appears to
confirm the view of those who hold that when the author wrote
the event had not taken place.

15—18. As in chap. vii., an interpretation of the vision is
supplied by an angel. וָאֲבַקְשָׁה בִינָה does not necessarily imply a
prayer to God, but is equivalent to צְבִית לְיַצָּבָה (chap. vii. 19).
The word גֶּבֶר is evidently used with reference to the name
גַּבְרִיאֵל. קוֹל אָדָם (*v.* 16) "*a human voice*", i.e. a voice speaking in
human language. בֵּין אוּלַי "*between (the two banks of the) Ulai*"—
a somewhat strange ellipse; for the idea cf. chap. xii. 6. גַּבְרִיאֵל
(Man of God), who among the later Jews was reckoned one of the
archangels, appears here for the first time. It is well known
that no names of angels are mentioned in any Jewish writing
older than the book of Daniel[1], whereas works of the period

[1] The ancient Israelites, as Ewald   283), assumed as a matter of course
observes (*Lehre der Bibel von Gott*, ii.   that an angel had no individual name,

immediately following, above all the book of Enoch, contain a highly developed angelology. To what influences this was due cannot, of course, be here discussed. הַלָּז, the shortened form of הַלָּזֶה (which occurs only in Gen. xxiv. 65; xxxvii. 19), is the etymological equivalent of the Arabic relative pronoun اَلَّ, shortened from the far commoner اَلَّذِى. Elsewhere הַלָּז, הַלָּזֶה, and the feminine הַלָּזוּ (Ezek. xxxvi. 35) are always appended to a determined noun (as is the case with הַזֶּה, הַהוּא etc.), except in I Sam. xiv. 1, where הַלָּז has the adverbial sense "there". For the construction of הָבֵן with לְ cf. chap. xi. 33. The terror with which Daniel is seized at the approach of Gabriel (v. 17) seems at first inconsistent with chap. vii. 16, but may be ascribed to the fact that Gabriel is no ordinary angel. Daniel is addressed as בֶּן־אָדָם, a phrase presumably suggested by the book of Ezekiel; he is bidden to mark well, "*for the vision is for the time of the end*", i.e. it refers to the final crisis of the world's history, and is therefore worthy of peculiar attention. Unless we are prepared to deny that the chapter refers to the time of Antiochus Epiphanes, this verse clearly shews that to the author the time of Antiochus was "the time of the end", or, in other words, that the Divine Kingdom was then to be established[1]. In v. 18 Daniel, who was already prostrate, loses consciousness on hearing the angelic voice, cf. the parallel passage chap. x. 9. The phrase עַל עָמְדִ (cf. chap. x. 11) after the verb עָמַד is peculiar to the post-exilic style (Neh. xiii. 11. II Chron. xxx. 16; xxxiv. 31 etc.); an older writer would here use פְּתְחִי (cf. I Sam. xiv. 9).

19—25. The interpretation of the vision is now given. The angel informs Daniel of what will take place "*in the last days of wrath*", i.e. at the end of the heathen domination, for the period of the subjection of Israel to the Gentiles is the period of the divine wrath (chap. xi. 36). כִּי לְמוֹעֵד קֵץ "*because*

---

i.e. he was merely one of a class (Gen. xxxii. 30), or else that his name was unutterable (Judges xiii. 18).

[1] Hävernick, who is forced to admit that "the little horn" of chap. viii. is Antiochus, endeavours to save his theory of the book of Daniel by explaining that "the time of the end" means only "one of the most important periods in the history of Israel"!

(*it is*) *for the time of the end*"; cf. *vv.* 17, 26, and chap. x. 14.
עֶת־קֵץ and קֵץ מוֹעֵד are identical terms, since עֵת bears much the
same relation to מוֹעֵד that שָׁבָת bears to מוֹשָׁב (cf. Ps. lxviii. 17 ;
cxxxii. 13)[1]. Verse 20 explains that the ram represents the
"kings", i.e. the empires, of the Medes and Persians, cf. chap.
vii. 17 where the Four Empires are called "four kings". In
v. 21 "king" is used in both senses ; the he-goat is the "empire"
of the Greeks, and the great horn is the first "king". הַשָּׂעִיר is
scarcely an epithet ("hairy"), but a synonym of הַצָּפִיר, added by
way of explanation. הַנִּשְׁבֶּרֶת (*v.* 22) is a *Nominativus pendens*,
"*and as for the horn that was broken, so that four arose in its
place*" etc. On the peculiar form מַלְכִיּוֹת see p. 30. Instead of
מִגּוֹי we should perhaps read מִגּוֹיוֹ, with Graetz, though the reading of the LXX. τοῦ ἔθνους αὐτοῦ proves very little ; the conjecture is supported by what follows, וְלֹא בְכֹחוֹ, where the suffix
obviously refers to Alexander (cf. ch. xi. 4). The form יַעֲמֹדְנָה is
rather to be regarded as an Aramaism than as a survival of
primitive Hebrew inflection—the only cases apparently analogous are Gen. xxx. 38. I Sam. vi. 12. The "four kingdoms",
which in *v.* 8 and chap. xi. 4 correspond to the four winds, are,
according to Porphyry, Macedonia, Syria, Asia, and Egypt—
according to Von Lengerke, Hitzig and others, Thrace (North),
Egypt (South), Syria (East), and Macedonia (West). But since
in chap. xi. the Seleucidae are called kings of the North, not
kings of the East, it is perhaps more probable that chap. viii. 22
refers to Syria, Egypt, Parthia, and Macedonia ; of the two latter,
with which the Palestinian Jews never came directly in contact,
the author may have had but a vague knowledge, so that we
need find no difficulty in the fact that the Parthian kingdom
was formed long after the other three. In *v.* 23 the phrase כְּהָתֵם
הַפֹּשְׁעִים is rendered by Von Lengerke and Hitzig, "*when the
sinners fill up their measure*". By "the sinners" are meant the
heathen oppressors. The LXX., Theodotion, and the Pĕshīttā
read "the sins" (הַפְּשָׁעִים), and this has been accepted by Ewald,
on account of chap. ix. 24. But if the author had meant "when

---

[1] I here assume that Delitzsch is
right in connecting עֵת with יָעַד.

Others have derived עֵת from עָדָה or
even from עָנָה.

the sins have come to the full", he would presumably have said כְּתֹם הַפְּשָׁעִים (cf. Is. xviii. 5). The objection which has sometimes been raised (e.g. by Meinhold) that the full measure of sin was not reached until after Antiochus had arisen, is hardly cogent, for the reign of Antiochus is obviously included in the אַחֲרִית מַלְכוּתָם, and all that the author intends, by inserting the words כהתם הפשעים, is to designate the *latter* days of Greek supremacy as the worst. "*A king insolent and skilled in double-dealing*"— חִידֹות has here a more general sense than "dark sayings", and means much the same as חֲלַקְלַקּוֹת in chap. xi. 21. Verse 24 contains several difficulties. וְלֹא בְכֹחוֹ signifies, according to Hävernick and others, "not by his own power, but by the permission of God". Von Lengerke more naturally explains "not by his strength, but by his intrigues" (cf. chap. xi. 23 וְעָלָה וְעָצַם בִּמְעַט־גּוֹי), כֹּחַ being used in a double sense. Very improbable is Ewald's interpretation, according to which the suffix in כֹחוֹ refers to Alexander the Great. Perhaps וְלֹא בְכֹחוֹ in *v.* 24 has been wrongly introduced from *v.* 22; in any case, if we strike out these words the sense is in no wise impaired. וְנִפְלָאוֹת יַשְׁחִית is rendered by almost all commentators, "*and he shall destroy wonderfully*"; in support of this Job xxxvii. 5 is quoted, but from such a passage no safe conclusion can be drawn. Graetz admits that ישחית is suspicious, but suggests no emendation. I venture to propose וְנִפְלָאוֹת יְשֹׂחֵחַ or וְנִפְלָאוֹת יָשִׂיחַ "*and he shall utter monstrous things*" (cf. יְדַבֵּר נִפְלָאוֹת chap. xi. 36). The verb שִׂיחַ is almost entirely confined to the poetical style, but the borrowing of poetical words is, as we have seen, characteristic of Daniel. The latter part of *v.* 24 must be discussed in connection with *v.* 25, which is usually translated "*and through his cunning he shall cause fraud to prosper in his hand*" etc.—contrary to all syntax. Graetz, following the LXX., reads וְעַל קְדֹשִׁים שִׂכְלוֹ— which we may safely accept. It has already been suggested (p. 53), in discussing the LXX. text of this passage, that the last words of *v.* 24 וְעַם קְדֹשִׁים are an interpolation occasioned by the beginning of *v.* 25. This view is confirmed by an examination of the context. We should scarcely be told first that Antiochus "destroyed the people of the saints", and afterwards that "his mind was against them". Accordingly it appears that

by the "many" (עֲצוּמִים) in *v.* 24 we are to understand, not the
Jews, but the political enemies of Antiochus, who, being a
usurper, naturally had many opponents among the upper
classes (see chap. xi. 22—24). It was not until he had firmly
established himself on the throne that his hatred of the Jewish
religion began to shew itself. Thus the author, having described
in *v.* 24 the political successes of Antiochus, passes on, in *v.* 25,
to describe the king's contest against Judaism, and fittingly
introduces the subject with the words וְעַל קְדֹשִׁים שָׂכְלוֹ "*and
against the Saints shall his mind be*", cf. וּלְבָבוֹ עַל־בְּרִית קֹדֶשׁ chap.
xi. 28. בִּלְבָבוֹ יַגְדִּיל is usually explained as "he shall be proud",
but it is rather, "*he shall devise great things*"; the Hiphil expresses the idea of *producing* something great, whether in the
way of deeds or thoughts. The destroying of many "unawares"
perhaps refers to the treacherous attack upon Jerusalem described in I Macc. i. 30; for the phrase בְּשַׁלְוָה see p. 31. The
"*Prince of princes*" is God, cf. chap. ii. 47. "*Without hand*"
means, of course, "not by human means, but by a special divine
intervention", cf. chap. ii. 34.

26, 27. The angel ends his speech with a solemn assertion
of the truth of "*the vision concerning the evening and the morning*", i.e. concerning the daily sacrifice (*v.* 14). Here for the
first time Daniel is commanded "to hide the vision", see chap.
xii. 4; the author of the book evidently intends by these words
to explain how the revelation made to Daniel had remained
hidden until the times of Antiochus Epiphanes. The ellipse in
כִּי לְיָמִים רַבִּים is precisely like that in *v.* 19. In *v.* 27 נִהְיֵיתִי and
the following ו are ignored by the LXX.; if the Masoretic text
be correct, נִהְיֵיתִי means "I came to an end" (cf. chap. ii. 1), i.e.
"I was exhausted", but it must be admitted that nowhere else
is נִהְיָה so used. The Pĕshīṭtā has *zā'ēth* "I trembled"—evidently a guess. The words וְאֵין מֵבִין "*and there was none who
understood*", do not, of course, imply that Daniel communicated
the vision to others, but the phrase must be taken as signifying
"and (I was) no understander (thereof)"; see what has been
said on וְאֵין נֹגֵעַ in *v.* 5, and for the idea cf. chap. xii. 8.

CHAPTER IX.

The two last visions of Daniel (chaps. ix—xii) differ from the preceding ones in that the events of history are no longer exhibited in the symbolical form of beasts, horns, etc., but are communicated to Daniel in direct terms. The vision in chap. ix. is dated from the first year of Darius, and is introduced by a long preface. The text of *v.* 2, interpreted in its most obvious sense, informs us that Daniel "understood by the Scriptures" the prediction of the prophet Jeremiah, according to which the desolation of Jerusalem was to last 70 *years.* Thereupon Daniel confesses before God the sins of Israel, acknowledges the justice of their punishment, and implores mercy. Whilst he is praying, the angel Gabriel appears with the announcement that 70 *weeks* are decreed for Israel, and that at the end of that period the sins of Daniel's people will be pardoned for ever.

This vision has been a subject of controversy, from a very early time, both among Jews and Christians. Ecclesiastical writers of the 3rd century differ widely from one another on the subject, and even so late as the time of Jerome there was no interpretation generally accepted in the Church. Similar disagreement prevailed among the medieval Rabbins, and in modern times the methods devised for solving the problem have been innumerable. To pass in review all the rival interpretations is therefore impossible; the utmost that can be attempted is to make a general classification, giving specimens of the principal types.

The main points to be discussed are (1) What is meant by a *week*? and (2) What events form the starting-point and the conclusion of the series?

As to the first of these questions, the great majority of interpreters, whether Jewish or Christian, ancient or modern, have held that a "week" is a period of *seven years.* Some early

Christians, however, according to Eusebius (*Demonstr. Evang.*
VIII.), explained the last week as a period of *seventy years,* while
admitting that the other sixty-nine weeks were periods of seven
years only.   To this very arbitrary assumption they were led
solely by the desire of making the 70th week cover the time
between the Crucifixion of Christ and the reign of Trajan.   A
notion still more extravagant has in modern times been defended
by Kliefoth, Keil, and others.   According to these writers the
"weeks" are "symbolical" "heavenly" or in plain language
unknown periods, and Keil proceeds to assure us that the incom-
prehensibility of the revelation is a striking proof of its divine
origin[1].   Every other interpretation, it seems, does violence to
the text; this alone satisfies all the conditions of the problem.
But in reality, this theory is more obviously at variance with
the text than any other that has been proposed.   Verses 22, 23,
and 25, certainly imply that the duration of the weeks was
definitely known; indeed, save upon this assumption, the speech
of the angel would be, from beginning to end, a piece of ela-
borate mockery.

Very much greater is the difference of opinion as to the
beginning and end of the 70 weeks.   On this subject no pre-
Christian interpretation has been handed down to us, for to
argue, with Hitzig and others, that the LXX. translator regarded
the 70 weeks as coming to an end in the time of Antiochus
Epiphanes, is unsafe, owing to the confused state of the Greek
text in this passage.   According to Jerome, the Jews of his age
made the 70 weeks to begin with the date of the vision, i.e. the
first year of Darius the Mede, and to end with the destruction
of Jerusalem by Hadrian.   The medieval Jews, on the other
hand, usually reckoned the weeks from the destruction of the
First Temple to the destruction of the Second, under Titus, the

[1] Lest it should be suspected that I have here exaggerated the absurdity of Keil's theory, I will cite his own words.   "Die Weissagung verliert dadurch, dass sie die Entwicklungszeiten der zukünftigen Vollendung des Gottesreichs und dieser Welt nach symbolischen nicht nach irdisch-chronologischen Zeitmaassen vorausverkündigt, nicht das Geringste von ihrem Offenbarungscharakter, sondern erweist dadurch erst recht ihren göttlichen über menschliches Meinen und Denken erhabenen Ursprung".   Keil, *Commentar,* p. 332.

first 7 weeks being the period of the Exile and the "Anointed
One" of *v.* 25 being Cyrus[1]. But Ben Ezra, while admitting
that the 70 weeks end with Titus, makes them to begin with
the date of the vision, the first seven weeks extending as far as
Nehemiah, who is the "Anointed One".

Early Christian theologians naturally endeavoured to find
in the passage a prediction of Christ, but the great discordance
between them sufficiently proves the difficulty of the task which
they undertook.

According to Julius Africanus (ap. Euseb.), the 70 weeks
begin with the decree of Artaxerxes, in the 20th year of his
reign (Neh. ii. 1—9), and end with the Crucifixion of Christ in
the 15th year of Tiberius. But as this amounts to 475 years
only, instead of 490, which is the number required, Julius Africanus attempts to get over the difficulty by saying that we are
to count by lunar, not by solar, years.

Hippolytus differs from Julius Africanus in that he recognizes a meaning in the division of the 70 weeks into $7 + 62 + 1$.
He makes the 7 weeks to extend from the date of Daniel's
vision to the Return of the Exiles under Joshua the high-priest,
Ezra, and Zerubbabel (*sic*), and the 62 weeks from the Return
of the Exiles to the birth of Christ. The 70th and last week
Hippolytus severs from the rest, and places at the end of the
world, in the time of the Antichrist (see the fragments of Hippolytus' *Commentary on Daniel,* in Migne's *Patrologia Graeco-
Latina,* Vol. x, and also *Das neu entdeckte vierte Buch des
Daniel-Kommentars von Hippolytus,* ed. Bratke, Bonn, 1891).

Eusebius (*Demonstr. Evang.* VIII.) dates the 7 weeks from
the Return of the Exiles in the 1st year of Cyrus to the completion of the Temple and the surrounding buildings in the 9th
year of Darius Hystaspis[2]. The 62 weeks he makes to extend
from the time of Darius to the taking of Jerusalem by Pompey,
in 63 B.C. He explains the "Anointed One" as a collective
term, referring to the Jewish high-priests from Joshua son of

---

[1] So Saadia the Gāōn (cited by Ben
Ezra), and Rashi.

[2] This Eusebius reckons as a period

of 49 years, whereas it amounted in
reality to 26 only (from 538 to 512
B.C.).

Jozadak to Alexander (Yannai), whose death (79 B.C.) he places 482 years after the accession of Cyrus[1]. Another view which Eusebius admits to be possible, is that the 70 weeks begin with the second year of Darius and that the 69th week ends with the death of the high-priest Hyrcanus II. (30 B.C.). The 70th week Eusebius, like Hippolytus, detaches from the others; but he does not regard it as still future. It extends, according to him, from the beginning of Christ's public ministry to the middle of the fourth year after the Crucifixion. The causing of the sacrifice and offering to cease (Dan. ix. 27) refers to the fact that upon the death of Christ the services in the Jewish Temple ceased to be recognized by God[2].

Apollinarius, according to Jerome, maintained that the 70 weeks did not begin till the birth of Christ; in the last week (from 483 to 490 A.D.) Elijah and the Antichrist were to appear. On this theory Jerome sagely remarks, *Periculose de incertis profert sententiam.*

It will be seen at once that the above patristic interpretations agree in nothing but in the attempt to establish a more or less fanciful connection between the 70 weeks and the rise of Christianity. Not one of them has any claim to be regarded as the interpretation current among the Christians of the Apostolic age, still less as an interpretation derived from a pre-Christian source. Here, as in so many other cases, a "traditional" explanation does not exist. The explanations given by the Rabbins and the Christian Fathers follow no definite system whatsoever, but are merely the random guesses of individuals, the gropings of men who lacked the clue to the book[3]. The endeavour made by modern apologists to obscure the subject by the introduction of dogmatic considerations is therefore alto-

---

[1] Strictly speaking therefore the 62 weeks (i.e. 434 years) should close at the death of the high-priest Alexander, not at the taking of Jerusalem by Pompey 16 years later.

[2] Some of the details of Eusebius' theory are uncertain, as the Latin translation by Jerome varies considerably from the present Greek text, but

any one who compares the two will, I think, admit that the abstract I have given is, in the main, correct.

[3] "*Scio de hac quaestione ab eruditissimis viris varie disputatum et unumquemque pro captu ingenii sui dixisse quod senserat*". Jerome, *Comm. in Dan.* cap. ix.

gether futile. If the question is to be decided at all, it must be decided on scientific grounds alone.

The first principle to be laid down for the interpretation of the vision is that it should be studied in close connection with what precedes. The prayer of Daniel and the revelation made to him are indissolubly linked together (*v.* 23). What then is the principal subject of Daniel's petition? Verse 20 supplies the answer—he prays on behalf of the "holy mountain" of God, that is, Jerusalem and the Temple. Accordingly we have a right to assume that Jerusalem and the Temple are also the subjects of the revelation; any interpretation which makes the speech of Gabriel to turn upon some different topic, must be unhesitatingly rejected. The 70 weeks, we are expressly told, concern, not the world in general, but the people and the holy city of Daniel (*v.* 24).

Another point to which special notice must be called is that the revelation sent to Daniel is intended "to give him clear understanding" (*v.* 22), he is to "understand and know" its contents (*v.* 25). We are therefore bound to suppose that the author of the chapter knew what was meant by a week, and knew from what point the 70 weeks were to be reckoned.

The 70 weeks obviously stand in connection with the 70 years of *v.* 2. Elsewhere in the Bible the word "week" always means a week of days (Dan. x. 2), but that this cannot be the case here is evident, and the idea of weeks of years therefore naturally presents itself. The institution of the sabbatical year proves that the *notion* of a week of years was quite familiar to the ancient Jews—the word Sabbath being applied indifferently to the 7th day and to the 7th year (Lev. xxv. 2, 4). It has often been noticed that, according to the author of the book of Chronicles, the 70 years of captivity foretold by Jeremiah corresponded to 70 sabbatical years (II Chron. xxxvi. 21 as compared with Lev. xxvi. 34, 35). Moreover if we believe the book of Daniel to have been composed in the Maccabean period, there is yet another reason for the connection between the 70 years and the 70 weeks of years. For, as I have before pointed out, the 2nd verse of this chapter states that the author understood by reading the Scriptures the number of the years fixed for the desolation of Jerusalem according to the prophecy of Jeremiah, i.e. he discovered in the Scriptures something which enabled him rightly to understand Jeremiah's prediction. But to what passage of Scripture does he here refer? Some light is thrown on the question by *vv.* 11 and 13, where the punishment that has come upon Israel is said to be "written in the law of Moses". All commentators are agreed that Lev. xxvi. 14 ff. is at least one of the passages which the author had in mind. But no one, so far as I am aware, has noticed that the *special* allusion is to Lev. xxvi. 18, 21, 24, 28, where it is emphatically declared that the Israelites are to be punished *seven times* for their sins. The 70 weeks become intelligible if we suppose that the author of Daniel combined Jer. xxv. 11; xxix. 10 with Lev. xxvi. 18 ff. The motive is obvious. Since he firmly believed in the infallibility of Jeremiah's prediction, and was at the same time painfully conscious that the prediction, in its literal sense, had received but a very partial fulfilment, it became necessary to seek for some new interpretation. This was supplied by the passage in Leviticus. The 70 years of Jeremiah were to be repeated 7 times, and at the end of the 490th year the long-promised deliverance might be confidently expected. In the exegesis of the later Jews such deductions, formed by artificially combining different passages of Scripture, were extremely common.

If therefore the 70 weeks are merely the 70 years of Jeremiah multiplied by 7, it is clear that the 70 weeks must begin in the time of Jeremiah. The question has often been discussed whether the *terminus a quo* is the date of Jeremiah's prediction, as is maintained by Hitzig, or the destruction of Jerusalem by Nebuchadnezzar, as is maintained by Von Lengerke, Ewald, and Schürer. It is probable, as Graetz remarks, that the author of Daniel did not separate these two events in his mind but regarded them as contemporaneous. To the post-exilic Jews what seemed important was the fact that Jeremiah, the prophet of the last days of the Judaean kingdom, had foretold 70 years of desolation. The precise date of the prophecy was immaterial. Accordingly in II Chron. xxxvi. 21 the 70 years are represented as beginning with the destruction of Jeru-

salem[1], and there is every reason to suppose that the author of
Daniel took the same view.

On the other hand, those modern interpreters who connect
the 70 weeks with the coming of Christ naturally endeavour to
place the *terminus a quo* much later. For this purpose two
principal theories have been proposed: that of Hengstenberg
who dates the 70 weeks from the 20th year of Artaxerxes I.,
and that of Auberlen who dates them from the 7th year of the
same king. In order to make the 490 years end at the time
required, Hengstenberg has recourse to the extraordinary assumption that Artaxerxes I. came to the throne in 474 B.C. (so
that his 20th year would begin in 455), and discovers, as we
might have expected, many wonderful confirmations of this idea.
But since it is now admitted by every one that Artaxerxes I.
began to reign in 465 or 464 B.C., Hengstenberg's theory has
been generally abandoned. With regard to the theory of
Auberlen, it is sufficient to remark that it contradicts the text,
for how could Daniel be said to "understand the vision", if the
terminus a quo, upon which the whole matter depended, were an
event that took place some 70 or 80 years after his death?
Are we to suppose that on some previous occasion, of which
nothing is recorded, the history of the reign of Artaxerxes had
been supernaturally revealed to him?

Since therefore the 70 weeks begin with the destruction of
Jerusalem, we may proceed to examine the division into
$7 + 62 + 1$. Great as are the obscurities of the text in some
matters of detail, the following facts stand out clearly. The
first 7 weeks date from "the going forth of the word" for the
building of Jerusalem, and end with the appearance of an
Anointed One, a Prince. The 62 weeks end with the cutting
off of an Anointed One. The one remaining week is divided into
halves—during the latter half "sacrifice and oblation" are suspended. All critical interpreters identify the second half of the
last week with the "time, times, and half a time" of chap.

[1] This is quite compatible with the
fact that the Chronicler seems to regard the Return of the Exiles under
Cyrus as the close of the 70 years
(II Chron. xxxvi. 22). Zechariah,
writing *circa* 519 B.C., evidently thought
that the 70 years were only just coming
to an end (Zech. i. 12).

vii. 25, so that the middle of this week must coincide with the
cessation of the daily sacrifice, by the order of Antiochus, near
the close of the year 168 B.C. (see p. 128, note), and the 70th
week therefore ends in 164. But here a difficulty arises. From
588 B.C. (the probable date of the destruction of Jerusalem) to
164 there are only 424 years. Of this fact various explanations
have been suggested. Ewald imagines that the full sum of
490 years was diminished, owing to an afterthought of the
writer, and even goes so far as to maintain that a passage, in
which this was stated, has fallen out at the end of the chapter.
The theory has, it need hardly be said, found few adherents.
Von Lengerke and Hitzig make the 7 weeks to run parallel
with the first 7 weeks in the next series (i.e. the 62 weeks),
instead of preceding them. But this interpretation, if less fantastic than Ewald's, is at least highly artificial and scarcely
reconcileable with the text. Finally, Graf, Nöldeke, and Cornill have given it as their opinion that the author of Daniel,
who lived amongst a people very imperfectly acquainted with
the chronology of remote ages, followed an incorrect computation. Schürer agrees with this view, and shews that a precisely similar error is found in other Jewish writers ; thus
Josephus places the reign of Cyrus some 40 or 50 years too
early (compare *Bell. Jud.* VI. 4, 8. *Antiq.* XIII. 11, 1 ; XX. 10),
while Demetrius, an Egyptian Jew who composed a work on
chronology about the end of the 3rd century B.C., places the
fall of Samaria (722 B.C.) 573 years before the accession of
Ptolemy IV. (222 B.C.)[1]. We cannot suppose that either Demetrius or Josephus was exceptionally ignorant of chronology, and
if professed historians could fall into such mistakes, it is absurd
to expect superior accuracy in an apocalyptic work such as
Daniel. The difficulty of calculating dates in the ancient
world was much greater than is usually imagined[2]. Until the
establishment of the Seleucid era, in 312 B.C., the Jews had no
fixed era whatsoever. Hence the length of the period between

[1] See Schürer, *Gesch. d. jüd. Volkes,*
II. p. 616.
[2] A curious instance of this is seen
in the fact that the Persians, under
the Sāsānian kings, reckoned only 266
years from Alexander the Great to the
overthrow of the Parthian dynasty
(228 A.D.).

Cyrus and Alexander could be discovered only by summing up the reigns of the Persian kings, and it may be doubted whether, in the Maccabean age, one Jew in ten thousand was acquainted even with the names and order of these kings, not to mention the length of their reigns, for the study of non-Biblical history was never a part of Jewish education.

It has sometimes been objected that since the author of Daniel recognizes only 4 Persian kings (see chap. xi. 2), and since the existence of the Seleucid era must have enabled him to compute approximately the date of Alexander, he cannot have made the interval between Cyrus and Alexander so great as the above interpretation would require. But this objection proceeds upon the unfounded assumption that all those chronological difficulties which occur to us must have occurred to the author of Daniel.

1—3. On Darius, son of Ahasuerus, see the Introduction to chap. vi. The name אחשורוש was possibly borrowed by the author from Ezra or from Esther, in both of which books it is spelt as in Daniel. But the form originally in use among the Jews was no doubt אחשירש (pron. *Aḥashyarsh* or *Aḥshayarsh*), for the native Persian form is *Khshayārshā*, and on an Aramaic stele found in Egypt and now preserved at Berlin, the name is written חשיארש (see the *Corpus Inscr. Sem.* Pt. 2, Nᵒ. 122). With בִּינֹתִי (*v.* 2) compare רִיבוֹת Job xxxiii. 13. These forms were regarded by Ewald as shortened from הֲבִינֹתִי and הֲרִיבוֹת, but Nöldeke has shewn, in the *Z. D. M. G.* XXXVII. p. 525 ff., that the dropping of the ה of the Hiphil, where there is no prefix, is impossible in Hebrew[1]. Accordingly בִּינֹתִי is either a Ḳal, inflected according to the analogy of the Hiphil and of such forms as סַבּוֹתִי, or else a mere scribal error for בַּנֹתִי, cf. בָּנְתָה Ps. cxxxix.

2. בִּינֹתִי בַּסְּפָרִים is rendered by Von Lengerke "*I sought to understand the Scriptures*", and by Hitzig "*I marked in the Scriptures the number of the years*" etc. But if the view suggested on p. 146 be correct, the sense must be "*I understood by the Scriptures*" etc.—the Scriptures being here the Pentateuch. With the form מַלֹּאות cf. מְלֹאות Jer. xxv. 12 and מְלֹאת Jer. xxix.

---

[1] See also Wright, *Comp. Gramm.* p. 244, where the same view is taken.

10. Such forms are combinations of the vulgar pronunciation מִלּוֹת, מִלּוֹה, with the etymologically correct מְלָא, מַלְּא ; see again chap. x. 3. In *v.* 3 "*to seek prayer and supplication*" is, of course, to apply oneself to them, cf. Zeph. ii. 3.

4—9. This prayer bears a striking resemblance to those in Neh. i. 5 ff.; ix. 6 ff., and to that in the Book of Baruch i. 15 ff.[1] It is commonly supposed that the author of Daniel copied from Nehemiah. But it is also possible that both writers were merely using current formulae, for the language of devotion is peculiarly liable to flow in traditional grooves, and how often must prayers such as these have been offered up by the devout Israelites during the long ages of Gentile oppression! Daniel here speaks as the representative of his people, and it is remarkable that in the whole prayer there is not a single verse which does not apply at least as well to the days of Antiochus Epiphanes as to the days of the Babylonian Exile. Nowhere does the speaker even hint that he is at a distance from Palestine; in *v.* 7 the phrase "*all Israel, those who are near and those who are afar off in all the lands whither Thou hast driven them*", can scarcely mean anything but "those Jews who are in Palestine and those who are in foreign countries", the speaker himself belonging to the former of these classes. The expression "*our kings*", in *v.* 8, does not, of course, assume the existence of a Jewish king at the moment, any more than it does in Neh. ix. 32. The speaker is here looking back upon the history of Israel, and he confesses that from of old his people have been transgressors.

10—14. For וַתִּתַּךְ see *v.* 27 and Jer. xlii. 18; xliv. 6. II Chron. xii. 7; the same metaphor occurs again in Ps. lxxix. 6 and Rev. xvi. "*The curse and the oath which is written in the law of Moses*" refers back to *v.* 2 and, as has before been said, to Lev. xxvi. 18 ff. In *v.* 12 "*judges*" is apparently a general term for "rulers" (Amos ii. 3. Ps. ii. 10). Ewald, believing that the author of Daniel copied from Baruch, considers this verse an abbreviated form of Bar. ii. 1, where the word "judges"

[1] Compare especially Dan. ix. 4 with Neh. i. 5 (which again is based upon Deut. vii. 9); Dan. ix. 7, 8 with Bar. i. 15—17; Dan. ix. 12, 13 with Bar. ii. 1, 2; Dan. ix. 14 with Neh. ix. 33. Bar. ii. 9; Dan. ix. 15 with Neh. ix. 10.

is evidently used in its special historical sense. For אֲשֶׁר "so that", in אֲשֶׁר לֹא־נֶעֶשְׂתָה, see I Kings iii. 12. Is. lxv. 16. To the pious Jews the outrages committed by Antiochus at Jerusalem appeared altogether unparalleled, as we can see from the terms, doubtless somewhat hyperbolical, which are employed in I Macc. i. 39, 40; ii. 7—12. In *v.* 13 the אֵת in אֵת כָּל־הָרָעָה הַזֹּאת is probably due to the preceding passive, כָּתוּב, cf. Num. xxxii. 5. I Kings ii. 21. לְהַשְׂכִּיל בַּאֲמִתֶּךָ is rendered by Von Lengerke "*to become wise through Thy truth*", and by Hitzig "*to have insight into Thy faithfulness* (einzusehen deine Treue)", i.e. to realize that God fulfils His threats; the original meaning of the root שׂכל is, of course, "to gaze", "to contemplate". With the phrase וַיִּשְׁקֹד יהוה עַל־הָרָעָה (*v.* 14) cf. Jer. i. 12.

15—19. Upon the confession of sin now follows the prayer for deliverance. "*And so Thou gattest to Thyself renown as at this day*", i.e. the memory of Thy deeds is still living among us, cf. Ps. xliv. 1 ff. That the recollection of God's acts in the remote past and, above all, of the Exodus from Egypt, contributed greatly to rouse the enthusiasm of the Jews in the Maccabean age, appears from many indications. In *v.* 16 צִדְקֹתֶךָ (with defective spelling, according to Baer) "*Thy righteous acts*", are the works which God has wrought for His people, cf. Judg. v. 11. I Sam. xii. 7. The words "*Jerusalem and Thy people are a reproach to all that are round about us*" exactly express the position of the faithful Jews under Antiochus, since in addition to the tyranny of the king they had to endure the taunts of their heathen neighbours, the Edomites, the Ammonites, etc. The word שָׁמֵם (*v.* 17) is chosen with special reference to שִׁקּוּץ שֹׁמֵם (chap. xii. 11), i.e. the heathen altar set up in the Temple. Instead of לְמַעַן אֲדֹנָי the LXX. has ἕνεκεν τῶν δούλων σου δέσποτα, i.e. למען עבדיך אדני, which gives a decidedly better sense. For though in this prayer the speaker several times passes from the second to the third person without any apparent reason, the words למען אדני, following immediately upon a petition, would be very harsh. Nor can it be objected that למען עבדיך is inconsistent with the confession of the utter unworthiness of Israel, for the same phrase occurs in Is. lxiii. 17, a passage of very similar import. The opening words of *v.* 18 are almost identical with II Kings xix. 16. Is. xxxvii. 17.

20—23. Though Daniel had already *understood* the meaning of Jeremiah's prophecy (*v.* 2), Gabriel appears, before the prayer is ended, to give him fuller and more explicit information. With הָאִישׁ "the man", as applied to Gabriel, cf. כְּמַרְאֵה גָבֶר chap. viii. 15 and also Acts i. 10. For בַּתְּחִלָּה "*previously*" see chap. viii. 1. The peculiar phrase מֻעָף בִּיעָף is rendered by Hävernick and Von Lengerke "*being caused to hasten with haste*", מֻעָף being taken as a participle Hophal from יָעַף, a verb which elsewhere is used only in the Kal, and which, it must be admitted, never means "tò hasten" but "to be weary". יָעֵף is a noun of the same form as יָקָר. Theodotion, the Pĕshīttā, and the Vulgate have here "*flying*", according to which interpretation מֻעָף would be from עוּף; but to this there are two objections, firstly that בִּיעָף would then become inexplicable, and secondly that nowhere in the Old Testament are angels represented as flying[1]. Meinhold takes מֻעָף בִּיעָף as referring to Daniel, and translates the clause, "*whom I had seen previously, when I was exhausted*", cf. chap. viii. 17, 18. נֹגֵעַ אֵלָי "*approaching me*", cf. Jon. iii. 6. Job iv. 5. "*About the time of the evening oblation*", see Acts iii. 1. The mention of the oblation doubtless refers to the suspension of the daily sacrifice—Daniel is praying for the holy mountain of his God at the hour when, in the usual course of things, the evening oblation would be offered. For וַיָּבֶן (*v.* 22) "*and he instructed (me)*", the LXX. and the Pĕshīttā read ויבא "*and he came*". The phrase לְהַשְׂכִּילְךָ בִינָה apparently signifies, not "*to cause thee to understand the meaning of the prophecy*" (Von Lengerke), but rather "*to give thee clear understanding*"— בינה being used adverbially, cf. אַל תִּתְגָּר בָּם מִלְחָמָה Deut. ii. 9, 24; phrases of this kind form the transition from the use of the abstract verbal noun as the object of the verb (as in וַיַּךְ בָּהֶם מַכָּה גְדוֹלָה I Sam. xix. 8) to the so-called accusative of manner (as in וְרָעוּ אֶתְכֶם דֵּעָה וְהַשְׂכֵּיל Jer. iii. 15). יָצָא דָבָר (*v.* 23) "*a word went forth*", i.e. the divine sentence, which now follows, was uttered. With the term חֲמוּדוֹת, applied to Daniel, we must

---

[1] Jacob's dream, in Gen. xxviii. 12, obviously assumes that angels are wingless.

compare אִישׁ חֲמֻדוֹת in chap. x. 11, 19; the expression is a peculiar one, for elsewhere חֲמֻדוֹת is used of things, never of persons (see Dan. x. 3; xi. 38, 43); the only passage in which the verb חמד has God as its subject is Ps. lxviii. 17, the object being *impersonal*. The LXX. has here ὅτι ἐλεεινὸς εἶ, and ἄνθρωπος ἐλεεινός in chap. x. 11, 19, i.e. the translator read חסדות (חֲסֻדוֹת) instead of חמדות, for ἔλεος is the most usual rendering of חֶסֶד. In favour of this reading it might be urged that אנשי חסידות "men of piety" actually occurs in the Palestinian Talmud (*Sōṭāh* ix., near the end). But, on the whole, the Masoretic text is here to be preferred, for singular as the expression אִישׁ חֲמֻדוֹת appears, it may have been suggested by some such phrase as יֶלֶד שַׁעֲשׁוּעִים Jer. xxxi. 19. With the use of the fem. plural חֲמוּדוֹת as "*an object of affection*", cf. בְּרָכוֹת "an object of blessings" Ps. xxi. 7. וּבִין בַּדָּבָר וְהָבֵן בַּמַּרְאֶה "*therefore heed the word, and give heed to the vision*"; בִּין is here the Imperat. Ḳal, of the same form as שִׂים (see what has been said on בִּינֹתִי *v.* 2), and apparently does not differ in meaning from הָבֵן, cf. רְשַׁעְנוּ *v.* 15 and הִרְשַׁעְנוּ *v.* 5.

24. This verse lays down the fundamental principle, which is afterwards explained in detail. The 70 years foretold by Jeremiah are to be understood as 70 weeks of years, and by the end of this period the redemption of Israel will be complete. It has already been remarked that elsewhere in the Old Testament שָׁבוּעַ always means "a week of days", here only "a week of years"; in this latter sense it is sometimes used in post-Biblical Hebrew, e.g. in the Mishnah, *Sanh.* v. 1. Instead of the Pl. שָׁבֻעִים, which occurs 6 times in Daniel, other Biblical writers employ שָׁבֻעוֹת (e.g. Exod. xxxiv. 22. Deut. xvi. 9. II Chron. viii. 13). On נֶחְתַּךְ "*have been decreed*", see p. 30; for the use of the singular form of the verb with a plural subject, cf. Gen. xxxv. 26. Job xxii. 9, in both of which cases the verb has, as here, a *passive* meaning. The expression "*thy people and thy holy city*" does not imply, as Jerome imagines, that Israel and Jerusalem are no longer recognized by God, but is used because Daniel represents the true Israel, cf. עַמֶּךָ chap. xii. 1 and the phrase בֵּית קָדְשֵׁנוּ וְתִפְאַרְתֵּנוּ Is. lxiv. 10. Von Lengerke rightly observes that the Infinitives which now follow

refer, not to the events which take place during the course of the 70 weeks, but to the blessings with which the 70 weeks conclude. לְכַלָּא stands for לְכַלּוֹת, as in Jer. xxxviii. 4 מָרַפֵּא stands for מְרַפֵּה, owing to the confusion (doubtless the result of Aramaic influence) between roots with final א and those with final י. Von Lengerke chooses to read לִכְלֹא, which he renders "to shut in" (einschliessen); but such a metaphor is very forced. In ולחתם חטאות the word ולחתם is no doubt a mistake for וּלְהָתֵם (Kĕrî), due to the ולחתם almost immediately following. Von Lengerke, however, prefers the Kĕthîb "to seal", although "to seal up sin" elsewhere signifies "to reserve it for punishment" (Job xiv. 17, cf. Deut. xxxii. 34), which cannot be the sense here. Instead of the Kĕthîb חטאות the Masoretes read חַטָּאת, for the sake of the parallelism, but this is unnecessary (see Micah i. 5). Hitzig translates this passage "to complete the transgression and to fill up the measure of sin" ("zu vollenden den Abfall und zu füllen das Sündenmaass"); it is however more in accordance with the context to understand כלא and התם in the negative sense, i.e. "to make an end of", "to abolish" (cf. Num. xxv. 11. Ezek. xxii. 15). The versions read as follows—LXX. συντελεσθῆναι τὴν ἁμαρτίαν καὶ τὰς ἀδικίας σπανίσαι (read σφραγίσαι)—Theod. τοῦ συντελεσθῆναι ἁμαρτίαν καὶ τοῦ σφραγίσαι ἁμαρτίας—Aquila, τοῦ συντελέσαι τὴν ἀθεσίαν καὶ τοῦ τελειῶσαι ἁμαρτίαν—Pĕsh. ܠܡܚܬܡ ܚܛܗܐ ܘܠܡܫܠܡܘ ܚܛܝܬܐ. The next clause וּלְכַפֵּר עָוֹן is, according to the accents, connected with what precedes, but it should rather be coupled with וּלְהָבִיא צֶדֶק עֹלָמִים, for the six acts here enumerated naturally fall into three pairs. The words כַּפֵּר and צֶדֶק are both legal terms, by the "atoning of sin" and the "bringing in of everlasting righteousness" is meant the termination of that controversy or suit (רִיב) which God has with His people (see Is. xxvii. 9). "To seal vision and prophet" is "to confirm" the predictions of the prophets (Von Lengerke, Hitzig), cf., in the New Testament, John iii. 33; vi. 27. The metaphor is taken from the affixing of a seal to a document in order to attest its genuineness (I Kings xxi. 8). The last act is "to anoint the most holy thing"—i.e. to consecrate the Altar in the Temple, which, when the author wrote, was given up to the heathen worship. Some early Christians and some medieval Jews discovered an allusion to the Messiah in this passage (see the Pĕshīṭtā and Ben-Ezra), but the phrase קֹדֶשׁ קֳדָשִׁים, which occurs more than forty times in the Old Testament, never refers to persons, always to things, and is used especially of the Altar of sacrifice (Exod. xxix. 36, 37 ; xxx. 29 ; xl. 10).

25—27. וְתֵדַע וְתַשְׂכֵּל is rightly pointed as indicating a command, "*and so thou art to know and to understand*". The "word" (דָּבָר) is of course the divine promise uttered by Jeremiah; for the phrase, cf. *v.* 23 and Is. lv. 11. That the expressions להשיב ולבנות and תשוב ונבנתה are meant to correspond to one another, is evident. Yet most commentators translate the former "*to restore* and to build", and the latter "shall be built *again*", taking the verb first in a literal and afterwards in a derived sense (so Ewald). Von Lengerke and Hitzig endeavour to avoid the difficulty by translating תשוב "*shall be restored*". But it appears much more probable that we should read לְהֹשֵׁב וְלִבְנוֹת "*to people* and to build", and תֵּשֵׁב וְנִבְנְתָה "shall be *peopled* and built"—cf. Isaiah xliv. 26. Jer. xxx. 18. Ezek. xxxvi. 10, 11, 33. If it be asked why the author says "to people and to build" rather than "to build and to people", the obvious answer is that the *repopulation* of Jerusalem necessarily preceded the *rebuilding*, and as a matter of fact we know from Nehemiah that nearly a century after the First Return most of the city was still in ruins (Neh. vii. 4). By the מָשִׁיחַ נָגִיד most modern interpreters (Von Lengerke, Hitzig, Schürer, Cornill) understand Cyrus, on account of Is. xlv. 1. Graetz however, agreeing with Eusebius, explains it as referring to the line of Jewish high-priests. This view appears to be supported by the following considerations. Firstly in *v.* 26 and in ch. xi. 22 the words מָשִׁיחַ and נָגִיד certainly seem to designate the High-Priest. Secondly, if the author were referring to Cyrus, he would surely not content himself with saying "till an Anointed One, a Prince", but would add something to indicate that this Anointed One was the liberator of the Jewish exiles. That the term מָשִׁיחַ may be applied to the High Priest is shewn by Lev. iv. 3, 5, 16 ; vi. 15, and with regard to נָגִיד Graetz has observed that it exactly corresponds to προστάτης, προστασία, used of the High Priest in his civil capacity (Ecclesiasticus xlv. 24. Josephus, *Antiq.* XII. 4. 2)[1]. It appears therefore that the first 7 weeks end with the reestablishment of the Jewish worship under Joshua son of Jozadak (Ezra iii. 2), who bore the title of High Priest even before the completion of the new Temple (Haggai i. 1. Zech. iii. 1). From that time till the reign of Antiochus Epiphanes there was always a מָשִׁיחַ נָגִיד at Jerusalem, and the city continued to be "peopled and builded". But what is meant by רְחוֹב וְחָרוּץ? Von Lengerke disconnects these two words and considers רְחוֹב to be the subject of the preceding verbs; he therefore renders, "*And as for 62 weeks—the street* (or, *public place) shall be restored and built*" etc. Others, following the Masoretic accentuation, take רְחוֹב וְחָרוּץ as a single phrase, and suppose that the subject of the preceding verbs is Jerusalem (so Hitzig). חָרוּץ is explained by Von Lengerke as "that which is determined", on account of נֶחֱרָצָה in *vv.* 26, 27; his rendering "*and it is determined, but in distress of times*"—is, however, quite impossible. Most recent interpreters (Ewald, Cornill and others) make חָרוּץ to mean "trench" or "moat", and in proof of this the term חריץ is cited, which occurs in the Mishnah (e.g. *Kil'ayim* II. 8; v. 3) and the Talmud. But it there seems to be used only of "ditches" (in fields or gardens), never of "trenches" for purposes of fortification. And why should "trenches" be mentioned here, for elsewhere we read of "walls" or "towers" as the bulwarks of Jerusalem? A city built on such uneven ground can be but very imperfectly defended by moats. Moreover the coupling together of רחוב וחרוץ "public places and trenches" would be very strange. Hitzig translates "nach Strasse und Hof", but for this rendering of חָרוּץ there is no authority. The renderings of the LXX. (εἰς πλάτος καὶ μῆκος) and of Theodotion (πλατεία καὶ τεῖχος) seem to be mere guesses. Graetz proposes רחוב וחיץ "*with public places and walls*", and thinks that this was the reading which lay before Theodotion. But neither in Ezek. xiii. 10, the only other pas-

---

[1] נָגִיד may also be compared to the Arabic *imām* (cf. נֶגֶד =*amāma*), which is applied both to temporal and spiritual leaders, but especially to the latter.

sage in the Old Testament where the word occurs, nor yet in post-Biblical Hebrew, so far as Graetz has shewn, does חָרִיץ signify the wall of a city, as the context would here require. Perhaps we should read רְחֹב וְחוּץ "*with public places and streets*", Pĕsh. ܘܫܘܩܐ ܘܦܬܝܐܬܐ, cf. Jer. v. 1. For the construction of רְחֹב וָחוּץ as an adverbial phrase, cf. וְהַשָּׁמַיִם הִתְקַדְּרוּ עָבִים וְרוּחַ I Kings xviii. 45. Instead of וּבְצוֹק הָעִתִּים the LXX. has καὶ κατὰ συντέλειαν καιρῶν and the Pĕshīttā ܘܒܫܘܠܡ ܙܒܢܐ, i.e. וּבְקֵץ הָעִתִּים. That the Pĕshīttā has here been influenced by the LXX. is improbable. The difficulties of the Masoretic reading are obvious, for, not to mention the fact that צוֹק occurs nowhere else, the notion of "troublous times" would surely be expressed, as Graetz remarks, by "times of trouble" not "trouble of times" (cf. עֵת צָרָה chap. xii. 1, עִתּוֹת בַּצָּרָה Ps. ix. 10; x. 1 and similar expressions). Such a phrase as צוֹק הָעִתִּים is altogether without analogy. Moreover the ו before בצוק seems to indicate that here a fresh clause begins; the rendering "*even in troublous times*" is extremely forced—the Pĕshīttā, feeling this difficulty, ignores the ו altogether. I therefore venture to think, with Graetz, that the words in question should be connected with what follows. Whether we should strike out the ו in וְאַחֲרֵי (*v.* 26), as Graetz proposes, or whether we should regard the words וְאַחֲרֵי הַשָּׁבֻעִים שִׁשִּׁים וּשְׁנַיִם as an interpolated gloss, is doubtful; in either case the sense remains the same. יִכָּרֵת מָשִׁיחַ "*an Anointed One shall be cut off*", refers, according to Von Lengerke, to the death of Seleucus Philopator (175 B.C.). Hitzig and others explain it as an allusion to the deposition of the High Priest Onias III., which took place early in the reign of Antiochus Epiphanes. This latter view appears decidedly the more probable (see chap. xi. 22). The words which follow, וְאֵין לוֹ, are very uncertain. The renderings which have been proposed "but not for himself", "and he shall have nothing (or no one)", "and he shall cease to be"—all present grave syntactical difficulties. The idea naturally suggests itself that we should read וְאֵינֶנּוּ "and he shall be no longer", but it is more likely that some word or words have fallen out. Graetz wishes to read וְאֵין עוֹזֵר לוֹ as in chap. xi. 45; since however the latter passage refers to the

death of Antiochus, not to the death of Onias III., the emendation is hardly probable. The latter half of *v.* 26 and the whole
of *v.* 27 are involved in such extraordinary difficulties that hardly
any two interpreters take the same view. Any attempt to con-
strue or emend the passage must be regarded as purely conjectural. As it is impossible to discuss the innumerable suggestions
that have been made, I must confine myself to points of special
importance. Von Lengerke, following the Masoretic text, translates, "*and the city and the sanctuary shall be devastated by
the people of a prince, who cometh and in the flood (shall be) his
end, and till the end (shall be) war and a decree of desolations*"
("und die Stadt und das Heiligthum wird verwüsten Volk
eines Fürsten, welcher kommt und in der Fluth sein Ende, und
bis aufs Ende Krieg und Beschluss der Wüsten"). The "prince",
according to Von Lengerke, is Antiochus Epiphanes; after his
"people" (i.e. his armies) have ravaged Jerusalem, he is to
"come" into Persia, and then "his end" will overtake him in
the midst of a "flood" (i.e. an armed multitude). Hitzig and
Ewald also make this "prince" to be Antiochus, whereas Graetz
identifies him with the "Anointed One" who is "cut off", i.e.
the High Priest Onias III. Instead of עַם Graetz reads עִם
(according to the LXX., Theod. and the Pĕsh.), and he explains
the sentence as meaning that the city and sanctuary are to
share in the ruin of Onias. For the words הַבָּא וְקִצּוֹ, Graetz
substitutes וּבָא קִצּוֹ (with the LXX.) "*and his end shall come*".
That the "prince" is Antiochus seems improbable from chap. xi.
22, but it is likewise unsafe to identify him with the "Anointed
One", for in that case the author would presumably have said
עַם הַנָּגִיד. I would therefore suggest, though with the greatest
diffidence, that we should read וְהָעִיר וְהַקֹּדֶשׁ יִשָּׁחֵת עִם־נָגִיד הַבָּא, "*and
the city and the sanctuary shall go to ruin, together with the
prince that shall come (after Onias)*". If נָגִיד does not refer to a
person previously mentioned, the omission of the article is possible (cf. Gen. i. 31. Ps. civ. 18). The "prince" would seem to
be Jason, the brother and successor of Onias III., and to him
therefore we may refer the suffix in קִצּוֹ; his miserable end is
described in II Macc. v. 7—10. Since the latter half of *v.* 26
anticipates the events of the 70th week, as is shewn by the

phrase וְעַד קֵץ, we need find no difficulty in the fact that the final overthrow of Jason took place about 170 B.C., i.e. after the 70th week had begun. The metaphor of a "flood", for "destruction", appears again in chap. xi. 22. "*And until the end shall be war (and) a sentence of desolations*"—קֵץ here means the end of the time of affliction (cf. chap. viii. 17, 19), and the "war" is that which is being waged by Antiochus against the Saints (chap. vii. 21). נֶחֱרֶצֶת is stat. constr. of נֶחֱרָצָה (*v.* 27 and chap. xi. 36), properly that which is "cut", "decided". For the present "a sentence of desolations" is being executed upon Jerusalem, but the time of deliverance is near. Verse 27 describes the last week, i.e. the period beginning in the year 171 B.C. Von Lengerke translates, "*A week shall make a firm covenant with the many, and during half the week he shall abolish sacrifice and oblation, and over the edge of abominations (cometh) the desolator; and (this shall be) till the consummation and (till) the sentence shall be poured out upon the desolator*". According to this interpretation, the "covenant" is the conspiracy of the apostate Jews against the religion of Israel; the "edge of abominations" is the Temple defiled by heathen rites, and the "desolator" is Antiochus. Hitzig agrees with Von Lengerke in taking שָׁבוּעַ אֶחָד to be the subject of the first clause, but he explains הִגְבִּיר as "make burdensome", and בְּרִית as the covenant of God with Israel, i.e. for a week those who adhere to the covenant are to be persecuted. Each of these interpretations is open to serious objection. In the first place, to speak of a period of time as "making a covenant", or "rendering a covenant burdensome" would be quite without analogy. Secondly, the meanings here ascribed to הִגְבִּיר cannot be proved; in the only other passage where the Hiphil of this verb occurs (Ps. xii. 5) it has a totally different sense. Ewald agrees with Von Lengerke as to the meaning of הִגְבִּיר, though he makes Antiochus, not the week, to be the subject of the verb. Graetz substitutes וְהֶעֱבִיר for וְהִגְבִּיר, and thinks that the sense is either, "*And he* (i.e. Antiochus) *shall abolish the covenant for the many*", or else "*And he shall cause the many to transgress the covenant*". Whether the words will admit of this latter rendering is extremely doubtful, and, in any case, if Graetz be right in supposing that hitherto

Antiochus has not been mentioned, it is very unlikely that the verb here refers to him. Perhaps the author may have written וְהֻפַר בְּרִית לָרַבִּים " *and the covenant shall be annulled for the many*", i.e. there is to be a period of general apostasy; cf. Jer. xxxiii. 21. The use of a masculine verb with a feminine subject is particularly common when the verb is *passive* (Judges xvi. 11. Is. xxi. 2. Jer. xxix. 22). The "many" are, of course, the majority of the Jewish people (cf. chap. xi. 33). In the latter half of the verse, the article of הַשָּׁבוּעַ shews that it is still a question of the 70th week, not of a subsequent period; thus we are to understand that during the latter half of the 70th week (from 168 to 164 B.C.) "sacrifice and oblation" cease. As it is impossible to discover a subject for the transitive יַשְׁבִּית (unless we take the "prince" of *v.* 26 to be Antiochus), we should perhaps read יִשְׁבֹּת. Of the clause וְעַל כְּנַף שִׁקּוּצִים מְשׁוֹמֵם innumerable interpretations have been proposed, besides that of Von Lengerke quoted above, but none of them is even plausible[1]. If the text be sound, it is clear that מְשׁוֹמֵם (so Baer reads, not מְשֹׁמֵם) must be taken as an epithet of שִׁקּוּצִים (see chaps. xi. 31; xii. 11), according to the very rare construction אֲדֹנִים קָשֶׁה Is. xix. 4. This at once disposes of all those renderings which make מְשׁוֹמֵם by itself to be the subject of the clause. For וְעַל כְּנַף it has been proposed to read וְעַל כַּנּוֹ " and instead thereof" (cf. chap. xi. 20, 21, 38)—an emendation which appears wellnigh certain (see Kuenen, *Historisch-critisch Onderzoek*, II. p. 472). In this case, the suffix in כַּנּוֹ refers to the זֶבַח וּמִנְחָה, which, as they together form the daily sacrifice, may be construed as a singular. משומם may be a corruption of שָׂמִים or מְשָׂמִים " set up", from שׂוּם, of which the Hophal perhaps occurs in Gen. xxiv. 33—see what has been said on chap. viii. 13. In the last clause of *v.* 27 the phrase כָּלָה וְנֶחֱרָצָה " *ruin and sentence (of judgment)*" is quoted from Is. x. 23; xxviii. 22. If כָּלָה וְנֶחֱרָצָה be, as seems natural, the subject of the verb תִּתַּךְ, we are almost obliged to read וְעַד (with Bleek), for when עַד introduces a verbal clause, the verb takes precedence of the subject (Gen. xxxviii. 11. Josh. ii. 22. II Sam. x. 5. Prov. vii. 23); a well-known case in which עַד has

---

[1] "Die Ausleger", says Hitzig, "sind hier selbst mit allerhand שִׁקּוּצִים in die Wochen gekommen".

been wrongly pointed as עָד is Job i. 18. שׁוֹמֵם, according to
Von Lengerke and Ewald, refers to Antiochus, on whom a divine
judgment is to be poured out. But to this there are two objections—firstly, that in chap. xii. 11 שֹׁמֵם refers to the שִׁקּוּץ, not to
Antiochus; secondly, that neither שׁוֹמֵם nor מְשׁוֹמֵם ever means
a "desolator". It is also remarkable, though the difficulty is
not an insuperable one, that שׁוֹמֵם has no article. I would venture to propose that for עַל־שׁוֹמֵם we should read עַל־שָׂמָם "upon
him that set them up" (according to the analogy of קָמֵי etc.),
the suffix referring to the שִׁקּוּצִים; cf. again chap. viii. 13.

For the convenience of the reader, I here repeat the last
four verses of the chapter, emended and translated according to
the suggestions made above.

24. *Seventy weeks are decreed for thy people and for thy
holy city, to make an end of transgression and to do away with
sins, to atone for iniquity and to bring in everlasting righteousness, to seal vision and prophet and to anoint the most holy thing.*

25. *Know therefore and understand (that) from the going
forth of the promise to people and to build Jerusalem until an
Anointed One, a Prince, (there are) seven weeks, and for sixty
and two weeks it* (i.e. Jerusalem) *shall be peopled and built,
(with) public places and streets:*

26. *And in the end of the times [after the sixty and two
weeks] an Anointed One shall be cut off and shall have no......
and the city and the sanctuary shall go to ruin together with the
Prince that shall come (after him), and his end (shall be) in
a flood (of destruction), and until the end (shall be) war, a sentence of desolations.*

27. *And the covenant shall be annulled for the many during
one week, and during half the week sacrifice and oblation shall
cease, and instead thereof (there shall be) abominations set up,
and afterwards ruin and a sentence (of judgment) shall be poured
out upon him that set them up.*

CHAPTERS X—XII.

The fourth of Daniel's visions is, from a historical point of view, by far the most important of all. The whole of chap. x., it is true, is little more than a prologue, but in chap. xi. we find a complete survey of the history from the beginning of the Persian period down to the time of the author. Here, even more than in the earlier visions, we are able to perceive how the account gradually becomes more definite as it approaches the latter part of the reign of Antiochus Epiphanes and how it then passes suddenly from the domain of historical facts to that of ideal expectations. Accordingly those interpreters who endeavour to find in the vision allusions to historical events later than the Maccabean period, have had to contend against the greatest difficulties. As it was impossible to deny that the description up to chap. xi. 21 referred to the predecessors of Antiochus Epiphanes, most of the Christian Fathers took refuge in the hypothesis that between *v.* 20 and *v.* 21 there is an interval of several centuries, although the opening words of *v.* 21, "And there shall arise *in his place* a contemptible man," clearly shew that in the mind of the author there was no interval whatever[1]. Nor have modern apologists been more fortunate. Kliefoth takes the liberty of assuming, without a shadow of proof, that a few thousand years elapse between chap. xi. 35 and what follows. Hävernick asks us to believe that chap. xi. 45 refers to the death of Antiochus Epiphanes, and that the next verse (which begins, "*At that time* shall Michael stand up") refers to a period still future.

In order to understand the vision it is of the utmost importance to determine, as nearly as possible, the date of its

[1] On chap. xi. 21 Jerome remarks "Hucusque ordo historiae sequitur, et inter Porphyrium ac nostros nulla contentio est. Caetera quae sequuntur usque ad finem voluminis, ille interpretatur super personâ Antiochi qui cognominatus est Epiphanes...Nostri autem haec omnia de Antichristo prophetari arbitrantur qui ultimo tempore futurus est",

composition, or in other words to discover the exact point at which the description ceases to be historical and becomes ideal. Von Lengerke thinks that the piece was written directly after the death of Antiochus, and that with chap. xii. 1 the author begins to describe his expectations. But there seems reason for believing that the transition takes place earlier, namely in chap. xi. 40. The arguments are briefly as follows. Although it is not certain how many times Antiochus invaded Egypt, one thing is tolerably clear—that in Daniel xi. *three* invasions only are mentioned, i.e. those in *vv.* 25—28, in *v.* 29, and in *vv.* 40—43. To suppose, with Hitzig and others, that *vv.* 22—25 refer to an invasion of Egypt, has been shewn by Hoffmann to be altogether illegitimate (*Antiochus IV. Epiphanes*, pp. 94—96). Both Hoffmann and Schürer (*Gesch. d. jüd. Volkes*, I. p. 130) are of opinion that the first Egyptian campaign took place in the summer of 170 B.C. This is no doubt the campaign described in Dan. xi. 25—28 and I Macc. i. 17—19[1]. Antiochus seems to have invaded Egypt again in 169 B.C., but the fact is not mentioned in Daniel, for the invasion spoken of in chap. xi. 29 must be that of the year 168 B.C. After this, it would appear, Antiochus never attacked Egypt again. We are thus led, with Cornill, to regard the invasion described in Dan. xi. 40—43 as one which the author expected but which never actually took place. The hypothesis of Von Lengerke and Hitzig that in *v.* 40 the author suddenly goes back to describe events anterior to 168 B.C., does violence to the plain sense of the text. But a difficulty still remains. Porphyry, quoted by Jerome, states that in the 11th year of his reign (i.e. in 165 B.C.) Antiochus again made war upon Egypt, and explains Dan. xi. 40—43 as referring to this campaign[2]. Several modern interpreters, e.g. Hävernick and Hoffmann, have accepted Porphyry's explanation. It is, however, quite incredible that the author of Daniel is here describing facts. A conquest of Egypt such as we read of in this passage, could not have been passed over

[1] In II Macc. v. 1 this campaign is called "the second", but the statement is probably erroneous.

[2] On Dan. xi. 40, 41, Jerome says, "Et haec Porphyrius ad Antiochum refert: quod undecimo anno regni sui rursus contra sororis filium Ptolemaeum Philometorem dimicaverit".

in silence by all the historians, for Egypt was at that time under Roman protection and an attack upon the country must therefore have at once produced a war with Rome. Nor can we suppose the campaign here described to have been so short that the Romans had no time to interfere. The text implies that it is of considerable duration, for not only is all Egypt at the feet of Antiochus but even the more distant Libyans and Ethiopians make their submission to him. It is a still more fatal objection to Porphyry's interpretation that it entirely contradicts what we know about Antiochus himself at this period. Nothing is more certain than that this king at the end of his reign—far from "having power over the treasures of gold and silver and all the riches of Egypt"—was reduced to great financial distress. We are therefore forced to conclude that Porphyry was here in error. Whether the mention of the "eleventh year" is due simply to the fact that Antiochus reigned eleven years, so that any event which was believed to have occurred at the end of his reign would naturally be placed in his eleventh year, or whether Porphyry has confounded the eleventh year of Antiochus with the eleventh year of Ptolemy Philometor (i.e. 170 B.C.), I do not venture to determine. In any case no historical argument can be built upon Porphyry's treatment of this passage, for it is evident (as Meinhold has observed) that when he describes Antiochus as pitching his tent "in the place called Apedno between the Tigris and the Euphrates", the narrative is based upon nothing but a false interpretation of Dan. xi. 45.

If the above reasoning be valid, these three chapters must have been composed before the death of Antiochus. Indeed it appears well-nigh certain that they were composed more than a year before his death, for they mention neither the great victories of Judas Maccabaeus nor the recovery and reconsecration of the Temple. The deliverance predicted in chap. xii. 1—3 is not to be brought about by human valour or policy but is of a wholly supernatural kind. It is therefore legitimate to conclude that the book of Daniel was finished at the time when the armed opposition of the Jews to Antiochus was in its earliest stage, and had as yet met with little success (chap. xi. 34).

x. 1—3. The third year of Cyrus is the latest date given
in Daniel's life; on the difficulty of reconciling this date with
chap. i. 21 see p. 63. Some commentators have spent much
time in discussing why Daniel remained in Babylonia until the
third year of Cyrus instead of availing himself of the opportunity to return to Palestine. If we regarded the narrative of
Daniel as historical it might be worth while to seek for an
explanation of the fact, but for those who believe Daniel to be
an ideal figure no explanation is needed. In *v.* 1 we find the
incorrect spelling בלמאשצר (so Baer) instead of בלטשאצר. The
latter half of the verse is rendered by Von Lengerke—"*And
truth is the revelation and (the) distress is great: and understand
thou the revelation, and understand it in the vision*". Both בין
and בינה he explains as Imperatives; the author, he supposes,
is here addressing the reader, and the suffix in לו refers to הַדָּבָר.
Much more probable is Hitzig's interpretation—"*And the word
is truth, and great distress; and he heeded the word and gave
heed to the vision*". But the meaning of צָבָא is here very uncertain. The proper sense of the word is "military service",
hence it is applied metaphorically to toil and sorrow (Is. xl. 2.
Job vii. 1); since however in Dan. viii. 13 צָבָא seems to mean
the "service" in the Temple, it is possible that here some such
thought may be present, namely that of an "obligation" or
"charge" laid upon Daniel. According to Hitzig, בין is a Perfect Hiphil, with dropping of the initial ה (see what has been
said on בִּינֹתִי chap. ix. 2), and בִּינָה is an abstract noun, with the
accent thrown back, as in קִינָה הִיא Ezek. xix. 14. Hävernick
makes בין to be an Infinitive used substantively, a view which
is certainly not favoured by the construction of the sentence.
Olshausen regards the word as a perfect Ḳal (*Lehrb. d. hebr.
Sprache*, p. 486). There remain two possibilities—בין may be
either a mistake for בָּן (Perfect), as J. D. Michaelis supposed, or
it may be an Infinitive used in the place of a Perfect (cf. סוֹר
chap. ix. 11). Instead of ובין both the LXX. and Aquila read
יבין, which is doubtless an error. In *v.* 2 we are not told for
what reason Daniel mourned, but from *v.* 12 we may conclude
that it was from anxiety as to the fate of Israel. For the phrase
שְׁלֹשָׁה שָׁבֻעִים יָמִים "*three full weeks*" cf. Gen. xli. 1. Deut. xxi. 13.

לֶחֶם חֲמֻדוֹת "*dainty bread*" (*v.* 3) is, as Hävernick remarks, the opposite of לֶחֶם עֹנִי (Deut. xvi. 3).

4—8. The vision which now follows took place on the 24th day of the 1st month (i.e. Abib or, as it was called by the post-exilic Jews, Nisan), the month of the Passover; Daniel, with some companions, was by the חִדֶּקֶל (Tigris), a river which is mentioned nowhere else in the Old Testament excepting in Gen. ii. 14. The form חִדֶּקֶל is peculiar, for the Tigris is in Syriac *Deḳlath*, in Arabic *Dijla*, and in Assyrio-Babylonian usually *Diglat*; but according to Schrader a form *Idiglat* is also found. Schrader supposes that the Hebrew and Syriac forms, with ק, follow the *Assyrian* pronunciation, whereas the Arabic *Dijla* is based upon the more primitive *Babylonian* form, with *g* (*Cuneif. Inscr.* p. 33). In *v.* 5 the description of the angel is probably taken from Ezek. ix. 2; he is "clothed with linen" like a Jewish priest (Lev. vi. 3), and his girdle is of the gold of Uphaz. This district, mentioned nowhere else but in Jer. x. 9, has never been identified. Ewald and others have suggested that אוּפָז is either a mistake for אוֹפִיר (Ps. xlv. 10), or a phonetic variation of the same name. In *v.* 6 תַּרְשִׁישׁ (cf. Exod. xxviii. 20. Ezek. i. 16; xxviii. 13) is usually supposed to be the chrysolith or topaz. מַרְגְּלוֹתָיו means, according to Von Lengerke, "*the place where his feet rested*", according to Hitzig "*his feet*" simply; the latter interpretation agrees better with the context, cf. Rev. i. 15 where this passage is imitated. The phrase כְּעֵין נְחֹשֶׁת קָלָל is borrowed from Ezek. i. 7, and is commonly rendered "*like the appearance of polished brass*". But although the use of the masc. form קָלָל with נְחֹשֶׁת would in itself offer no difficulty (see I Kings vii. 45. Ezra viii. 27), the text of Ezek. i. 7 is very suspicious; Cornill suggests that we should there read כְּעֵין נְחֹשֶׁת וְכַנְפֵיהֶם קַלּוֹת according to the LXX. The corruption, if it exists, must of course be older than the book of Daniel; what meaning the author attached to קָלָל it is impossible to say. That קָלָל has anything to do with קִלְקַל "to shake" (Ezek. xxi. 26. Eccles. x. 10) appears extremely improbable. וְקוֹל דְּבָרָיו כְּקוֹל הָמוֹן "*and the sound of his words was as the sound of a deep murmur*"; since הָמוֹן is quite a general term, applying to any deep sound, it is unnecessary to limit its meaning here to a "multitude" or the "sea". In v. 7 בְּהֵחָבֵא seems to mean "*seeking to hide themselves*", lit. "in the act of hiding themselves"—we should rather have expected לְהֵחָבֵא (cf. I Kings xxii. 25). The phrase (v. 8) וְהוֹדִי נֶהְפַּךְ עָלַי לְמַשְׁחִית "*and my comeliness was turned in me to corruption*" is the Hebrew equivalent of וְזִיוִי יִשְׁתַּנּוֹן עֲלַי chap. vii. 28 (cf. also v. 9); somewhat similar is the language in which Habakkuk describes the effect of a divine revelation (Hab. iii. 16). For the use of מַשְׁחִית in the abstract sense cf. Ezek. xxi. 36. II Chron. xx. 23; xxii. 4. On עָצַרְתִּי כֹּחַ see p. 29.

9—11. As in chap. viii. 18, Daniel becomes unconscious; וַאֲנִי הָיִיתִי נִרְדָּם וגו' "*after I had fallen into a slumber*" etc., seems to be a circumstantial clause inserted parenthetically, the apodosis beginning with v. 10. It has been much discussed whether the being who touches Daniel in v. 10 and who speaks in the following verses, is identical with the being described in vv. 5 and 6. Von Lengerke regards them as distinct, and supposes that the angel of vv. 10 ff. is Gabriel. Hitzig, on the other hand, identifies the angel of vv. 5 and 6 with that of vv. 10 ff., but denies that Gabriel is intended. The question is fortunately not of any great importance, as it concerns the form only, not the substance, of the vision. וַתְּנִיעֵנִי עַל־בִּרְכַּי וְכַפּוֹת יָדָי is usually explained as a *constructio praegnans*, i.e. "and caused me to tremble upon my knees and the palms of my hands", meaning "*and set me upon my knees and hands which were trembling*". On אִישׁ חֲמֻדוֹת (v. 11) see chap. ix. 23, and on עֹמֵד עַל־עָמְדֶךָ chap. viii. 18. מַרְעִיד is here intransitive, as in Ezra x. 9.

12—14. The angel now proceeds to reveal what has been passing in heaven. From the beginning of the three weeks, when Daniel set himself "*to attain to understanding*" (as to the destiny of Israel) and to humble himself before God, his petition had been accepted. וַאֲנִי בָאתִי בִּדְבָרֶיךָ "*and I am come by reason of thy words*", cf. ובדבריך (*Kĕrī* וּבִדְבָרֶךָ) I Kings xviii. 36. The coming of the angel was delayed for a while (v. 13) by the opposition of "*the prince of the kingdom of Persia*", i.e. the guardian angel of the Persian Empire—not Cyrus, as Hävernick and others have imagined. The belief in the guardian angels of nations is perhaps assumed in Is. xxiv. 21 and Ps. lxxxii.;

since however both passages are not only very obscure but of
unknown date, we have no means of discovering at what period
the idea arose among the Jews. The fact that in Dan. x. this
belief is rather presupposed than definitely stated shews that
the author is here dealing with a conception already familiar to
his readers, and hence nothing can be more absurd than to
argue from Ecclesiasticus xvii. 17 that Ben-Sīrā must have
borrowed the idea from Daniel. The guardian angel of the
Jews is Michael (see chap. xii. 1), who is here described as one
of "*the chief princes*", i.e. the archangels, and who comes to the
aid of the speaker. נוֹתַרְתִּי is variously explained as "*I obtained
the precedence*" (Gesenius, Hävernick, Von Lengerke), "*I remained*", i.e. I was delayed (Hitzig), and "*I was superfluous*"
(Ewald). But nowhere else does the verb bear any one of these
meanings. Graetz proposes to read וְאֹתוֹ הוֹתַרְתִּי "*and him I
left*", alleging the authority of the LXX. and Theodotion. But
the words καὶ αὐτὸν ἐκεῖ κατέλιπον are probably a mere guess,
and do not presuppose any variant, for the insertion of αὐτὸν
and the substitution of a transitive for an intransitive verb are
quite in the manner of the LXX. translator. Perhaps, retaining
the traditional text, we may take וַאֲנִי נוֹתַרְתִּי וגו as a circumstantial clause describing the previous situation of the speaker,
"*whereas I had been left (alone) there, (contending) with the
kings of Persia*", cf. Jer. ii. 21; xxiii. 32. Ezek. xiii. 7. מַלְכֵי
פָרָם "*the kings of Persia*" seems to be an intentionally vague
phrase for "the Persian dynasty" or "the power of the Persian
Empire". It is quite unnecessary to suppose, with Bertholdt,
that the word שַׂר has fallen out before מַלְכֵי, for the rendering of
the LXX. (μετὰ τοῦ στρατηγοῦ τοῦ βασιλέως Περσῶν) is probably an expansion of the original, just as in *v.* 20 עִם שַׂר פָרָם is
translated μετὰ τοῦ στρατηγοῦ βασιλέως τῶν Περσῶν. It is of
course impossible to say what was the author's conception as to
the nature of the contest between this angel and the angel of
the Persian Empire. Von Lengerke suggests that the passage
refers to some change in the policy of the Persian government
towards the Jews, but this is to import into the book ideas
which are nowhere expressed in it, for Daniel's solicitude on
behalf of his people is described in perfectly general terms,

without any hint that his anxiety was due to special circumstances. With וּבָאתִי לַהֲבִינֶךָ (*v.* 14) compare the parallel passage
in chap. ix. 23 וַאֲנִי בָּאתִי לְהַגִּיד; the following words were apparently suggested by Gen. xlix. 1 וְאַגִּידָה לָכֶם אֵת אֲשֶׁר־יִקְרָא אֶתְכֶם
בְּאַחֲרִית הַיָּמִים. The Masoretes read יִקְרֶה, instead of יִקְרֶה, in order
to assimilate the two passages. The phrase כִּי עוֹד חָזוֹן לַיָּמִים is
rendered by Von Lengerke "*since the vision is still for these
days*", i.e. for the aforesaid אַחֲרִית הַיָּמִים; but if this were the
meaning, we should expect כִּי עוֹד לַיָּמִים הֶחָזוֹן. Hitzig substitutes
לַיָּמִים for לְיָמִים, on account of כִּי לְיָמִים רַבִּים in chap. viii. 26. It
is perhaps more natural to translate, retaining the Masoretic
vocalization, "*since there is yet a vision for the days*", i.e. there
is one vision more, relating to the days before mentioned.

15—xi. 1. נָתַתִּי פָנַי אָרְצָה "*I bent my face towards the earth*"
does not imply that Daniel again fell prostrate. The "one like
the sons of men" (*v.* 16), who touches Daniel's lips, must be the
angel who has spoken previously. When at length Daniel
speaks, he seeks to excuse his confusion, "*My lord, by reason of
the vision my pangs came upon me, and I retained no strength;
and how should a servant of my lord speak with my lord?*" The
expression נֶהֶפְכוּ צִירַי עָלַי is a metaphor borrowed from childbirth (I Sam. iv. 19); such comparisons are used elsewhere to
describe the prophetic excitement (Is. xxi. 3). On the Aramaic
form הֱיִד see p. 29, note. In *v.* 17 זֶה is a demonstrative particle
added by way of emphasis (cf. Gen. xxvii. 21), and corresponds
in meaning to the German *da*; in English we have no exact
equivalent. The latter half of *v.* 17, if the Masoretic text be
correct, must be a continuation of Daniel's speech—"*and as for
me henceforth there remains in me no strength, nor is any breath
left in me*". Von Lengerke takes these words as part of the
narrative, but though in German we may say "von nun an" in
speaking of the past, the Hebrew מֵעַתָּה always refers to the present. Von Lengerke's objection that since Daniel has already
said לֹא עָצַרְתִּי כֹּחַ in *v.* 16, it is needless for him to make a similar
statement in *v.* 17, proves very little, for terror and perplexity
may naturally lead to repetitions. But however we take the
passage, it must be owned that מֵעַתָּה is very strange in this connection—the Pĕshīṭtā omits the word, and the LXX. has ἠσθέ-

νησα (i.e. מְשַׂדְתִּי, cf. Ps. xviii. 37). Possibly מְעַתָּה may be a corruption of מִבְּעָתָה "from terror", cf. נִבְעַתִּי chap. viii. 17; the root בעת is applied specially to supernatural alarm or panic (Is. xxi. 4. Job vi. 4; xviii. 11 etc.). In *v.* 18 the expression כְּמַרְאֵה אָדָם "*one who wore a human form*" is the subject of the preceding verbs, cf. כִּדְמוּת בְּנֵי אָדָם in *v.* 16. For חֲזַק וַחֲזָק (*v.* 19) the LXX. has ἀνδρίζου καὶ ἴσχυε, the Pĕshĭṭtā ܐܬܚܝܠ ܘܐܬܐܫܪ, apparently reading חזק ואמיץ (Deut. xxxi. 7, 23. Josh. i. 6, 7, 9, 18. I Chr. xxii. 12; xxviii. 20). חֲזַק וַחֲזַק is at least exceptional, for when the Imperative is repeated, the conjunction is not used (Judg. v. 12. II Sam. xvi. 7. Is. li. 9; lii. 1, 11; lvii. 14. Ezek. xxxiii. 11. Ps. cxxxvii. 7). Instead of וּבְדַבְּרוֹ, which is found in the ordinary printed texts, the best MSS. have וּבְדַבְּרוֹ. The first clause of *v.* 20 is an affirmation put into the form of a question, for Daniel has already been informed as to the reason of the angel's coming (*v.* 14), cf. I Sam. ii. 27. Ezek. xx. 4. The train of thought in *vv.* 20 and 21 may appear at first sight to proceed "in a zig-zag" (Hitzig), but the connection is probably as follows—"I am come to bring thee a revelation, but cannot linger, for I must return at once (עַתָּה) to contend against the enemies of Israel; I will however (אֲבָל) stay long enough to unveil the future to thee, although during my absence from the strife there is no one but Michael to defend the right cause". וַאֲנִי יוֹצֵא is explained by Von Lengerke, "and I go forth (to fight with the angel of Persia)"; Bertholdt and Hitzig more naturally interpret "and as soon as I come forth (from the contest with the angel of Persia), the angel of Greece will appear (to oppose me)"—i.e. as soon as the Persian supremacy is over, another enemy will arise. The "writing of truth" is the book of divine decrees, cf. Ps. cxxxix. 16. On the phrase מִתְחַזֵּק עִמִּי "*helping me*", see p. 29. עַל־אֵלֶּה "*against these*" refers doubtless to the angel of Persia and the other hostile powers. The first verse of chap. xi. must be examined in connection with what precedes. As the text stands, it presents great difficulties, and those difficulties are further complicated by the wide disagreement between the ancient versions. Von Lengerke renders, "*But I also, in the first year of Darius the Mede, stood by him as helper and defender*". He explains the verse as alluding to the conquest of Babylon, and makes the suffix in לֹו refer to Michael. Others, e.g. Hävernick, refer the suffix to Darius. But the statement that the speaker had helped Michael, or Darius, some years earlier, has nothing to do either with the verse preceding or with the verse following. Moreover the use of עָמְדִי, "my standing", in the place of עָמַדְתִּי is scarcely justified by such a passage as Job ix. 27. The LXX. reads—Καὶ ἐν τῷ ἐνιαυτῷ τῷ πρώτῳ Κύρου τοῦ βασιλέως εἶπέν μοι ἐνισχῦσαι καὶ ἀνδρί-ζεσθαι. There is here no trace of אֲנִי, and even the καὶ does not necessarily presuppose a conjunction in the Hebrew[1]. Thus the Hebrew basis of the LXX. appears to have been [ו]בשנת אחת לכורש [המלך] אמר למחז[י]ק ולמעוז לי. Here אמר is presumably a corruption of עמד. The Pĕshīttā comes nearer to the Masoretic text, but attaches ואני to chap. x. 21, and reads עמד for עמדי and לי for לֹו. Hence the reading לי is supported by the combined testimony of the LXX. and of the Pĕshīttā, and the Masoretic reading עמדי is supported by neither. Prof. Robertson Smith has suggested that the words בשנת אחת לדריוש המדי are a fragment of a heading which was wrongly introduced here by a scribe (cf. the headings in chaps. vii. 1; viii. 1; ix. 1; x. 1). After the words had been incorporated with the text, ואני may have been added in order to make sense. This hypothesis would account for the absence of ואני in the LXX. If we read עמד for עמדי, and לי for לֹו, the latter part of the verse may be understood as a continuation of chap. x. 21, ואין אחד מתחזק עמי על אלה כי אם מיכאל שרכם עמד למחזיק ולמעוז לי, i.e. "*there is none that helpeth me against these, save that Michael your prince standeth as a strengthener and a defence to me*".

2—4. The revelation properly speaking now begins. There are to be three more Persian kings after Cyrus, and the fourth Persian king, that is, the last of the three above-mentioned, will be richer than all his predecessors. In this last king all commentators recognize Xerxes, the two preceding kings being probably Darius and Artaxerxes. Nor is it any valid objection to this interpretation that in reality there were many more than four Persian kings after Cyrus, and that the first Artaxerxes

---

[1] Cf. chap. vii. 19 שניה καὶ ἰδοὺ οἱ ὀδόντες αὐτοῦ; ix. 19 תאחר אל καὶ μὴ χρονήσῃς.

reigned after, not before, Xerxes. For in the Old Testament,
which was doubtless the principal source of information accessible to the author of Daniel, only four names of Persian kings
happen to occur, viz. Cyrus, Darius, Xerxes and Artaxerxes, and
as to the order in which the last two reigned nothing is positively stated. That the Darius mentioned in Neh. xii. 22 is a
different person from the Darius mentioned elsewhere, may
easily have escaped the notice of readers in the 2nd century B.C.
וּבְחֶזְקָתוֹ בְעָשְׁרוֹ " *and when he shall have grown strong by reason of
his wealth*" (so Hitzig), cf. II Chr. xii. 1; xxvi. 16 ; חֶזְקָה is here
a verbal noun like יִרְאָה. The phrase יָעִיר הַכֹּל אֵת מַלְכוּת יָוָן is very
obscure. Von Lengerke renders " *he will stir up all, (even) the
kingdom of Greece*" ; but if the clause refers, as it apparently
does, to the war of Xerxes *against* Greece, such an expression
would be meaningless. More natural is the interpretation of
the Vulgate, which is followed by Bertholdt and De Wette, " *et
concitabit omnes adversum regnum Graeciae*". It is true that, as
Von Lengerke objects, אֵת nowhere else means "against"—excepting where some such word as נִלְחַם or מִלְחָמָה precedes (Gen.
xiv. 9. I Chr. xx. 5)—but since עִם is so used (Ps. xciv. 16), the
thing cannot be pronounced absolutely impossible. Hitzig
explains אֵת as indicating motion "towards". Perhaps יָעִיר הכל את
may be a corruption of יערך לִ[קר]את, " *he shall array (his armies)
against the kingdom of Greece*", cf. I Sam. iv. 2. II Sam. x. 9,
10, 17. The expression " the kingdom of Greece" shews, as
Hitzig remarks, that the author imagined Greece to have been
a monarchy, like the Oriental states. The " mighty, or warlike,
king", who appears in *v.* 3, is doubtless Alexander the Great.
The beginning of *v.* 4 is usually translated, " *and when he has
stood up*", but probably we should read, with Graetz, וּבְעָצְמוֹ " *and
when he has become strong*", according to the parallel passage,
chap. viii. 8. The corruption may easily be explained by the
וְעָמַד of *v.* 3. Much less plausible is Hitzig's interpretation, " *and
when he dies*" (taking עָמְדוֹ as equivalent to עֲנָדוֹ), for the verb ענד
" to die", though common in Syriac, is unknown in Jewish
Aramaic, as well as in Hebrew. With תִּשָּׁבֵר מַלְכוּתוֹ " *his kingdom shall be broken up*", cf. נִשְׁבְּרָה הַקֶּרֶן הַגְּדֹלָה chap. viii. 8. The
form וְתֵחָץ, " *and it shall be divided*", is peculiar, for we should

expect וְתִחְצֶה, since the Imperfect is here used in the sense of a simple Future; similar are וַיַּעַשׂ in *v.* 16, וְיָשֵׂם (not וְיָשִׂים) in *v.* 17, וְיָשֹׁב (not וְיָשׁוּב) in *v.* 28, etc. Prof. Driver supposes that in all these cases the apocopated form is used incorrectly "without any recollection of its distinctive signification" (*Tenses*, p. 247). The latter half of *v.* 4 seems to mean, "*and (it shall) not (belong) to his posterity, nor (shall it be) according to the rule which he had ruled, for his Empire shall be overthrown and (shall belong) to others, besides these*". After וְלֹא לְאַחֲרִיתוֹ and after וְלַאֲחֵרִים we must understand הִיא or תִּהְיֶה, cf. chap. viii. 19, 26, as well as Ps. xvi. 8. The rule of Alexander's successors is to be feebler than that of Alexander himself (cf. וְלֹא בְכֹחוֹ chap. viii. 22). To whom אֵלֶּה refers is not clear. Von Lengerke, following Jerome, makes it apply to the first successors of Alexander, i.e. his empire was first to be divided among his generals, and afterwards was to be still further broken up. According to this view, the אֲחֵרִים would be the dynasties which arose in Cappadocia, Armenia, and other countries, during the century and a half that followed upon the death of Alexander. Hitzig, on the other hand, translates "*to others, to the exclusion of these*", referring אֲחֵרִים to the first successors of Alexander, and אֵלֶּה to his posterity (אַחֲרִיתוֹ), i.e. his two sons who were murdered in their infancy; but מִלְּבַד elsewhere means "in addition to", not "to the exclusion of", which would rather be תַּחַת (Gen. iv. 25. I Kings xx. 24).

5, 6. From this point onwards the history is confined to the kingdoms of the South and the North, i.e. the kingdom of the Ptolemies and that of the Seleucidae. These two dynasties successively dominated Palestine, and therefore occupy the attention of the author. During the greater part of the 3rd century B.C. the country was under the Ptolemies, but about the end of that century it was permanently incorporated with the Seleucid empire. The king of the South, in *v.* 5, is Ptolemy Soter, son of Lagus, who having long been master of Egypt, assumed the title of king in 306 B.C. The verse is usually rendered, "*And the king of the South shall be strong, and one of his captains (shall be strong likewise), but he (i.e. the latter) shall become stronger than he (i.e. the former), and shall rule, a great*

domain shall be his dominion". Probably, however, the Masoretic accentuation is here erroneous, and the words וּמִן־שָׂרָיו
should be taken, as Hitzig proposes, with what follows, so that
the sense will be, "*And the king of the South shall be strong;
but as for one of his captains he shall become stronger than he*"
etc. It is unnecessary to read יֶחֱזַק for וְיֶחֱזַק, with Meinhold, since
the construction is the same as in chap. vii. 20 וְקַרְנָא דִכֵּן וְעַיְנִין לַהּ.
For the omission of אֶחָד "one", before מִן, cf. Exod. vi. 25. Neh.
xiii. 28. The suffix in שָׂרָיו refers to Ptolemy Soter; the captain
in question is Seleucus Nicator, who served in the army of
Ptolemy and afterwards, in 306 B.C., became independent sovereign of Northern Syria, Babylonia, and the other eastern provinces of Alexander's empire. Seleucus' son and successor,
Antiochus Soter, is here passed over in silence. Verse 6
describes the relations between Ptolemy II. (Philadelphus) and
Antiochus Theos, son of Antiochus Soter. About 250 B.C.
Ptolemy Philadelphus gave his daughter Berenice in marriage
to Antiochus Theos, on condition that the latter should divorce
his former wife Laodice and that the posterity of Berenice
should succeed to the throne of the Seleucidae. When after
two years Ptolemy died, Antiochus took back his former wife
and divorced Berenice. Laodice, however, fearing that her husband might change his mind, poisoned him. Berenice and her
infant son were soon afterwards murdered near Antioch. Von
Lengerke translates, "*And at the end of some years they shall
make an alliance together, and the daughter of the king of the
South shall come to the king of the North, to establish an agreement. But she will not retain any power of support, and neither
he will abide nor his support, and she shall be given up, and those
who have made her a bride, and he who begat her, and he who
obtained possession of her in those times*". For the phrase
לְקֵץ שָׁנִים cf. II Chr. xviii. 2. The verb יִתְחַבָּרוּ refers, of course,
to the king of the South and the king of the North; the author
however, considers it unnecessary to state that the kings in this
verse are not the same individuals as those mentioned in *v.* 5.
מֵישָׁרִים elsewhere means that which is "right" or "fitting",
hence it is used for "an equitable arrangement"; Hitzig compares the use of δίκαια in I Macc. vii. 12. As זְרוֹעַ is employed

metaphorically in *vv.* 15, 22, 31, we may take it so here; since
however the notion of an "army" is inappropriate in this verse,
הַזְּרוֹעַ may signify the political "support" which Berenice gave
to her father Ptolemy. But Von Lengerke's rendering of וְלֹא
תַעְצֹר כּוֹחַ הַזְּרוֹעַ, "aber sie wird Kraft des Beistandes nicht be-
haupten", is syntactically open to objection. Wherever else the
phrase עצר כח occurs, כח is in the absolute state, and, as Graetz
has noticed, the analogy of II Chr. xiii. 20 is certainly in favour
of regarding הַזְּרוֹעַ as the subject of the clause. וְלֹא יַעֲמֹד וּזְרֹעוֹ is
understood by Von Lengerke as meaning "neither Ptolemy will
abide, nor his support Berenice". But if the preceding הַזְּרוֹעַ
refers to the support afforded by Berenice, it is very unlikely
that זְרֹעוֹ refers to Berenice herself. More probably we should
read, with Hitzig, וְלֹא יַעַמְדוּ זְרֹעָיו (see *vv.* 15, 31), "*nor shall his
arms abide*". But the suffix in זְרֹעָיו can scarcely refer to the
feminine הַזְּרוֹעַ, as Hitzig supposes—it is far more natural to
explain it as referring to Ptolemy. Thus the sense of these two
clauses would seem to be, "neither shall that support (which is
afforded by Berenice) be of any avail, nor shall his (other) sup-
ports prove effectual". The remainder of this verse presents
such insuperable difficulties that there is every reason for believing the text to be corrupt. To interpret תִּנָּתֵן as "she shall
be given up to destruction" is to assign to the verb a sense
which it bears nowhere else, for in Is. li. 12 חָצִיר יִנָּתֵן need mean
no more than "which shall be made as grass"; when נתן is construed with ל or בְּיַד, we may of course render it by "give up" or
"deliver over", but תִּנָּתֵן by itself signifies only "she shall be
given". מְבִיאֶהָ (so the best MSS. read, with defective spelling)
is referred by some, as Ewald, to "those who accompanied"
Berenice from Egypt to Syria, and by Von Lengerke to "those
who concluded her marriage", i.e. her father and her husband.
Hitzig understands it of her husband only, the Plural being
used for the Singular (cf. בְּעֲלַיִךְ Is. liv. 5). הַיֹּלְדָהּ, if correctly
pointed, must be Ptolemy; for the use of the article before
a participle with suffix compare הַמְּכֵּהוּ Is. ix. 12. מַחֲזִקָהּ is referred by Von Lengerke to Antiochus, the verb having the
same sense as in *v.* 21; Ewald and Hitzig explain מַחֲזִקָהּ as "he
who strengthened her" or "he who upheld her", and refer the

word to Ptolemy. בְּעִתִּים may perhaps be equivalent to בָּעִתִּים הָהֵם (*v.* 14), just as in chap. x. 14 לַיָּמִים? seems to mean " for those days". But on the whole it is more probable that here something has fallen out.

7—9. The three verses which now follow describe the reigns of Ptolemy III. (Euergetes) and of Seleucus Callinicus, eldest son and successor of Antiochus Theos. Ptolemy Euergetes, at the beginning of his reign, avenged the murder of Berenice by invading Syria and Babylonia, whence he carried off an immense booty. מִנֵּצֶר שָׁרָשֶׁיהָ is usually explained as " *one of the offshoots of her roots*", the מִן being partitive, as in *v.* 5, and נֵצֶר being a collective noun. Possibly however we should read נֵצֶר מִשָׁרָשֶׁיהָ (LXX. φυτὸν ἐκ τῆς ῥίζης αὐτοῦ), see Is. xi. 1. כַּנּוֹ evidently has the same meaning as עַל־כַּנּוֹ *vv.* 20, 21, i.e. "*instead of him*". With כַּנּוֹ used thus abverbially, cf. the Arab. *maḳāmahu*; the indiscriminate use of עַל־כַּנּוֹ and כַּנּוֹ is like the indiscriminate use of בְּבֵית הָאֱלֹהִים (II Chr. iv. 11 ; xxii. 12) and בֵּית הָאֱלֹהִים (I Chr. ix. 26 ; II Chr. iv. 19) " in the house of God". The suffix in שָׁרָשֶׁיהָ obviously refers to Berenice, and the suffix in כַּנּוֹ to Ptolemy Philadelphus. Thus there is to arise in the place of Ptolemy Philadelphus an offshoot of the roots whence Berenice had sprung, i.e. her brother, Ptolemy Euergetes, will succeed to the throne of Egypt. וְיָבֹא אֶל־הַחַיִל is explained by Von Lengerke, Ewald, and Hitzig, as "*and he shall come to the army*", i.e. he shall place himself at the head of his army in order to invade Syria. But it is not easy to see why the king should be described as coming *to* his army rather than *with* it (see *v.* 13). Hävernick's rendering "*and he shall come into power*" is wholly unsupported by usage. Perhaps we should read וְיָבֹא [אֱלֵהֶ[ם] חַיִל " *and he shall bring an army against them*", i.e. against the Syrians; for the use of אל instead of על, see chap. viii. 7. Hitzig is probably right in making מָעוֹז in this verse refer to the fortified city of Seleucia, on the Mediterranean coast. According to Polybius (v. 58), Seleucia was taken by Ptolemy during this war and remained for many years afterwards in the power of Egypt. וְעָשָׂה בָהֶם וְהֶחֱזִיק " *and he shall do as he wills with them and act valiantly*" (cf. וְעָשׂוּ יַחֲזִקוּ *v.* 32, also Neh. ix. 24)—the suffix in בָהֶם refers to the Syrians, as do also

the suffixes in אֱלֹהֵיהֶם and the following words (*v.* 8). נְסִבֵיהֶם
certainly means "*their molten images*", and unless it be merely
a mistake for נִסְבֵּיהֶם, is from a Singular נָסִיךְ synonymous with
נֶסֶךְ (Is. xlviii. 5); similarly we find פְּסִילִים "graven images" used
as a virtual plural of פֶּסֶל. Jerome relates, presumably on the
authority of Porphyry, that among the spoils which Ptolemy
brought away with him were the statues of Egyptian gods
carried off by Cambyses some 280 years earlier. Hence, it is
said, the Egyptians gave to Ptolemy the title of Euergetes.
With כְּלֵי חֶמְדָּתָם "*their costly things*" cf. II Chr. xxxii. 27; xxxvi.
10. The words כֶּסֶף וְזָהָב can scarcely stand in apposition to
כְּלֵי חֶמְדָּתָם, for in that case we should expect הַכֶּסֶף וְהַזָּהָב, the
preceding nouns being defined by the suffix. It is better to
take כֶּסֶף וְזָהָב as a term of specification (Arab. *tamyīz*), "*in silver
and gold*"; cf. הַכְּרוּבִים זָהָב I Chr. xxviii. 18. The last clause of
v. 8 is interpreted by Von Lengerke, Hitzig, and Ewald, "*and
for some years he will refrain from (attacking) the king of the
North*"; see Gen. xxix. 35. II Kings iv. 6. Others explain,
"*and he shall continue alive some years longer than the king of
the North*". In *v.* 9 the verbs בא and שׁב must refer to the king
of the North. Some years after Ptolemy's invasion of Syria,
Seleucus Callinicus made an expedition against Egypt. He
was totally defeated, and returned with a small remnant of his
army to Antioch.

10—12. The next ten verses are occupied with the times of
Antiochus III., known as Antiochus the Great. Seleucus Callinicus left two sons, Seleucus Ceraunus and Antiochus. The
former was killed, after a reign of two years, during a campaign
in Asia Minor. Antiochus, who succeeded to the throne, soon
afterwards made war upon Ptolemy Philopator, son and successor of Ptolemy Euergetes, and conquered Syria as far as Gaza.
Thereupon Ptolemy marched from Egypt and defeated him
with severe loss at Raphia, about twenty miles to the south
west of Gaza. Antiochus having retreated northward, Palestine
was again annexed to the empire of Ptolemy. In *v.* 10 בָּנָיו "*his
sons*" refers to Seleucus Ceraunus and Antiochus. Von Lengerke has observed that though Seleucus Ceraunus never
actually made war upon Egypt, his expedition into Asia Minor

may be regarded as a prelude to an intended attack upon the
Ptolemaic Empire.   Hence it may be said of him and of his
brother, "*they shall war and gather together a multitude of great
forces*"—but the following words must describe events subsequent to the death of Seleucus[1].   For the placing of the Infinitive absolute בּוֹא after the Perfect, see Num. xxiii. 11; xxiv. 10.
The words וּבָא בוֹא וְשָׁטַף וְעָבָר are referred by Von Lengerke and
Hitzig to Antiochus; Ewald more naturally refers them to the
multitude (המון) mentioned before.   Thus we may render, "*and
it* (i.e. the army of Antiochus) *shall come onward and shall
sweep away (all before it) and overflow (the land); then it shall
return again (to the attack), and they shall war even to his stronghold*".   The word וְיָשֹׁב seems to allude to the fact that after the
conquest of part of Coele-Syria, the army of Antiochus retired
northward to winter in the neighbourhood of Seleucia, garrisons
having been left in the conquered cities (Polybius v. 66); in
the following spring the army "returned again" to complete the
conquest.   For the Plural יתגרו the *Kĕrī* substitutes the easier
יִתְגָּרֶה.   Von Lengerke refers יתגרו to Antiochus and Ptolemy
Philopator.   Since however the next verse represents Ptolemy
as "coming forth" to fight, it is more natural to suppose that
יתגרו (assuming it to be the original reading) refers to the army
of Antiochus, which may be treated either as a Singular or a
Plural.   The word מָעֻזֹּה "*his stronghold*" is explained by Von
Lengerke as meaning the stronghold of Ptolemy, viz. Raphia;
Hitzig interprets it as the stronghold of Antiochus, viz. Gaza.
This latter view may at first appear irreconcileable with *v.* 7,
where מָעוֹז מֶלֶךְ הַצָּפוֹן seems to designate Seleucia; but since in
v. 19 we read of מָעוּזֵּי אַרְצוֹ, there is no reason why several places
should not be called by this title.   That Pelusium (סִין), described
by Ezekiel as מָעוֹז מִצְרַיִם (Ezek. xxx. 15), cannot here be meant,
is obvious, for Antiochus never advanced so far during this cam-

---

[1] The words of Jerome—"*Post fu-
gam et mortem Seleuci Callinici, duo
filii ejus Seleucus cognomento Ceraunus
et Antiochus qui appellatus est Magnus,
provocati spe victoriae et ultione paren-
tis, exercitu congregato adversus Pto-*
lemaeum Philopatorem arma corripiunt"
—are apparently nothing but a deduction drawn from this passage of Daniel,
for in reality Seleucus Ceraunus died
before the accession of Ptolemy Philopator.

XI. 11, 12. 179

paign. In *v.* 11 Ptolemy appears upon the scene. At first he made no attempt to arrest the progress of Antiochus, but was at length induced by his ministers to advance with a large force. For יִתְמַרְמַר see chap. viii. 7, and also p. 30. The latter half of *v.* 11 means, according to Von Lengerke, " *And he* (i.e. Ptolemy) *shall raise a great army, and the army shall be placed under his command*". So also Hitzig, excepting that he prefers to read וְנָתַן " *and he shall place*", rather than וְנִתַּן. But in either case it is extremely doubtful whether the text will bear the above sense; the passages cited by Hitzig (II Kings xviii. 23. Ps. x. 14) are far from conclusive. It is certainly more in accordance with Hebrew usage to translate " *the multitude shall be given into his hand*" (i.e. it shall be defeated by him), cf. I Kings xx. 28. But since הֶהָמוֹן must refer to the הָמוֹן רָב immediately preceding, it becomes necessary to take the verb וְהֶעֱמִיד as having Antiochus for its subject. Hence we may interpret, " *And he* (i.e. Antiochus) *shall raise a great multitude, but the multitude shall be given into his* (i.e. Ptolemy's) *hand*". This view is confirmed by *v.* 13, where the " multitude greater than the former one" evidently means the army of Antiochus. Verse 12 is interpreted both by Von Lengerke and Hitzig, " *And the multitude shall stand up* (*to fight*), *their courage being raised, and he* (i.e. Ptolemy) *shall cast down myriads, but he shall not shew himself strong*". According to this explanation, נִשָּׂא has the same sense as in Is. xxxiii. 10, and יָרוּם לְבָבוֹ is a circumstantial clause. But if, as has been before suggested, the הָמוֹן of *v.* 11 is the army of Antiochus, the הָמוֹן of *v.* 12 must refer to the same thing. Accordingly the first half of *v.* 12 appears to mean, " *And the multitude shall be swept away* (i.e. routed), *and his* (i.e. Ptolemy's) *heart shall be puffed up with pride*" (reading וְרָם according to the *Ķĕrī*). For this use of נשׂא see chap. ii. 35 and Is. xl. 24; xli. 16; lvii. 13. The term רִבֹּאוֹת " myriads" must be understood in a rhetorical sense. According to Polybius (v. 86), the losses of Antiochus at Raphia amounted to nearly 10000 infantry and 300 cavalry, besides 4000 taken prisoners. וְלֹא יָעֹז " *but he shall not shew himself strong*", accurately describes the conduct of Ptolemy on this occasion. Instead of following up his success, he contented himself with the acquisition of Coele-

Syria, and made peace with Antiochus as soon as possible (Polybius v. 87).

13—16. About 12 years after the battle of Raphia, Ptolemy
Philopator died leaving an infant son, who succeeded to the
crown and is known as Ptolemy Epiphanes. Antiochus soon
took the opportunity of again attacking the Ptolemaic Empire.
In v. 13, וְשָׁב is adverbial, "*And again the king of the North shall
raise a multitude, greater than the former one...*". In the latter
half of this verse, שָׁנִים is explained by Von Lengerke as being
in apposition to הָעִתִּים, i.e. "*at the end of the time (consisting of)
some years*"—in which case the presence of הָעִתִּים is altogether
unnecessary and even disturbing to the sense. Ewald translates, "*At the end of the times he will come repeatedly* (יָבוֹא בוֹא)
during some years;" but for this we should expect שָׁנָה בְשָׁנָה (see
Neh. x. 36) rather than שָׁנִים. Perhaps שָׁנִים may have been
added by a scribe in order to explain the vague term הָעִתִּים, in
accordance with וּלְקֵץ שָׁנִים in v. 6. For the placing of the Infinitive Absolute בוֹא after the Imperfect, cf. II Kings v. 11. רְכוּשׁ
which here seems to mean "implements of war" (so Hitzig,
Ewald) and which in v. 24 means "possessions" in general, is a
word peculiar to the Pentateuch and to post-exilic writings. In
v. 14, the "many" who "stand up against the king of the
South" may be taken as a reference to Philip, king of Macedon,
the ally of Antiochus, and to the rebellions which at this time
broke out in the provinces subject to Ptolemy. The rest of the
verse evidently alludes to events which took place in Palestine.
According to the usual interpretation, the בְּנֵי פָּרִיצֵי עַמְּךָ, "*the
sons of the violent among thy people*" are those Jews who took
part with Antiochus. The author, it is supposed, hating the
Syrian rule, here expresses his disapprobation of those who
helped to bring Palestine under the Seleucidae. Before discussing this theory, it is necessary to examine the words which
follow, לְהַעֲמִיד חָזוֹן, which are commonly rendered, "*so as (thereby) to fulfil the prophecy*", i.e. the conduct of the Jews who sided
with Antiochus, though in itself blameworthy, was necessary for
the fulfilment of the Divine predictions. Against this it may
fairly be urged that the author cannot here be speaking of an
attempt which *succeeded*, but rather of an attempt which *failed*

(וְנִכְשָׁלוּ). Accordingly Graetz wishes to render לְהַעֲמִיד חָזוֹן " *to cause the Law to totter*" (um das Gesetz wankend zu machen), cf. Ezek. xxix. 7. He explains the verse as referring to an attempt on the part of the Hellenizing faction among the Jews to abolish the Mosaic law. That such attempts were made at the period in question is quite possible, but חָזוֹן means " vision ", " prediction ", and is never used as an equivalent of תּוֹרָה or בְּרִית. Hence there seems to be no choice but to take לְהַעֲמִיד חָזוֹן in its literal and obvious sense—the author speaks of persons who " lift themselves up *for the purpose of fulfilling prophecy* ", but the attempt fails, " they are overthrown " (וְנִכְשָׁלוּ). But who are the בני פריצי עמך ? The phrase, as it stands, is very singular, for " the violent among thy people " would surely be expressed by בְּנֵי עַמְּךָ הַפָּרִיצִים or פָּרִיצֵי בְנֵי עַמְּךָ. We can no more say בְּנֵי פָּרִיצִים for " violent persons " than we could say בְּנֵי צַדִּיקִים for " righteous persons ". Perhaps we should read בֹּנֵי פִּרְצֵי עַמְּךָ " *those who build up the breaches of thy people* ", cf. Amos ix. 11 and the somewhat analogous phrase מַחֲזִיקֵי בִדְקֵךְ Ezek. xxvii. 9. Our total ignorance as to the internal history of the Jews at this period makes it impossible to say what event the author of Daniel has here in view, but it may be suggested as at least not improbable that at the time when the Ptolemaic dynasty was losing its hold upon Judaea some of those who aimed at a restoration of Israel may have entertained hopes of throwing off the foreign yoke altogether and thereby of fulfilling the predictions of the prophets[1]. Such hopes were of course doomed to disappointment. The opening clause of *v.* 15, "*And the king of the North shall come*", is understood by Von Lengerke as a mere repetition of the statement in *v.* 13, since *v.* 14 is of the nature of a parenthesis. Hitzig, on the contrary, refers *v.* 15 to a campaign subsequent to that mentioned in *v.* 13. Although the details of the war between Antiochus and Ptolemy Epiphanes are obscure, there can be no doubt that it lasted several years.

[1] It hardly requires to be said that the account given by Josephus (*Antiq.* xii. 3. 3, 4) of the help which Antiochus received from the Jews—even if it be strictly true—does not necessarily apply to the whole nation. We have also to remember that Josephus always does his best to conceal the hatred with which the Jews regarded the Gentile rule.

The fate of Palestine was virtually settled by the great victory which Antiochus gained at Mount Panium, near the Bāniyās source of the Jordan, over Ptolemy's general Scopas (Polybius XVI. 18; XXVIII. 1). According to Jerome, Scopas afterwards sought refuge, with an army of 10000 men, in the fortress of Sidon, which Antiochus besieged and took[1]. To this there seems to be an allusion here, "*And he shall cast up earth-works and take a fortified city*". Instead of מִבְצָרוֹת we elsewhere find the Plural מִבְצָרִים, as in *v.* 24. Theod. and the Pĕsh. appear to have read עָרִים בְּצֻרוֹת. The following words describe the total collapse of the Egyptian power in Syria. "*And the forces of the South shall not withstand (Antiochus), nor (even) his* (i.e. Ptolemy's) *chosen men, and there shall be no strength to withstand.* (*v.* 16) *And he* (i.e. Antiochus) *who shall come against him* (i.e. Ptolemy) *shall do as he wills, and none shall withstand him, and he shall stand in the land of Glory, with destruction in his hand*". זְרֹעוֹת, for which *v.* 31 has זְרֹעִים, is a general term including not only armies but all means of offence or defence, cf. בְּאֶדְרָע וְחָיִל Ezra iv. 23. The phrase עַם מִבְחָרָיו is peculiar, but may be compared to כְּלֵי מַחֲמֻדֶּיהָ II Chr. xxxvi. 19. Whether the suffixes in מִבְחָרָיו and אֵלָיו refer to Ptolemy or to "the South" is not quite clear; the sense in either case is the same. On אֶרֶץ הַצְּבִי, as a name for Judaea, see chap. viii. 9. The rendering given above for וְכָלָה בְיָדוֹ is that adopted by Hitzig. Von Lengerke and Ewald translate, "*and it* (i.e. the land) *shall be wholly in his hand*", taking כָּלָה as an adverb (Gen. xviii. 21). But, as Hitzig remarks, if this be the meaning we must at least read וְכָלֹּה, with Bertholdt. Von Lengerke's objection that the idea of "destruction" is here out of place because the Jews were on the side of Antiochus, has no weight, for even if the Jews sided with Antiochus (as Josephus states), it is still possible that this clause may refer to the "destruction" of the Egyptian armies.

---

[1] " Antiochus enim volens Judaeam recuperare et Syriae urbes plurimas, Scopam ducem Ptolemaei juxta fontes Jordanis, ubi nunc Paneas condita est, inito certamine fugavit, et cum decem millibus armatorum obsedit clausum in Sidone. Ob quem liberandum misit Ptolemaeus duces inclytos Eropum et Menoclem et Damoxenum. Sed obsidionem solvere non potuit: donec fame superatus Scopas manus dedit et nudus cum sociis dimissus est". Jerome, *Comm. in Dan.* XI. 15.

17—19. "*And he shall set his face to come with the power
of his whole kingdom, but he shall make an agreement with him*"
etc. Hävernick and Von Lengerke refer the suffix in מַלְכוּתוֹ to
Ptolemy, and accordingly explain, "*He* (i.e. Antiochus) *shall set
his face to come against the power of his* (i.e. Ptolemy's) *whole
kingdom*". But after the description of the utter defeat and
helplessness of Ptolemy (*vv.* 15, 16) it would be very unnatural
to speak of "the power of his whole kingdom". Ewald's translation, "*to come into possession of his kingdom*", assumes for the
word תֹּקֶף a sense which it bears nowhere else. It is therefore
much more probable that the suffix in מַלְכוּתוֹ refers to Antiochus (so Hitzig). The author seems to mean that after the
conquest of all Syria, Antiochus determined to apply his strength
to the conquest of Egypt itself, but thought it advisable, for the
moment, to come to terms with Ptolemy. Instead of וְעָשֹׂה we
should no doubt read יַעֲשֶׂה (so Hitzig and others), according to
the LXX. καὶ συνθήκας μετ᾽ αὐτοῦ ποιήσεται. יְשָׁרִים is either
a mistake for מֵישָׁרִים (see *v.* 6) or else a word of exactly the same
meaning; in the latter case it would be a Plural of יָשָׁר. The
suffix in עִמּוֹ must refer to Ptolemy. The latter half of *v.* 17 is
obscure. "*The daughter of women*" seems to be Cleopatra,
daughter of Antiochus, whom he betrothed and some years
afterwards married to Ptolemy. With the singular phrase בַּת
הַנָּשִׁים Hitzig compares בֶּן־אֲתֹנוֹת Zech. ix. 9. The LXX. has
θυγατέρα ἀνθρώπου, the Pĕsh. ܒܪܬ ܐܢܫܐ, but whether this
proves the existence of a reading בת אנשים may be doubted. The
suffix in לְהַשְׁחִיתָהּ is referred by De Wette, Hävernick, and Von
Lengerke, to מַלְכוּתוֹ, i.e. "*and he shall give to him* (i.e. Ptolemy)
the daughter of women, to destroy it (i.e. the Empire of Egypt)".
Von Lengerke supposes that the object of Antiochus, in giving
his daughter in marriage, was to excite against Ptolemy the
resentment of the Romans. But if מַלְכוּתוֹ means the kingdom
of Antiochus, the suffix in לְהַשְׁחִיתָהּ must refer to Cleopatra herself, i.e. he will give her in marriage "*to her ruin*". Perhaps,
however, we should read לְהַשְׁחִית (with Hitzig), i.e. "*in order to
work ruin*". The verbs תַּעֲמֹד and תִּהְיֶה should probably be taken
impersonally (see Is. vii. 7), "*but it shall not avail, nor shall he*

attain it (i.e. his object)". In *v.* 18 the *Kĕthīb* וישׂב is preferable to the *Kĕrī* וְיָשֵׂם (LXX. καὶ δώσει) since it is a question, not of a purpose (as in *v.* 17), but of actual motion (as in *v.* 19). *"And he shall turn his face towards the isles and shall take many"* etc. אִיִּים, as elsewhere, has the general sense of "lands by the sea". In the year 197 B.C. Antiochus made an expedition, by sea and land, against Asia Minor. For a while he met with great success; at length, in 190 B.C., he was severely defeated by the Roman general Lucius Scipio near Magnesia, and made peace on the most humiliating conditions. To this catastrophe the latter half of *v.* 18 probably alludes. Von Lengerke translates, *"But a Commander shall put an end to his insults, nothing but his insults shall he repay to him"*. The first לֹו Von Lengerke explains as meaning "to his hurt" (cf. Jer. xlviii. 35. Ruth iv. 14). The word קָצִין seems to be derived from קצה (Ar. قَصَى "to decide", "to pronounce a legal sentence"), in which case the grammatical formation would be quite unique in Hebrew. As קָצִין is elsewhere used both of civil and military officials, it may well be applied here to Scipio. But the latter part of the verse presents great difficulties. Nowhere in the Old Testament does בִּלְתִּי mean "only", "nothing but" (Von Lengerke, Hitzig), and to appeal to Is. x. 4 is to elucidate the obscure by means of the more obscure. Equally unproven is the meaning "and moreover" (ausserdem dass), proposed by Hävernick. Graetz's emendation בלחי, "on the cheek", is ingenious, but though "to *smite* on the cheek" is a familiar Hebrew metaphor (Micah iv. 14. Ps. iii. 8. Job xvi. 10), such a phrase as "to requite an insult upon the cheek" is unknown. Perhaps some help may here be derived from the LXX. which has καὶ ἐπιστρέψει ὀργὴν ὀνειδισμοῦ αὐτῶν ἐν ὅρκῳ κατὰ τὸν ὀνειδισμὸν αὐτοῦ ἐπιστρέψει [αὐτῷ· καὶ ἐπιστρέψει] τὸ πρόσωπον αὐτοῦ κ.τ.λ. The words in square brackets I have supplied from conjecture—their omission is easily explained by the homoioteleuton. Instead of והשבית קצין the translator appears to have read והשיב קצף, but here the Masoretic text is obviously preferable. In the words immediately following there is a wide divergence between the two texts. It is possible that the original reading may have

been שְׁבְעָתַיִם חֶרְפָּתוֹ יָשִׁיב לוֹ " *he shall requite his insults sevenfold*",
cf. Ps. lxxix. 12. This hypothesis at least will account both for
the present Masoretic text and for the variations of the LXX.
לוֹ בִלְתִּי may have arisen out of שבעתים, since in some forms of
the older alphabet ל and ו are little more than vertical strokes.
On the other hand the LXX., in which the first לוֹ is absent,
may have confused שבעתים with שְׁבֻעָה, ὅρκος. Verse 19—"*And
he shall turn his face towards the strongholds of his (own) land,
and shall be overthrown and fall and disappear*". After his
discomfiture Antiochus retreated to the lands east of the
Taurus, and was at length killed in the attempt to plunder
the temple of Bel in Elymais.

20. This verse describes in a few words the reign of Seleucus Philopator, son of Antiochus the Great. The usual rendering
is, "*and there shall arise in his place one who shall cause an
exactor to pass through the glory of the kingdom*" etc., (so Von
Lengerke). This is supposed to refer to the mission of Heliodorus for the purpose of robbing the Jewish Temple (II Macc.
iii. 7), and by "the glory of the kingdom", the author, it is said,
means Judaea. With this view Hitzig substantially agrees, but
he renders "*towards* the glory of the kingdom", and explains
הֶדֶר מַלְכוּת to be Jerusalem. In either case the usage of Hebrew
would require a preposition before הֶדֶר (cf. Zech. ix. 8). Moreover it would be very strange to call Judaea or Jerusalem the
glory of a *heathen* kingdom, and in *v.* 21 הוד מַלְכוּת evidently
means "royal honour". Since הוד and הָדָר are so frequently
coupled together, we may assume that הֶדֶר מַלְכוּת and הוד מַלְכוּת
express much the same idea, הֶדֶר being a mere phonetic variation of הָדָר. For these reasons Graetz inserts בְּלִי before הֶדֶר,
"*there shall arise one who shall cause an exactor to pass (through
the land), without royal dignity*" etc. But the words מַעֲבִיר נוֹגֵשׂ,
without further specification, would be scarcely intelligible—
not to mention the boldness of adding בְּלִי. It appears to me
simpler and more satisfactory to read נוֹגֵשׂ מַעֲבִיר instead of מעביר
נוגש, i.e. "*And there shall arise in his place an exactor who shall
cause the royal dignity to pass away*" etc. For this use of הֶעֱבִיר
see II Sam. xii. 13. Esth. viii. 3. The suffix in כַּנּוֹ naturally
refers to Antiochus the Great. By the "exactor" would be

meant Seleucus, who made himself unpopular by his avarice;
Livy speaks of this king's reign as "otiosum, nullis admodum
rebus gestis nobilitatum" (Bk. XLI. 19). Such a prince, following
immediately upon Antiochus the Great, might well be described
as "causing the royal dignity to pass away". "*And in a few
days he shall be broken*"; for יָמִים אֲחָדִים cf. Gen. xxvii. 44; xxix.
20. "To be broken" is "to be ruined", not necessarily "to
be slain" (cf. *v.* 26). Those who find in the preceding words an
allusion to the mission of Heliodorus, generally explain the
"few days" as the time which elapsed between that mission
and the death of Seleucus. Rosenmüller thinks that the whole
reign of Seleucus, which lasted 12 years, is here called "a few
days", as contrasted with the much longer reign of Antiochus
the Great. Perhaps the author may mean no more than that
the fall of Seleucus will be sudden and unexpected. The last
words of the verse are usually translated "*but not in wrath* (i.e.
by open violence), *nor in war*". But for this we should expect
בְּאַף rather than בְּאַפַּיִם. Graetz plausibly suggests בַּאֲנָפִים "*in
battle array*", cf. Ezek. xvii. 21; xxxviii. 6, 9, etc. It has been
already mentioned, in the Introduction to Chap. vii., that
Seleucus Philopator is said to have been murdered, and that
the author of Daniel seems to have attributed the murder to
the intrigues of Antiochus Epiphanes, who at the time was on
his way back from Rome to the East.

21—24. "*And there shall arise in his place a contemptible
man, upon whom they have not conferred royal dignity, but he
shall come in unawares and shall seize the kingdom by guile.*"
In the "contemptible man" all modern commentators recognize
Antiochus Epiphanes, younger son of Antiochus the Great.
The words וְלֹא נָתְנוּ עָלָיו הוֹד מַלְכוּת are best understood as a relative clause, אֲשֶׁר being omitted; cf. Ps. xxii. 30, where וְנַפְשׁוֹ לֹא
חִיָּה stands for וַאֲשֶׁר נַפְשׁוֹ לֹא חִיָּה. The subject of נָתְנוּ is "men"
in general (cf. I Kings i. 1, 2); for the phrase, see I Chr. xxix.
25. The meaning is that Antiochus Epiphanes had never been
treated as heir apparent to the throne. On בְּשַׁלְוָה and חֲלַקְלַקּוֹת,
see pp. 31, 32. Verses 22—24, as we have seen, are understood
by many, from Porphyry onwards, to refer to the campaigns of
Antiochus against Egypt. This view is accepted by Von Len-

gerke, who explains *v.* 22, as follows—"*And the overwhelming forces* (lit. the arms of the flood, viz. the forces of Egypt) *shall be overwhelmed from before him and shall be broken, and also an allied prince*" (viz. Ptolemy Philometor, son and successor of Ptolemy Epiphanes). But since Egypt is nowhere expressly mentioned until we come to *v.* 25, it seems much more probable that *vv.* 22—24 describe events which took place in Syria during the first five years of Antiochus' reign, i.e. between 175 and 170 B.C. Moreover the phrase זְרֹעוֹת הַשֶּׁטֶף would be a singularly inappropriate designation for the armies *defeated* by Antiochus—שׁוֹט שׁוֹטֵף (Is. xxviii. 15), which is cited as a parallel, evidently describes a *victorious* army. Also the use of נְגִיד בְּרִית, instead of בַּעַל בְּרִיתוֹ (Gen. xiv. 13) or אִישׁ בְּרִיתוֹ (Obad. 7), is quite anomalous. I would therefore propose to read הַשֶּׁטֹף, instead of הַשֶּׁטֶף, and to render, "*And forces shall be utterly overwhelmed before him, and shall be broken, and likewise a Prince of the Covenant*". The word זְרֹעוֹת may be used absolutely, like זְרֹעִים in *v.* 31, and in all probability refers to Heliodorus and the other domestic enemies whom Antiochus had to overcome at the beginning of his reign; מִלְּפָנָיו corresponds to מִן־קֳדָמַיהּ in the parallel passage, chap. vii. 8. The "Prince of the Covenant" seems to be the Jewish High Priest Onias III. (so Hitzig), who was deposed by Antiochus about 174 B.C., and some years afterwards murdered near Antioch (II Macc. iv. 33—36)[1]. On the term נָגִיד, as applied to the High Priest, see chap. ix. 25. בְּרִית (here, as in *v.* 32, without the Article) is the "covenant" of God with Israel, and hence Israel itself as a religious community, cf. בְּרִית קוֹדֶשׁ *v.* 30; similarly, in Syriac, *kĕyāmā* "covenant" or *kĕyāmā kaddīshā* "holy covenant", is used for "the clergy" (see Hoffmann's *Julianos der Abtrünnige*, p. 62, line 5, and p. 63, line 25). Verse 23—"*And from the time when they shall ally themselves with him he shall practise fraud, and shall rise and become strong with (but) few men*". Thus all who ally themselves with Antiochus are outwitted. מִן is here used as

---

[1] According to II Macc. iv. 7—10, the deposition of Onias III. was due to his brother Jason (named originally Jesus, see Josephus, *Antiq.* xii. 5. 1), who by bribing Antiochus obtained the High-Priesthood for himself. About 171 B.C. Jason was deposed in favour of a certain Menelaus.

in chap. ix. 25; the form הִתְחַבְּרוּת, in which the abstract ending is added to the Infinitive, may be compared to הַשְׁמָעוּת Ezek. xxiv. 26, although in the latter case the vocalization is not above suspicion. The subject of הִתְחַבְּרוּת is unexpressed, cf. Ps. xlii. 4 בֶּאֱמֹר אֵלַי "when they say to me", for which v. 11 of the psalm has בְּאָמְרָם אֵלַי. גּוֹי seems here to be used in the sense of עַם. The "few men" are the partisans of Antiochus, i.e. those by whose help he was able to rise to power (וְעָלָה וְעָצַם) and over-come his rivals. The word בְּשַׁלְוָה (v. 24) Von Lengerke connects with v. 23; מִשְׁמַנֵּי מְדִינָה he explains as referring to Lower Egypt, invaded by Antiochus. Ewald, following the Masoretic text, translates, *"He shall come unawares even into the fattest provinces"*—by which provinces Ewald understands Galilee. But to describe Lower Egypt or Galilee as "the fattest parts of *a province*" (מְדִינָה Singular) would be a strange figure of speech; the phrase אֶבְיוֹנֵי אָדָם (Is. xxix. 19), which Hitzig here cites, is no real parallel, since אָדָם is a collective and cannot form a Plural. Graetz explains, *"In peace and with the honour-able men of the land he will present himself"*—taking מִשְׁמַנֵּי according to Is. x. 16. Ps. lxxviii. 31. But even if we admit such a use of מְדִינָה, why should this connection between Antiochus and "the honourable men" be specially mentioned? Perhaps we should read וּבְשַׁלְוָה בְמִשְׁמַנֵּי וגו׳ *"And by stealth he shall assail the mightiest men of (each) province"*. For בָּא בְ in the sense of "to come against", "to attack", see v. 30. This agrees moreover with chap. viii. 25, וּבְשַׁלְוָה יַשְׁחִית רַבִּים. The מִשְׁמַנֵּי מְדִינָה are presumably included in the עֲצוּמִים of chap. viii. 24, i.e. the "many" foes whom Antiochus contrived to ruin. The following words describe his marvellous success—*"And he shall do what his fathers have not done, nor the fathers of his fathers; spoil and plunder and riches shall he scatter among them, and against strongholds shall he devise his devices, but (it shall be only) for a time"*. The root בזר appears nowhere else in the Old Testament but Ps. lxviii. 31. The suffix in לָהֶם is referred by Von Lengerke, Hitzig, and Ewald to the מִשְׁמַנֵּי מְדִינָה, i.e. to the *inhabitants* of the regions in question, but if the מִשְׁמַנֵּי מְדִינָה are the enemies of Antiochus, the suffix in לָהֶם must refer to his adherents; this vague use of the Plural is particularly com-

mon in Daniel (e.g. בָּהֶם v. 7, יַחְשְׁבוּ v. 25). By the "strongholds"
we should probably understand the frontier of Egypt; it is
here a question, not of invasion, but merely of ambitious plot-
ting (cf. I Macc. i. 16 καὶ ὑπέλαβε βασιλεῦσαι τῆς Αἰγύπτου).
This state of things, however, is to last only for a time.

25—28. These four verses describe the war of Antiochus
against Ptolemy Philometor in 170 B.C. "*And he shall rouse his
might and his courage against the king of the South, with a great
army; and the king of the South shall engage in the war with an
army great and numerous exceedingly, but he* (i.e. Ptolemy) *shall
not stand, for they shall devise devices against him*". For this
use of יָעֵר cf. Ps. lxxviii. 38. The "king of the South" in this
verse is supposed by Hitzig to be Ptolemy Euergetes II. (commonly known by the nickname Φύσκων, younger brother of
Ptolemy Philometor), who in the course of this war was proclaimed king at Alexandria[1]. But since the "two kings" in v.
27 are certainly Antiochus and Ptolemy Philometor, it may be
assumed that also in vv. 25, 26, Ptolemy Philometor is meant[2].
In spite of his great resources, Ptolemy could not maintain the
contest, owing to the treachery of his adherents (יַחְשְׁבוּ עָלָיו
מַחֲשָׁבוֹת). He was defeated by Antiochus near Pelusium, and at
length fell into the power of the Syrian king. This is further
explained in what follows (v. 26) "*And those who eat of his
dainties shall ruin him, and his army shall be swept away, and
many shall fall down slain*". By "those who eat of his dainties"
(cf. chap. i. 5) are meant the courtiers of Ptolemy, perhaps in
particular Eulaeus and Lenaeus, two men who, after the death
of his mother Cleopatra (about 174 B.C.), had complete influence
over him (see Polybius XXVIII. 21, and Jerome on Dan. xi.
21 ff.). Instead of יִשְׁטוֹף we should probably read יִשְׁטֵף, according to v. 22. In v. 27, Ptolemy is in the hands of Antiochus.

---

[1] ""Αρχει μὲν γὰρ ὁ Φιλομήτωρ πρό-
τερος ἔτεσιν ἔνδεκα μόνος. 'Αντιόχου δ'
ἐπιστρατεύσαντος Αἰγύπτῳ καὶ περιελόν-
τος αὐτοῦ τὸ διάδημα, οἱ 'Αλεξανδρεῖς τῷ
νεωτέρῳ ἐπέτρεψαν τὰ πράγματα, καὶ
διώξαντες 'Αντίοχον ἐρρύσαντο τὸν Φιλο-
μήτορα" κ.τ.λ. Porphyry, quoted by
Eusebius in his *Chronicle*, ed. Schoene,

i. p. 162.

[2] A commentary on this passage is
furnished by I Macc. i. 18, 19—the
author of I Macc. here speaks of one
Ptolemy only (i.e. Philometor), ignor-
ing Physcon altogether, which confirms the interpretation given above.

"*And as for the two kings, their minds (shall be bent) on mischief, and at one table they shall speak lies, but it shall not avail, for there is yet a limit (fixed) for the time*". After the defeat of the Egyptians, Antiochus allied himself with Ptolemy Philometor, on the pretext of helping him against his younger brother (who, as we have seen, was now reigning at Alexandria); but the league was a hollow pretence—while feasting together, each was planning the ruin of the other. מְרָע, pausal form of מֵרָע, is an abstract noun from the root רעע, cf. מֵסָב from סבב. The subject of תִּצְלָח is indefinite, cf. תַעֲמֹד and תִהְיֶה in *v.* 17. The "time" (מוֹעֵד) is the time during which Antiochus is suffered to domineer over Egypt. Whether he was driven out or left of his own accord, *v.* 28 does not tell us. "*And he shall return to his land with great riches, and his mind (shall be set) against the Holy Covenant; so he shall do (his will) and return to his land*". On his march northwards, Antiochus found Jerusalem in a state of tumult. A report had gone forth that he was dead, in consequence of which Jason, the deposed High Priest, had seized the opportunity to reinstate himself by force, and had massacred many of the partisans of his rival Menelaus (II Macc. v. 5). Antiochus, not unnaturally, regarded this as a rebellion against his royal authority, entered Jerusalem with his army, and put great numbers of Jews to death. He then marched to Antioch, carrying with him the spoils of the Temple (I Macc. i. 20–24. II Macc. v. 11–21).

29, 30. "*At the time appointed he shall return and enter into the South, but it shall not be in the latter time as in the former time. And there shall come against him ships from Kittim, so shall he be cowed, and shall return and be wroth against the Holy Covenant, and shall do (his will), and return and have regard unto them who forsake the Holy Covenant*". In the spring of 168 B.C. Antiochus again invaded Egypt. Ptolemy Philometor and his brother, who at this time were reigning conjointly, had already despatched embassies to Achaia and to Rome, to ask for help against the Syrians (Polybius XXIX. 23. Livy XLIV. 19; XLV. 11). On this occasion Antiochus fared much worse than before—the latter expedition was not as the former one. For the construction כְּרִאשֹׁנָה וְכָאַחֲרֹנָה cf. Josh. xiv.

11. Ezek. xviii. 4. The phrase צִיִּים כִּתִּים, in which כִּתִּים is, of
course, an adjective, seems to have been suggested by Numb.
xxiv. 24. Originally כִּתִּים meant the inhabitants of Cyprus, but
among the later Jews it was used for all the western maritime
countries (I Macc. i. 1; viii. 5. Josephus, *Antiq.* I. 6. 1). The
allusion here is to the Romans, who sent Caius Popilius Laenas
to Egypt, summarily demanding that Antiochus should quit the
country. The king, thoroughly humiliated, was forced to obey[1].
The Niphal נִכְאָה is from a root which occurs frequently in
Syriac, but which appears nowhere else in the Old Testament
except in Ps. cix. 16 and possibly in Ezek. xiii. 22. Job xxx. 8.
The double וְשָׁב in *v.* 30 is taken by Von Lengerke in an adverbial sense, i.e. " and he shall *again* be wroth"—"and he shall
again have regard"; but, as Hitzig remarks, the first וְשָׁב probably refers to the march of Antiochus from Egypt towards
Judaea, the second וְשָׁב to his march from Judaea towards
Antioch. Whether Antiochus, after leaving Egypt, came in
person to Jerusalem, is not clear, for I Macc. i. 29, which
describes the events of this time, speaks only of an official sent
by the king with an army. But it is certain that in the
autumn of 168 B.C. Jerusalem was plundered by the king's
order, many Jews were slain, and a systematic attempt was
begun to suppress the Jewish religion. For the use of עָשָׂה cf.
וְהִצְלִיחַ וְעָשָׂה chap. viii. 24. "*He shall have regard unto them who*

[1] Ὅτι τοῦ Ἀντιόχου πρὸς Πτολεμαῖον
ἕνεκεν τοῦ Πηλούσιον κατασχεῖν ἀφικο-
μένου, ὁ Ποπίλιος ὁ τῶν Ῥωμαίων στρα-
τηγός, τοῦ βασιλέως πόρρωθεν ἀσπαζομένου
διὰ τῆς φωνῆς καὶ τὴν δεξιὰν προτείνοντος,
πρόχειρον ἔχων τὸ δελτάριον, ἐν ᾧ τὸ τῆς
συγκλήτου δόγμα κατατέτακτο, προύτει-
νεν αὐτῷ, καὶ τοῦτ' ἐκέλευε πρῶτον ἀνα-
γνῶναι τὸν Ἀντίοχον, ὡς μὲν ἐμοὶ δοκεῖ,
μὴ πρότερον ἀξιώσας τὸ τῆς φιλίας σύν-
θημα ποιεῖν πρὶν ἢ τὴν προαίρεσιν ἐπι-
γνῶναι τοῦ δεξιουμένου, πότερα φίλιος ἢ
πολέμιός ἐστιν. ἐπεὶ δ' ὁ βασιλεὺς ἀνα-
γνοὺς ἔφη βούλεσθαι μεταδοῦναι τοῖς φί-
λοις ὑπὲρ τῶν προσπεπτωκότων, ἀκούσας
ὁ Ποπίλιος ἐποίησε πρᾶγμα βαρὺ μὲν δο-
κοῦν εἶναι καὶ τελέως ὑπερήφανον· ἔχων

γὰρ πρὸ χειρῶν ἀμπελίνην βακτηρίαν
περιέγραφε τῷ κλήματι τὸν Ἀντίοχον, ἐν
τούτῳ τε τῷ γύρῳ τὴν ἀπόφασιν ἐκέλευσε
δοῦναι περὶ τῶν γεγραμμένων. ὁ δὲ
βασιλεὺς ξενισθεὶς τὸ γινόμενον καὶ τὴν
ὑπεροχήν, βραχὺν χρόνον ἐναπορήσας ἔφη
ποιήσειν πᾶν τὸ παρακαλούμενον ὑπὸ
Ῥωμαίων. οἱ δὲ περὶ τὸν Ποπίλιον τότε
τὴν δεξιὰν αὐτοῦ λαμβάνοντες ἅμα πάντες
ἠσπάζοντο φιλοφρόνως. ἦν δὲ τὰ γεγραμ-
μένα λύειν ἐξ αὐτῆς τὸν πρὸς Πτολεμαῖον
πόλεμον. διὸ καὶ δοθεισῶν αὐτῷ τακτῶν
ἡμερῶν οὗτος μὲν ἀπῆγε τὰς δυνάμεις εἰς
τὴν Συρίαν, βαρυνόμενος μὲν καὶ στένων,
εἴκων δὲ τοῖς καιροῖς κατὰ τὸ παρόν".
Polybius XXIX. 27. The last words
strikingly correspond to Dan. xi. 30.

forsake the Holy Covenant", i.e. he will henceforth fix his attention upon the apostate Jews, and in every way further their designs (cf. *v.* 37, also Job xxxi. 1).

31. "*And forces sent by him shall prevail, and they shall desecrate the sanctuary, the stronghold, and abolish the daily sacrifice, and set up the abomination*". יַעֲמֹדוּ is rendered by Von Lengerke, "*shall arise*", i.e. shall be set on foot, and by Hitzig "*shall remain*", i.e. shall be left to garrison the fortresses of Judaea, after the departure of Antiochus. But the analogy of *vv.* 15, 25, is in favour of the meaning "*shall prevail*". The desecration of the Temple was the work of the Syrian soldiery, abetted by a party among the Jews. הַמָּעוֹז is in apposition to הַמִּקְדָּשׁ—both before and after this period the Temple at Jerusalem appears to have had fortifications. As to the precise date of the abolition of the daily sacrifice, I Maccabees tells us nothing; but we are informed that on the 15th of Chisleu, i.e. near the end of December, 168 B.C., a heathen altar was built upon the stone platform which in the post-exilic Temple served as the place of sacrifice (I Macc. i. 54; cf. iv. 42–47). Ten days later, i.e. on the 25th of Chisleu, sacrifices were offered on the new altar. According to II Macc. vi. 2, the Temple was at this time dedicated to the Olympian Zeus. Hence almost all commentators are agreed in explaining "the abomination" (הַשִּׁקּוּץ) to be the heathen altar mentioned above. But as to the term מְשֹׁמֵם there has been considerable difference of opinion. As it is impossible to draw any conclusion from the corrupt passages viii. 13 and ix. 27, we must be guided chiefly by chap. xii. 11, where we read of a שִׁקּוּץ שֹׁמֵם. The oldest exegetical tradition on the subject is that contained in the LXX. which has βδέλυγμα ἐρημώσεως (chap. xi. 31) and τὸ βδέλυγμα τῆς ἐρημώσεως (chap. xii. 11). The phrase βδέλυγμα ἐρημώσεως is used also in I Macc. i. 54, and seems to have been borrowed from Daniel—whether from chap. xi. 31 or chap. xii. 11 it is impossible to say. This does not prove that מְשֹׁמֵם and שֹׁמֵם were used as abstract nouns, but only that they were connected with the *idea* of desolation. Most modern commentators translate מְשֹׁמֵם "desolating", and explain שֹׁמֵם in chap. xii. 11 as an equivalent form. But a Poel שֹׁמֵם "to desolate" is not known to

exist. Hitzig interprets both מְשֹׁמֵם and שֹׁמֵם as "an object of horror", but without any valid proof. Great light seems to me to have been thrown on this question by Nestle, in the *Zeitschrift für alttestamentliche Wissenschaft*, 1883. He thinks that שִׁקּוּץ שֹׁמֵם is an intentional disfigurement of בַּעַל שָׁמַיִם (in Phoenician inscriptions בעל שמם or בעשמם, in Aramaic בעלשמין or בעלשמן), the Semitic equivalent of the Greek Ζεύς[1]. The only objection which can be raised against Nestle's theory is that in Daniel שִׁקּוּץ שֹׁמֵם means, not the god, but the altar of the god. This however is of no great consequence, for when once the phrase was formed it might easily be applied to everything connected with the worship of Zeus, just as among the later Jews עֲבוֹדָה זָרָה meant either "idolatry" or "an idol". If therefore שִׁקּוּץ שֹׁמֵם is a term coined in order to connect the worship of בַּעַל שָׁמַיִם with the idea of "desolation" (ἐρήμωσις), it must appear very unlikely that the author of Daniel used שמם and משמם indifferently. It is at least remarkable that in *both* passages where משמם (משומם) occurs, it produces a syntactical construction which, if not impossible, is at all events open to grave suspicion, for in chap. ix. 27 we should expect מְשׁוֹמֵמִים and in chap. xi. 31 הַמְשֹׁמֵם. On the whole the most probable hypothesis is that in chap. ix. 27 מְשׁוֹמֵם is an error, and that in the verse before us משמם was inserted by a scribe who wished to assimilate the two passages.

32—35. "*And those who bring guilt upon the Covenant he shall make apostates by treacherous means, but a company who know their God shall be valiant and do exploits. And the teachers of the people shall give understanding to the multitude, and they shall fall by sword and by flame, by captivity and by*

---

[1] In addition to the proofs given by Nestle may be mentioned a passage of Philo of Byblus, cited by Eusebius (*Praep. Evang.* I. 10. 7), "Τοῦτον γὰρ Θεὸν ἐνόμιζον μόνον οὐρανοῦ κύριον, Βεελσαμὴν καλοῦντες, ὅ ἐστι παρὰ Φοίνιξι κύριος οὐρανοῦ, Ζεὺς δὲ παρ' Ἕλλησι". Moreover in a bilingual Palmyrene inscription of the year 134 A.D. the words לבעלשמן מרא עלמא are rendered by Διι μεγιστω κεραυνιω (see *Z. D. M. G.* xv. p. 16, and De Vogüé, *Syrie Centrale*, p. 50, note). How easily the play upon the word שָׁמַיִם might occur to a Jew is shewn by a passage in the בראשית רבא (sect. 4, near the end), where the sky is said to be called שָׁמַיִם because people are *astonished* at it (שהבריות משתוממים עליהן).

spoil (many) days. And when they are falling they shall be holpen with a little help, and many shall join themselves unto them—treacherously. But (when) certain of the teachers shall fall, (it shall be) in order to purge them and cleanse and make white, until the time of the end, for it is yet for the time appointed". מַרְשִׁיעֵי בְּרִית is usually rendered "*those that sin against the Covenant*" (Ewald). Von Lengerke translates "die Frevler des Bundes", i.e. *the sinners among the covenanted people*, and Hitzig "*those who condemn* (i.e. renounce) *the Covenant*". But it is more natural to suppose that the מַרְשִׁיעֵי בְּרִית, "those who bring guilt upon the covenanted people", stand in opposition to the מַצְדִּיקֵי הָרַבִּים of chap. xii. 3. The subject of the verb יַחֲנִיף is, of course, Antiochus. Those Jews who already had leanings towards heathenism he induced by specious promises (בַּחֲלַקּוֹת) openly to apostatize from the religion of Israel (see I Macc. ii. 18). Elsewhere in the Old Testament החניף is "to defile" the earth with bloodshed etc. (Numb. xxxv. 33. Jer. iii. 2); here the object is personal. חֲלַקּוֹת evidently has the same meaning as חֲלַקְלַקּוֹת (*vv.* 21, 34); if the pointing be correct, it is formed like קְטַנּוֹת, but elsewhere we find חֲלָקוֹת (Is. xxx. 10. Ps. xii. 3, 4). In contrast to the apostate Jews stand those "who know their God", i.e. those who have a practical knowledge of His ways (Jer. ix. 23). עַם is not in the construct state, but in apposition to יֹדְעֵי אֱלֹהָיו, cf. Ps. xcv. 10. Ezek. iii. 5. The suffix in אֱלֹהָיו refers to עַם (Jer. vii. 28). In *v.* 33 מַשְׂכִּילֵי עָם is rendered by some "*the wise of the people*" (so Von Lengerke), as also הַמַּשְׂכִּילִים in *v.* 35 and chap. xii. 3, 10. Ewald and Hitzig translate by "*teachers*", according to chap. ix. 22. The probability is that the author uses מַשְׂכִּילִים in a *double* sense, i.e. it includes both the possession of wisdom and the imparting of it; similarly יָבִינוּ is here active, "shall give understanding", whereas in the parallel passage, chap. xii. 10, we have to render "shall understand". In any case it is clear that a special class, or rather party, is here meant, viz. the leaders of the anti-Hellenistic movement, who were known as the "pious" (חֲסִידִים, see I Macc. ii. 42; vii. 13. II Macc. xiv. 6). Around these enthusiasts gathered a great multitude of their co-religionists, who till then had been halting between two opinions. The subject of נִכְשְׁלוּ may be either the רַבִּים (Hitzig) or the עַם מַשְׂכִּילֵי (Von Lengerke). The latter is perhaps the more probable view, as those who "fall" in v. 33 must be identical with those to whom "many join themselves" in v. 34. That the verb וְנִכְשְׁלוּ does not imply the extermination of the מַשְׂכִּילִים is obvious from what follows. The "*little help*" (v. 34), in the midst of adversity, refers doubtless to the first successes of the pious party, headed by Mattathias (I Macc. ii. 42–48), before any of the great battles had been fought. The ruthless severity which "the pious" displayed, produced its natural effect—many joined them from mere terror and were ready at any moment to turn traitors. Verse 35 should probably be taken as an explanation of what precedes. לִצְרוֹף בָּהֶם is literally "to purge amongst them", i.e. to perform a purifying process in their midst. The suffix in בָּהֶם, to judge by chap. xii. 10, must refer to the people at large, not only to the מַשְׂכִּילִים; the meaning therefore seems to be that the death of some of "the teachers" is no excuse for despair, but is necessary in order that their adherents, "the many", may be duly tested. לְלַבֵּן, if correctly pointed, is a contraction of לְהַלְבֵּן, which again stands for לְהַלְבִּין (cf. הַנְחֵל Deut. xxxii. 8, for הַנְחִיל); similar are לַעְשֵׂר Deut. xxvi. 12 and בַּעְשֵׂר Neh. x. 39. But more probably we should read לְלַבֵּן, with Hitzig. The Piel of לבן does not indeed occur in the Old Testament (for from Ps. ix. 1, to which Hitzig appeals, no conclusion can be drawn), but is common in post-Biblical Hebrew.

36—39. "*And the king shall do according to his own will, and shall exalt and magnify himself above every god, and against the God of gods shall he speak monstrous things; so shall he prosper until the wrath is over, for a sentence hath been executed. And to the gods of his fathers he shall have no regard, nor to the Desire of women, nor shall he have regard to any god, but shall magnify himself above all*". After describing the sufferings of the faithful Israelites, the angel returns to the subject of Antiochus, who is called, not "the king of the North", but "the king" simply. The portrait of Antiochus here given, as one who "magnifies himself above every god", and who "has no regard to the gods of his fathers", certainly does not appear at first sight to agree with the accounts of the western historians;

both Polybius and Livy speak with admiration of the honour
which Antiochus paid to the gods. We must, however, remember that though he acquired a reputation for piety among the
Greeks by his splendid presents to temples etc., his conduct may
have produced a very different impression upon his Oriental
subjects, both heathens and Jews. Indeed Polybius himself
tells us that men differed greatly in their opinion of the king's
character—some thinking him a good-natured easy-going man,
others a maniac (Fragm. of Bk. XXVI.). His waywardness and
his contempt for established customs were peculiarly calculated
to shock Oriental conservatism. When to this we add his
persecution of the Jews, it is not surprising that in Daniel he
should be represented as a marvel of impiety. "*The God of
gods*" (*v.* 36) is the God of Israel, cf. אֱלָהִין אֱלָהּ chap. ii. 47. The
phrase נֶחֱרָצָה כָלָה וְעַם is borrowed from Is. x. 25. On נֶחֱרָצָה see chap.
ix. 26, 27. The Perfect נֶעֱשָׂתָה expresses certainty, i.e. the sentence of punishment must first have been executed before the
divine wrath (זַעַם) is over. In *v.* 37, "*the gods of his fathers*"
are the deities whose worship was officially recognized in the
Seleucid Empire. In what manner Antiochus shewed his dis-
respect for "the gods of his fathers" we are not here told, but it
is by no means improbable that his attempts to centralize his
empire by the abolition of local usages (see I Macc. i. 41, 42)
may have spread the notion that he despised all established
religions. "*The Desire of women*" must, to judge by the context, be some object of worship. Most modern interpreters, following Ephraim Syrus, explain this as a reference to the goddess
Nanaia, whose temple in Elymais the king endeavoured to
plunder shortly before his death[1]. But to this view there are
two objections. Firstly, the attack upon the temple of Nanaia
cannot have been heard of in Judaea till the year 164 B.C.
Secondly, there is no reason why Nanaia should be designated
as the Desire of women. Even if her worship was, as has
been supposed, of a voluptuous character, this would scarcely
give rise to such an appellation. It appears therefore much
more probable that Ewald is right in explaining the Desire

[1] See Polybius XXXI. 11 where this goddess is called Artemis, and Appian, *Syr.* 60, where she is identified with Aphrodite.

of women as Tammuz (Adonis), whose cult had been popular in Syria from time immemorial, especially amongst women (Ezek. viii. 14). The meaning of *v.* 38 is doubtful. Von Lengerke interprets, "*But the god of strongholds shall he honour upon his pedestal, and a god whom his fathers have not known shall he honour with gold and with silver and with precious stones and with costly things*". The "god of strongholds" and the "god whom his fathers have not known" Von Lengerke takes to be designations of Jupiter Capitolinus, in whose honour Antiochus began to erect a temple, profusely adorned with gold, at Antioch (Livy XLI. 20). But why should it be mentioned that Antiochus honoured Jupiter "upon his pedestal"? It is decidedly preferable to translate עַל־כַּנּוֹ "*instead thereof*" (with Gesenius), the suffix referring to בֵּל in the preceding verse, cf. *vv.* 20, 21— the meaning "instead" is the only one which will suit all three passages. But as to אֱלֹהַּ מָעֻזִּים there has been much difference of opinion. The Pĕshiṭtā has ܐܠܗܐ ܥܫܝܢܐ "a mighty god". Some moderns (e.g. Keil) have thought that "the god of strongholds" is War personified. Hitzig reads מָעוֹז יָם instead of מָעֻזִּים, and interprets as follows—"*But the god of the stronghold of the sea* (i.e. the Tyrian god Melḳart, see Is. xxiii. 4, where מָעוֹז הַיָּם means Tyre) *shall he honour in his place* (i.e. in his temple at Tyre)". But by "the god whom his fathers have not known" Hitzig understands Jupiter Capitolinus. The obscurity of this passage may be due to the fact that the author is alluding to some report which was current among the Jews but which perhaps had little real foundation. The beginning of *v.* 39, as it stands in the Masoretic text, is quite unintelligible, for to translate, "*And he shall act towards the strong fortresses as towards the strange god*" (Ewald), or "*And so shall he act towards the strong fortresses, together with strange gods*" (Von Lengerke) is unnatural in the extreme. Probably we should read עַם instead of עִם, with Hitzig, so that the sense will be, "*And he shall procure for the strong fortresses the people of a strange god*", referring to the fact that Antiochus settled heathen colonists in the fortified cities of Judaea, especially in Jerusalem (I Macc. iii. 36, 45). For this use of עָשָׂה see II Sam. xv. 1. I Kings i. 5, and with עַם אֱלֹהַּ נֵכָר cf. עַם כְּמוֹשׁ Numb. xxi.

29. The following words are explained by Von Lengerke, " *Whosoever shews recognition* (Anerkennung übt), *on him he shall bestow great honour*", the word הכיר being used as in II Sam. iii. 36. Ps. cxlii. 5. The passage, according to Von Lengerke, refers to the apostate Jews. Somewhat fantastic is the view of Ewald, who interprets " Whosoever recognizes the fortresses as deities", etc. Hitzig more naturally takes הכיר as having Antiochus for its subject—" *Whomsoever he favours he shall raise to great honour, and shall make them rule over the many, and the land he shall portion out for gain*", i.e. the favourites of Antiochus are to be made rulers of the country, and the lands of " the pious", who have been slain or ejected, will be sold in order to fill the royal treasury. For the use of הִכִּיר " to have regard", " to shew favour", see Deut. xvi. 19 ; xxi. 17 ; xxxiii. 9. Ruth ii. 10. For הכיר the *Kĕrî* substitutes יַכִּיר, but this correction is unnecessary, since the clause אשר הכיר is virtually hypothetical ("if he shall have favoured any one"), and therefore may take the Perfect, while the verb of the apodosis is in the Imperfect (cf. אֲשֶׁר בֵּרַכְךָ יהוה אֱלֹהֶיךָ תִּתֶּן־לוֹ Deut. xv. 14).

40—45. With regard to these verses there are, as we have seen, three rival hypotheses, viz. (1) that they relate historical facts which took place *after* those already mentioned, i.e. after the year 168 B.C., (2) that they give a general sketch of the course of events from about 171 B.C. to the death of Antiochus, (3) that they describe, not real facts, but merely the expectations of the author. A careful examination of the details will, I think, shew that the third hypothesis alone is tenable. The opening words of *v.* 40, "*And at the time of the end*", indicate that what follows is *subsequent* to the persecutions described in *v.* 35, which are to last " until the time of the end ". The king of the South, i.e. Ptolemy Philometor, will go to war (lit. will exchange thrusts) with Antiochus ; for the metaphor, see chap. viii. 4. Antiochus will come against him like a whirlwind, with a vast armament. Verse 41 describes his march through Palestine (ארץ הצבי cf. *v.* 16). רַבּוֹת is taken by Hitzig as "*many lands*", referring to אֲרָצוֹת in the preceding verse. But the analogy of *v.* 12 (וְהִפִּיל רִבֹּאוֹת) is certainly in favour of reading

רְבּוֹת *"myriads of men"*, as De Wette proposes, cf. Neh. vii. 71.
That the Edomites and the chiefs of the Ammonites should not
be among the victims of Antiochus, is perfectly natural, for
both these peoples seem to have helped him against the Jews
(I Macc. iv. 61; v. 3—8). Why the Moabites, who had long
disappeared, should be specially mentioned, is not obvious.
Ewald supposes that Edom, Moab, and Ammon are not to be
understood literally, but are terms of reproach applied to the
apostate Israelites. More probably the mention of Moab is a
mere reminiscence of the older writings, in which Moab and
Ammon so frequently appear together[1]. In *vv.* 42, 43, Antiochus
subjugates Egypt. The word מכמנים, "hidden things", i.e.
"treasures", occurs here only. The Aramaic root כמן (in the
Targums כְּמַן, in Syriac *kĕmen*), whence is derived the late
Hebrew הִכְמִין "to place in ambush"—means, it is true, "to lie
in wait", and is never actually used for "storing up", but that
the same root *may* have both senses is shewn by the Hebr. צָפַן
(Prov. i. 18; ii. 7)[2]. The phrase *"the Libyans and Ethiopians
shall be in his train"* evidently implies that these peoples sub-
mit themselves to Antiochus. To suppose, with Hoffmann
(*Antiochus IV.* p. 103), that the passage refers merely to certain
Libyans and Ethiopians who happened to be in Egypt at the
time, is very far-fetched. The omission of the Article in לְבִים
וְכֻשִׁים is quite in accordance with analogy (cf. צִידֹנִים Deut. iii. 9;
I Kings xi. 5). With בְּמִצְעָדָיו cf. the synonymous בְּרַגְלָיו Judg.
iv. 10. The last two verses of the chapter close the story of
Antiochus. What the *"tidings from the East and North"* may
be, we can only guess, but since Antiochus is now in Egypt the
tidings presumably refer to events in Palestine. If, as has been
suggested in the Introduction to chap. viii., the author expected
the Temple service to be restored some months before the end
of the time of affliction, this passage may possibly mean that
the king, while in Egypt, will hear of the recovery of Jerusalem
by the Jews. That such news should move his bitterest resent-

---

[1] Compare the list of hostile nations
in Ps. lxxxiii., which very many commentators assign to the Maccabean
period.

[2] The Arab. *kamin* "ambush" is borrowed from the Aramaic (see Fraenkel,
Die aram. Fremdwörter, p. 243).

ment, would be natural. He goes forth (from Egypt) to destroy
and to exterminate many. *"And he shall plant his palace-tents
between the seas and the glorious holy mountain; so shall he
come to his end, and none shall help him"*. אפדן, in Syriac
āphadhnā, is from the Old Persian *apadāna* "palace"[1]. "The
tents of his palace" are the tents which form his head-quarters.
יַמִּים is here, as in Judg. v. 17, equivalent to הַיָּם, i.e. the Mediterranean. Thus Antiochus will encamp between the sea and
Jerusalem (הַר צְבִי קֹדֶשׁ). The notion of some commentators, e.g.
Hävernick, that by the "seas" are meant the Caspian Sea and
the Persian Gulf, and by the "glorious holy mountain" the
temple of Nanaia in Elymais, may be dismissed at once, for how
could a strict Jew designate a heathen temple as צְבִי קֹדֶשׁ? Von
Lengerke and Hitzig, while fully admitting that the beginning
of *v.* 45 describes Antiochus as encamped in Palestine, suppose
that in the latter half of the verse the author suddenly passes
on (overleaping several years) to relate the death of Antiochus
in Persia; they therefore explain וּבָא עַד־קִצּוֹ as meaning, *"And
he shall go (into Persia) to meet his end"*. But by this hypothesis the first half of the verse is deprived of all meaning.
What connection can there be between the fact that Antiochus
encamped in Palestine in 168 B.C. and the fact that he "came
to his end" in Persia four years later? It is much more reasonable to assume that the author describes the king as encamping
in Palestine because it is in Palestine that he is to "come to
his end". That Palestine, the scene of his greatest crimes,
should also be the scene of his final overthrow, was, from the
point of view of the persecuted Jews, a very natural expectation.
No details are here given, but since in chap. viii. 25 we read
that Antiochus will "be broken without hand", we must suppose that the author looked forward to some divine intervention
by which the great enemy would perish "with none to help
him."

xii. 1—3. The opening words of *v.* 1, *"And at that time"*,

---

[1] The Arab. *fadan* is, of course, a loan-word. See Nöldeke, *Beiträge zur Kenntniss der Poesie der alten Araber*, p. 138—*Fadanun yuṭīfu bihi-n-Nabīṭu muraffaʿū*, "a lofty palace which Naba-teans encompass", i.e. such as Syrians inhabit.

clearly shew that what follows will take place at the time of the
overthrow of Antiochus. Michael, the guardian angel of Israel
(chap. x. 13), will arise to defend the Saints. The precise
nature of the coming time of affliction is left undetermined,
but, as has been before remarked, the author of Daniel probably
looked forward to a gathering together of the heathen nations
against Jerusalem (Zech. xiv. 2 ff.). The conception of a great
battle in which the assembled Gentile powers are to be defeated, appears elsewhere both in Jewish and Christian apocalypses (Enoch xc. 16. Rev. xvi. 14; xix. 19). With the words,
"*And there shall be a time of affliction*" etc., cf. Jer. xxx. 7.
By עַמְּךָ "*thy people*" is meant, of course, the *true* Israel, "*all
who are found written in the book*". The metaphor of a "book",
in which the names of the righteous are inscribed, occurs also
in Exod. xxxii. 32. Ps. lxix. 29. cf. Mal. iii. 16. Verse 2 introduces the resurrection of the dead. To what extent this belief
existed among the Jews in pre-Maccabean times, cannot here
be discussed, but this is in any case the earliest passage where
the belief is unambiguously set forth. Here, however, the resurrection is far from being universal; it includes "many", not
all, of the dead. That only Israelites are raised is not expressly
stated, but appears probable from the context. The phrase
אַדְמַת עָפָר is very peculiar; we should expect rather עֲפַר הָאָרֶץ[1].
Those who awake are divided into two classes, corresponding to
the division in chap. xi. 32. חַיֵּי עוֹלָם "*everlasting life*", like the
חַיֵּי עָלְמָא of the Targums (Lev. xviii. 5. Ezek. xx. 13), evidently
means individual immortality, and is thus distinguished from
חַיִּים עַד־הָעוֹלָם Ps. cxxxiii. 3, which implies nothing more than the
perpetual existence of Israel (cf. Ecclesiasticus xxxvii. 25;
xliv. 13). The wicked who are raised will be objects of reproach
and abhorrence for ever. דִּרְאוֹן, constr. of דֵּרָאוֹן, seems to have
been suggested by Is. lxvi. 24, the only other passage where the
word is found. As to הַמַּשְׂכִּלִים (*v.* 3) see what has been said on
chap. xi. 33. Here, as before, "the teachers" are distinguished

---

[1] It has been suggested to me by
Prof. Robertson Smith that in Ps. xlix.
12 אדמות may be a corruption of
ארמות "cairns" (Arab. *iram*, Pl. *ārām*
or *urām*). If this were so, we might
read אַרְמֹת עָפָר in Daniel. But the
word in question has not hitherto been
found in Hebrew or Aramaic.

from the rest of the faithful Israelites—they not only live for ever but are eternally glorified.   זֹהַר "*splendour*" occurs also in Ezek. viii. 2; the verb הִזְהִיר "to shine" is found nowhere else in the Old Testament, but the root זהר often has this sense in the Aramaic dialects and in Arabic.   Whether the Biblical הִזְהִיר "to warn" comes from the same root, does not seem certain, though it is generally assumed[1].   "*Those that justify the multitude*" are apparently identical with "the teachers".   For the phrase, see Is. liii. 11.   As to the meaning of "justification" cf. the Mishnah, *Ābōth* v. 26, 27, "If a man makes the many righteous, sin cannot prevail over him, but if a man makes the many to sin, he is deprived of the power of repentance.   Moses was righteous and made the many righteous, and the righteousness of the many depended upon him" (משה זכה וזיכה את הרבים וזכות הרבים תלויה בו), etc.

4.   As in chap. viii. 26, the vision ends with an express command to "hide" the revelation.   By הַסֵּפֶר "*the book*" are meant all the revelations that have been made to Daniel (so Hitzig); see chap. vii. 1.   It is quite gratuitous to suppose, with Hävernick and Von Lengerke, that "the book" includes only the last vision, for no reason can be given why this vision should be more carefully concealed than the others.   It may indeed be asked by what means Daniel could prevent the unsealing of the book before "the time of the end", but the difficulty, however obvious to us, did not necessarily occur to the author's contemporaries.   In their eyes the passage would satisfactorily account for their previous unacquaintance with the work.   The latter half of the verse is extremely difficult.   Of the word יְשֹׁטְטוּ there are two common interpretations, "many shall *wander to and fro*" (Von Lengerke), and "many shall *peruse* the book" (Hitzig, Ewald).   According to the former view, the phrase refers to the *difficulties* of the prophecy; it was only

---

[1] Possibly הִזְהִיר "to warn" may be ultimately connected with the root זור "to turn aside from the way", which is common to Hebrew and Arabic— cf. the roots נור and נהר, زور and زهر. This would explain why הזהיר means "to divert" a person from a path of danger (II Kings vi. 10. Ezek. iii. 18), and the common ܐܙܕܗܪ ܡܢ "to beware of", in Syriac. Hence might be derived the more general sense of "teaching" (Exod. xviii. 20).

after many generations had been *perplexed* by it that its true
sense would be understood (וְתִרְבֶּה הַדָּעַת). According to the
latter view, which is the more popular, יְשֹׁטְטוּ refers to the zeal
with which the book would be studied. But neither view
agrees with the other passages in which שֹׁטֵט is used (Jer. v. 1.
Amos viii. 12. Zech. iv. 10. II Chr. xvi. 9). The verb seems
always to denote rapid motion, and especially motion hither
and thither. Everywhere else the motion is meant in a literal
sense, and it is therefore very bold to apply it to "mental perplexity" or the "perusal" of a book. And how do the above
interpretations agree with the beginning of the verse? It is
natural to suppose that the clause which follows the words
"Seal the book till the time of the end" will explain the reason
of the command, just as in chap. viii. 26 the angel adds כִּי לְיָמִים
רַבִּים. That in the present case the particle כִּי is omitted, proves
nothing to the contrary—cf., for example, אַל־תִּירָא אֲנִי עֲזַרְתִּיךָ Is.
xli. 13 with the parallel passage אַל־תִּירָא כִּי גְאַלְתִּיךָ Is. xliii. 1.
But to say "Seal the book—many are to peruse it", or "Seal
the book—many are to be perplexed by it", would be altogether
meaningless. The most probable solution of the difficulty is to
be found in the LXX., which instead of ותרבה הדעת has καὶ
πλησθῇ ἡ γῆ ἀδικίας, i.e. ותרבה הָרָעת "and many shall be the
calamities". For the use of the verb in the feminine singular
with the subject in the feminine plural, see Is. xxxiv. 13. Jer.
iv. 14. Zech. vi. 14. Neh. xiii. 10. This reading appears to be
signally confirmed by I Macc. i. 9, where it is said of the successors of Alexander (i.e. with reference to the very period which
the author of Daniel has here in view) καὶ ἐπλήθυναν κακὰ ἐν
τῇ γῇ "and they multiplied evils in the earth"[1]. That the
author of I Maccabees elsewhere quotes the book of Daniel is
generally admitted, and even if we hesitate to regard I Macc.
i. 9 as a quotation, it shews at all events with what feelings the

[1] Perhaps the original Hebrew text of I Macc. had וירבו הרעת, which may be read וַיַּרְבּוּ καὶ ἐπλήθυναν—but also וַיִּרְבּוּ, which would make the resemblance to Daniel even closer. It is remarkable that in the 1st chapter of I Macc. there are several other passages which seem to be reminiscences of the latter part of Daniel, cf. v. 15 with Dan. xi. 30, v. 17 with Dan. xi. 40, v. 18 with Dan. xi. 26.

Jews looked back upon the period in question. The meaning
of the verse would therefore seem to be, "*And do thou, Daniel,
hide the words and seal the book till the time of the end—many
shall rush hither and thither, and many shall be the calamities*",
i.e. the revelation must remain concealed, because there is to
ensue a long period of commotion and distress.

5—7. The speech of the angel is now ended, and Daniel
perceives two figures, doubtless angels also, standing on opposite
banks of the Tigris, which is here called, not הַנָּהָר as in chap. x.
4, but הַיְאֹר (see p. 32). Why *two* angels are here introduced, is
explained by *v.* 7, since for an oath, as for any other fact, two
witnesses are necessary (Deut. xix. 15). In *v.* 6 it is very doubtful who is the speaker. That "the man clothed in linen" is
identical with the being described in chap. x. 5, 6, cannot be
questioned. His position "above the waters of the river" agrees
with chap. viii. 16, where an angelic voice speaks from "between
(the banks of the) Ulai". Von Lengerke, as we have seen,
identifies with Gabriel the being who brings his speech to an
end in *v.* 4, and he supposes that Gabriel is also the speaker in
v. 6. The view of Hitzig, viz. that the angel who has been
speaking previously is "the man clothed with linen", and that
the speaker in *v.* 6 is one of the two angels mentioned in *v.* 5,
appears, upon the whole, more probable. We should indeed
have expected, in this case, ויאמר אחד מהם, or some such phrase,
instead of the simple ויאמר, but the use of a verb or suffix without any distinct indication of the person referred to is found
elsewhere in Daniel. The reading of the LXX. καὶ εἶπα, וָאֹמַר,
has not the appearance of genuineness, for the analogy of chap.
viii. 13 favours the view that it is an angel, not Daniel, who
asks the question, "*How long (will it be till) the end of the
marvels?*" By הַפְּלָאוֹת "the marvels" are meant the events
which have been foretold (cf. Is. xxix. 14), as is evident from
the oath which follows in *v.* 7. The lifting up of the hand
in swearing is mentioned in Gen. xiv. 22. Exod. vi. 8; here
both hands are lifted for the sake of greater emphasis. The
angel swears "by Him who liveth for ever" (cf. חַי עָלְמָא chap. iv.
31) that the end will come "after a time, times, and half (a
time)", i.e. after three years and a half; see chap. vii. 25. In

לְמֹועֵד the prep. לְ expresses the idea of limitation, cf. לְשִׁבְעַת הַיָּמִים, "after the seven days", Gen. vii. 10. The three years and a half begin with the abolition of the daily sacrifice (see *v.* 11). To the author of Daniel and to his readers the length of this period was a matter of vital interest, and it is therefore not without reason that the book closes with the most emphatic statements on the subject. The last words of *v.* 7 are obviously a further specification of what precedes, and cannot refer, as Hävernick imagines, to some period subsequent to the 3½ years. Von Lengerke renders, "*And when the scattering of a portion of the holy people should come to an end, all this should be ended*". So also Hitzig, except that he reads וְכִכְלֹות נֵפֶץ, which is certainly more in accordance with Hebrew syntax. By the "portion of the holy people" the writer, it is supposed, means the Israelites in exile. But even if we admit as possible this use of יד, the difficulty remains that the verse, so construed, is tautological. It is surely unnecessary for the angel to assert in so solemn a manner that all these visions are to be fulfilled "when the Israelites are no longer dispersed". The final deliverance of Israel, to which all the visions in Daniel lead up, naturally includes the gathering together of the dispersed of the holy people. Some other commentators, e.g. Ewald, render, "*when they shall cease to break in pieces* (or scatter) *the power of the holy people*". But this is no less tautological than the former interpretation, not to mention the strangeness of the metaphor נַפֵּץ יד. In view of these difficulties the correctness of the text becomes very doubtful. The LXX. has ὅτι εἰς καιρὸν καὶ καιροὺς καὶ ἥμισυ καιροῦ ἡ συντέλεια χειρῶν ἀφέσεως λαοῦ ἁγίου καὶ συντελεσθήσεται πάντα ταῦτα[1]. Here the words ἡ συντέλεια χειρῶν ἀφέσεως are so totally meaningless that we have every reason to regard them as a literal rendering, i.e. the translator read יד נפץ instead of נפץ יד. The substitution of the Plural (χειρῶν) for the Singular (יד) is, of course, of no consequence. If therefore we read וְכִכְלֹות יַד נֹפֵץ עַם קֹדֶשׁ, the passage

---

[1] That the Syro-Hexaplar has ܪܟ݂ܐ̇ܗ܊ܕ ܟܚܡܡܒܠ does not prove that Paul of Tellā read ἀφέσεως χειρῶν but merely that he took the words to mean "the hands' releasing" and was obliged to invert the order, owing to the exigencies of Syriac syntax.

will signify, "*And when the power of the Shatterer of the holy people should come to an end, all these things should be ended*". For this use of נפץ cf. Judg. vii. 19. Jer. li. 20 ff. Ps. ii. 9, and for ככלות יד cf. בְּכלוֹת כֹּחֵי Ps. lxxi. 9, בְּכְלוֹת בְּשָׂרֵךְ Prov. v. 11, as well as the common application of כלה to "failing" of the eyes. This reading seems moreover to be supported by chap. vii. 25, "they shall be given into his power (בְּיָדֵהּ) until a time, and times, and half a time". By "the Shatterer of the holy people" would be meant Antiochus Epiphanes, and, so understood, the passage is no longer tautological, its object being to assure the readers of the book (who naturally comprehended the allusion) that this great oppressor was to be last oppressor of all—when *his* power ceased, the sufferings of the holy people would be ended for ever.

8—13.   That Daniel is represented as not understanding the angel's words, shews that those words must contain a special reference to the time of the author, for to suppose that *v.* 7 was meant to be unintelligible to the *readers* would be absurd.   On Daniel's inquiry, "*What is the end of these things?*" he is dismissed by the angel (*v.* 9), who reminds him that the words are to be "hidden and sealed till the time of the end"[1] (see *v.* 4), i.e. the revelations are really intended, not for Daniel himself, but for readers in the distant future.   In *v.* 10 the coming time is briefly described—it is to be a time in which "many" (Israelites) are purified (by afflictions), while others will only plunge themselves more deeply in guilt.   The words לֹא יָבִינוּ Von Lengerke explains as "shall not understand the end of these things" (see *v.* 8).   But there appears no reason for this limitation of the sense, and it is more natural to interpret, with Hitzig, "*but the wicked are all without understanding*", i.e. they are acting blindly, whereas "the teachers" possess true wisdom. In *vv.* 11, 12 the limits of "the time of the end" are given. "*And from the time when the daily sacrifice is taken away and the abomination of desolation is to be set up, are 1290 days. Blessed is he that waiteth and cometh to 1335 days*".   הוּסַר is

---

[1] That people who believe "the time of the end" to be still future should write commentaries on the Book of Daniel is one of the most singular examples of the irony of history.

probably to be taken as a Perfect; for the syntax cf. מִיּוֹם דִּבַּרְתִּי אֵלֶיךָ Jer. xxxvi. 2 and וּבְעֵת הֵחֵלּוּ II Chr. xx. 22. The לְ in לָתֵת expresses a purpose (cf. chap. ii. 16). That the 1290 days and the 1335 days date from the same moment, is generally agreed; we have therefore here two events, one of which is to happen 1290 after the desecration of the Temple, and the other 45 days later. Hävernick and Von Lengerke suppose that the 1290 days end with the re-consecration of the Temple, and the 1335 with the death of Antiochus. Hitzig, on the other hand, places the death of Antiochus at the end of the 1290 days. It is impossible here to discuss the chronological difficulties to which these hypotheses lead. I have before endeavoured to shew that the book of Daniel was finished some time before the re-consecration of the Temple, which, according to I Macc. iv. 52, took place exactly three years after its profanation, i.e. near the end of the year 165 B.C. If this be so, the end of the 1290 days, and *a fortiori* the end of the 1335 days, must have been still future when the author wrote. It is therefore impossible for us to guess what particular events are here contemplated, and why the numbers 1290 and 1335 are chosen —but it would appear from the context that at the end of the 1290 days some great deliverance is to be wrought, and that at the end of the 1335 days the period of complete blessedness is to begin. "*And do thou depart to (await) the end, and so thou shalt rest and stand up to (receive) thy portion, at the end of the days*". The last verse of Daniel is one of the most obscure. That קֵץ here means "the end of Daniel's life" (Von Lengerke) is scarcely probable, for in that case we should expect לְקִצְּךָ (cf. chap. xi. 45. Ps. xxxix. 5). Still more objectionable is Hitzig's rendering, "*go to the goal*", i.e. go thy way; in Hab. ii. 3, to which Hitzig appeals, קֵץ does not refer to the "purpose" or "goal" of a person, but to the "accomplishment" of a prediction. Prof. Robertson Smith supposes that the first לַקֵּץ was wrongly introduced by a scribe, whose eye, passing from the preceding לְ, caught the last letters of לְגֹרָלְךָ in the second half of the verse. The sense would then be, "*And do thou depart and take thy rest*", etc. Most commentators, e.g. Von Lengerke and Ewald, explain וְתָנוּחַ וְתַעֲמֹד as meaning "*and so thou shalt rest (in thy grave) and rise (from the dead)"*, etc. To this Hitzig objects that in no Semitic dialect does עמד mean "to rise from the dead". But those who find here an allusion to the resurrection can reply that if this belief were new in the days of the author, a fixed technical term may have been wanting. Even in later times, when the resurrection was a familiar idea, several quite distinct words were used for it—the Rabbins usually said תְּחִיַּת הַמֵּתִים, the Syrian Christians *kĕyāmtā* or *nuḥ-ḥāmā*, the Mohammedans *ḳiyāma, baʻth*, or *ḥashr*. However this may be, קֵץ הַיָּמִין can scarcely differ in meaning from אַחֲרִית הַיָּמִים chap. x. 14; it is contrary to all analogy to explain it, with Hitzig, as "the end" of Daniel's earthly life.

APPENDICES.

APPENDIX I.

THE PALMYRENE DIALECT.

OF all the Aramaic dialects spoken by the heathens of Syria that which has left the most considerable remains is the dialect of Palmyra (in Greek Πάλμυρα, in the Old Testament תַּדְמֹר, II Chr. viii. 4, in the native inscriptions תדמור or תדמר[1], and in Arabic تَدمُر). The Palmyrene inscriptions were mostly set up during the first three centuries of the Christian era, and are of various kinds, honorific, funereal, religious, etc. They are written in a character which, like the present Hebrew character, is a modification of the old Aramaic Alphabet[2]. Many Palmyrene inscriptions are accompanied by Greek translations. The largest collection is that made by the Count De Vogüé in his great work *La Syrie Centrale*, Paris, 1868—1877. Most of the Greek texts have been published by Waddington in his *Inscriptions grecques et latines de la Syrie*, Paris, 1870. From these works the following specimens have been taken, with the exception of No. III. and the Greek text of No. I. I have availed myself also of Nöldeke's " Beiträge zur Kenntniss der ara- mäischen Dialecte" in the *Z. D. M. G.* Vol. XXIV., and Mordt- mann's " Neue Beiträge zur Kunde Palmyra's" in the *Sitzungs- berichte der königl. bayer. Akademie der Wissenschaften*, Munich, 1875.

---

[1] According to Josephus, *Antiq.* VIII. 6. 1, the Syrian pronunciation was Ta- damor (Θαδαμορα).

[2] To express *numbers* the Palmyrenes use the following signs—Simple strokes for units up to 4—Y for 5—⊃ for 10 —3 for 20. A number followed by ⊃ expresses *hundreds*, e.g. ⊃/// = 300.

*Words and letters which are uncertain or which have been
supplied conjecturally are enclosed in square brackets.*

I.

(De Vogüé, No. 36 *b*, p. 41)

(1) דכרנא דנה די הו יקר בת עלמא בנא ימלכו בר

מקימו די מתקרא אקליש בר מלכו בר בלעקב

(2) תדמריא ליקר בנוהי ובני בנוהי עד עלמא בירח ניסן

שנת ///ᒋ3333ᒋ////

(*Greek text*, publ. by Mordtmann, "Neue Beiträge zur Kunde
Palmyra's", p. 27)

(1) ΜΝΗΜΕΙΟΝ ΑΙΩΝΙΟΝ ΓΕΡΑΣ ΩΚΟΔΟ

(2) ΜΗΣΕΝ ΙΑΜΛΙΧΟΣ ΜΟΚΕΙΜΟΤ ΤΟΤ ΚΑΙ

(3) [ΑΚ]ΚΑΛΕΙΣ[ΟΤ] ΤΟΤ ΜΑΛΧΟΤ ΤΟΙΣ ΤΕΚ-
[ΝΟΙΣ]

(*Translation of Palmyrene text*)

(1) This memorial, which (is) a sepulchre of honour, was
built by Yamliku, son of Mokīmu, who (was) called Aḳḳalīsh,
son of Māliku, son of Bēl-ʿaḳab,

(2) the Palmyrene, to the honour of his sons and his sons'
sons, for ever. In the month Nīsān (*i.e. April*), the year 394
(*of the Seleucid era, i.e. 83 A.D.*).

(*Notes*)

(1) דֻּכְרָנָא (according to the Syriac pronunciation) corresponds to
the Bibl. Aram. דִּכְרוֹנָה (Ezra vi. 2), דָּכְרָנַיָּא (id. iv. 15); in Christian
Palestinian we find דיכרון (pron. דִּכְרוֹן), and in a Ḥaurān inscription

דכרון (De Vogüé, No. 2)[1]. יְקָר בֵּת עָלְמָא lit. "the honour of an eternal abode"—in Syriac also ܒܝܬ ܚܠܡܐ means "sepulchre" (Apocryphal Acts, ed. Wright, p. ܡܩܒ), cf. בֵּית עֹלָמוֹ in Eccles. xii. 5. ימלכו, like many other Arabic names in these inscriptions (e.g. מקימו, מלכו etc.), has the Arabic termination u, which in classical Arabic is the sign of the nominative case. The name מלכו appears in Greek either as ΜΑΛΧΟΣ or ΜΑΛΙΧΟΣ, and therefore seems to be the common Arabic مَالِكٌ. בלעקב (Gr. ΒΗΛΑΚΑΒΟΣ) apparently means "Bel has granted issue, posterity". The occurrence of the Babylonian deities Bel and Nebo in Palmyrene names shews how wide and how lasting an influence was exercised by Babylonia over Syrian religion.

II.

(De Vogüé, No. 123 a, I—p. 73)

(1) [ב]ירח אלול שנת ///צ/3333צ/Y/

(2) חמנא דנה ועלתא ד[נה]

(3) [ע]בדו וקרבו לשמש וזביד[א]

(4) בני מלכו בר יריעבל בר נשא

(5) די מתקרא בר עבדבל די מ[ן]

(6) פחד בני מג[ד]ת לשמש[א]

(7) אלה בית אבוהן על ח[ייוהי]

(8) [ו]חייהון וחיי אחיד[ון]

(9) ובניהון

(*Translation*)

(1) In the month Ilūl (*i.e. September*), the year 396 (i.e. 85 A.D.),

(2) this Sun-pillar and this altar

---

[1] In the 11th ed. of Gesenius' *Handwörterbuch*, s.v. דִּכְרוֹן, this form is wrongly given as Palmyrene.

(3)   were made and consecrated by Lishmash and Zebīdā

(4)   the sons of Māliku son of Yarī'bēl son of Neshā

(5)   who (was) called son of 'Abdibel, who (was) of

(6)   the clan of the Sons of .... — to the Sun,

(7)   the god of the house of their father, for his welfare

(8)   and their welfare and the welfare of their brethren

(9)   and their sons.

(*Notes*)

(2)   חַמָּן "Sun-pillar" is used in Biblical Hebrew in the Plural only, unless הֶחָסֹן in Is. i. 31 be a corruption of החמן, as De Lagarde has suggested. עֲלָתָא "altar" is common in Syriac. For the feminine of "this" the Palmyrene dialect uses either דנה or דה (= דָּא in Daniel).

(3)   לשמש signifies "(consecrated) to the Sun", and זבידא "given", "bestowed (by God)", cf. the Hebr. זָבוּד I Kings iv. 5.

(4)   The name יריעבל is explained by De Vogüé (p. 59) as "quem Bel gratum habebit", from the verb רעה; but this does not satisfactorily account for the form יריע. Perhaps יריעבל may mean "Bel causes to thrive", from the Arabic verb رَاعَ, Imperf. يَرِيعُ "to thrive".

(6)   פחד is the Arabic فَخِذ lit. "thigh", hence "clan", as sprung from a single ancestor. The word presupposes male kinship, just as بَطن (Hebr. בֶּטֶן), when used for "tribe", presupposes female kinship. The name מנדת is uncertain, since in this inscription ד and ר are not distinguished, as they usually are in Palmyrene, by the diacritical point.

III.

(See De Vogüé, "Inscriptions palmyréniennes", in the *Journal Asiatique* for 1883, and Sachau "Ueber den palmyrenischen Νόμος τελωνικός" in the *Z. D. M. G.* XXXVII. pp. 562 ff. Of this long inscription, which is grievously mutilated in parts, only the beginning is here given.)

(1) דגמא די בולא בירח [ניסן] יום ≤Y/// שנת
////≤33Y/// בפלהדרותא די בונא בר

(2) בונא בר חירן וגרמטיא די אלכסדרס בר אלכסדרס
בר פלפטר גרמטוס די בולא ודמס וארכוניא

(3) מלכו בר עליי בר מקימו וזבידא בר נשא כד הות
בולא כנישא מן נמוסא אשרת

(4) מדי כתיב מן לתחת בדילדי בזבניא קדמיא בנמוסא
די מכסא עבידן שגין חיבן

(5) מכסא לא אסקו והוו מתגבין מן עידא במדעם די
הוא מתכתב באגוריא די

(6) מכסא [י]הוא גבא היך בנמוסא ובעידא ומטל כות
זבנין שגין על צבותא אלן

(7) סרבנין הוו ביני תגרא ליני מכסיא אתחזי לבולא
די ארכוניא אלן ולעשרתא

(8) די יבקן מדעם די לא מסק בנמוסא ויכתב בשטר
אגריא חדתא ויכתב למדע[ם]

(9) מדעמא מכסה די מן עידא ומדי אשר לאגורא [י]כתב
עם נמוסא קדמיא בגלל[א]

(10) די לקבל היכלא די רבאסירא ויהוא מבטל לארכוניא
די הון בזבן זבן ועשר[תא]

(11) [ו]סדרקיא די לא יהוא גבא אגורא מן אנש מדעם
יתיר

(*Greek text*)

(1) ΕΤΟΤΣ Η͞Μ͞Τ͞ ΜΗΝΟΣ ΞΑΝΔΙΚΟΤ Ι͞Η͞ ΔΟΓΜΑ ΒΟΤΛΗΣ

(2) ΕΠΙ ΒΩΝΝΕΟΤΣ ΒΩΝΝΕΟΤΣ ΤΟΤ ΑΙΡΑΝΟΤ ΠΡΟΕΔΡΟΤ ΑΛΕΞΑΝΔΡΟΤ ΤΟΤ ΑΛΕΞΑΝΔΡΟΤ ΤΟΤ

(3) ΦΙΛΟΠΑΤΟΡΟΣ ΓΡΑΜΜΑΤΕΩΣ ΒΟΤΛΗΣ ΚΑΙ ΔΗΜΟΤ ΜΑΛΙΧΟΤ ΟΛΑΙΟΤΣ ΚΑΙ ΖΕΒΕΙΔΟΤ ΝΕΣΑ ΑΡΧΟΝΤΩΝ

(4) ΒΟΤΛΗΣ ΝΟΜΙΜΟΤ ΑΓΟΜΕΝΗΣ ΕΨΗΦΙΣΘΗ ΤΑ ΤΠΟΤΕΤΑΓΜΕΝΑ ΕΠΕΙΔΗ ΕΝ ΤΟΙΣ ΠΑΛΑΙ ΧΡΟΝΟΙΣ

(5) ΕΝ ΤΩ ΤΕΛΩΝΙΚΩ ΝΟΜΩ ΠΛΕΙΣΤΑ ΤΩΝ ΤΠΟΤΕΛΩΝ ΟΤΚ ΑΝΕΛΗΜΦΘΗ ΕΠΡΑΣΣΕΤΟ ΔΕ ΕΚ ΣΤΝΗΘΕΙΑΣ ΕΝ

(6) ΓΡΑΦΟΜΕΝΟΤ ΤΗ ΜΙΣΘΩΣΕΙ ΤΟΝ ΤΕΛΩ-ΝΟΤΝΤΑ ΤΗΝ ΠΡΑΞΙΝ ΠΟΙΕΙΣΘΑΙ ΑΚΟΛΟΤΘΩΣ ΤΩ ΝΟΜΩ ΚΑΙ ΤΗ

(7) ΣΤΝΗΘΕΙΑ ΣΤΝΕΒΑΙΝΕΝ ΔΕ ΠΛΕΙΣΤΑΚΙΣ ΠΕΡΙ ΤΟΤΤΟΤ ΖΗΤΗΣΕΙΣ ΓΕΙΝΕΣΘΑΙ ΜΕΤΑΞΤ ΤΩΝ ΕΜΠΟΡΩΝ

(8) ΠΡΟΣ ΤΟΤΣ ΤΕΛΩΝΑΣ ΔΕΔΟΧΘΑΙ ΤΟΤΣ ΕΝΕΣΤΩΤΑΣ ΑΡΧΟΝΤΑΣ ΚΑΙ ΔΕΚΑΠΡΩΤΟΤΣ ΔΙΑ-ΚΡΕΙΝΟΝΤΑΣ

(9) ΤΑ ΜΗ ΑΝΕΙΛΗΜΜΕΝΑ ΤΩ ΝΟΜΩ ΕΝΓΡΑ-ΨΑΙ ΤΗ ΕΝΓΙΣΤΑ ΜΙΣΘΩΣΕΙ ΚΑΙ ΤΠΟΤΑΞΑΙ ΕΚΑ-ΣΤΩ ΕΙΔΕΙ ΤΟ ΕΚ

(10) ΣΤΝΗΘΕΙΑΣ ΤΕΛΟΣ ΚΑΙ ΕΠΕΙΔΑΝ ΚΤΡΩΘΗ ΤΩ ΜΙΣΘΟΤΜΕΝΩ ΕΝΓΡΑΦΗΝΑΙ ΜΕΤΑ ΤΟΤ ΠΡΩ-ΤΟΤ ΝΟ

(11) ΜΟΤ ΕΝ ΣΤΗΛΗ ΛΙΘΙΝΗ ΤΗ ΟΤΣΗ ΑΝΤΙ-ΚΡΤΣ ΙΕΡΟΤ ΛΕΓΟΜΕΝΟΤ ΡΑΒΑΣΕΙΡΗ ΕΠΙΜΕ-ΛΕΙΣΘΑΙ ΔΕ ΤΟΤΣ ΤΤΓΧΑ

(12) ΝΟΝΤΑΣ ΚΑΤΑ ΚΑΙΡΟΝ ΑΡΧΟΝΤΑΣ ΚΑΙ
ΔΕΚΑΠΡΩΤΟΤΣ ΚΑΙ ΣΤΝΔΙΚΟΤΣ [ΤΟΤ] ΜΗΔΕΝ
ΠΑΡΑΠΡΑΣΣΕΙΝ ΤΟΝ ΜΙΣΘΟΤΜΕΝΟΝ.

(Translation of Palmyrene text)

(1)   Decree of the Council, in the month Nīsān, the 18th day, the year 448 (*i.e.* 137 *A.D.*), during the Presidency of Bōnnē son of

(2)   Bōnnē son of Ḥairān and (during) the Secretaryship of Alexander son of Alexander son of Philopator, Secretary of the Council and of the People—and the Archons (being)

(3)   Māliku son of Olai son of Moḳīmu, and Zebīdā son of Neshā. When the Council had been assembled according to law, it decreed

(4)   what is written below — Whereas in former times in the law of taxation many articles subject to

(5)   taxation were not included, and (so) they used to be charged according to custom in (pursuance of) what was written in the contract, (namely) that

(6)   the tax-collector should charge according to law and custom, and (whereas) in consequence of this many times upon these subjects

(7)   disputes arose between the merchants and the tax-collectors—it seemed good to the Council of these Archons and to the Ten

(8)   that they should examine whatever was not included in the law, and (that) it should be written down in the new document of contract, and (that) there should be written down for each

(9)   article its tax which (is) according to custom, and (that) after it had been ratified by the contractor, it should be written, together with the former law, on the stele

(10)   which (is) opposite the Temple (called) Rabasīrē, and (that) care should be taken by the Archons who are (in office) at any time, and (by) the Ten,

(11)   and (by) the Syndics, that the contractor do not demand any extra charge from any man.

(Notes)

(1)   פלהדרותא is the Greek προεδρία, but with the Aramaic termination.

(3)   אִשְׁתְּרַת lit. "certified", from the root שרר.

(4)   מָדִי, in Bibl. Aram. always מָה דִי (Dan. ii. 28, etc.).   מַכְסָא "tax", as distinguished from מָכְסָא "tax-collector" in lines 6 and 7. With עֲבִידָן compare עֲבִידְתָּא Dan. ii. 49.   Instead of שנין (pron. שַׁגִּין) we find also שניאן (pron. שַׁגִּיאָן, De Vogüé, No. 15) and even סניאן (ibid.), with the substitution of ס for שׁ—which substitution is exceptional in Palmyrene, as in Biblical Hebrew.   The syntactical construction חַיָּבֶן מַכְסָא, where the Adj. in the absol. state is made to govern a direct object, occurs often in Syriac; cf. the Hebr. בָּתִּים מְלֵאִים כָּל־טוּב Deut. vi. 11.

(5)   אסקו (Causative of the verb סלק) may be read either as active אַסְקוּ, or as passive אָסְקוּ.   הֲוַו or הֲווֹ is properly masc. plur. but is here used with a fem. subject.   עידא pron. עֵידָא.   מִדְּעַם "something", "anything", is common in Jewish Aramaic; in Syriac it becomes meddem.   אַגוּרְיָא (μίσθωσις) is an abstract noun from the verb אגר.

(6)   גבא pron. גָּבֵא (Participle).   מִטֻּל כְּנָת "because of this" (corresponding to Hebr. עַל־כֵּן) does not seem to occur in the other Aramaic dialects; in Jewish Aramaic כְּנָת means "like", "as".   זבנין, in the sense of so many "times" (French, fois), is feminine, as usually in Syriac.   צבותא (probably צְבְוָתָא) is Plural of צְבוּתָא (see Dan. vi. 18).

(7)   סרבנין pron. סָרְבָנִין (so Sachau).   תַּגְרָא is shortened, as in Syriac, from תַּגְּרָיָא; similarly we find מלכא for מלכיא "kings" (De Vogüé, No. 28).   It is possible that in the spoken language this shortening was much commoner than would appear from the writing. עשרתא is stat. emphat. of עֲשְׂרָא "ten".

(8) יִבְקוֹן, for יִבְקוֹן, from the verb בקא. מְסַק (according to the analogy of Hebrew and Arabic) or מַסַּק (according to the Syriac)[1] is the passive participle of the Causative conjugation. יִכְתֵּב, Imperfect passive of the Peal. אגריא is for אנוריא (see line 5).

(9) מְדִי is here "when" (ἐπειδάν), like Syr. ܡܶܕ ܕ. אשר pron. אֲשׁר, passive of אשׁר (see line 3). אגורא pron. אֲגוֹרָא.

(10) מְבְטַל or מַבְטַל lit. "made to be a care". הון pron. הָוֵוּ Pl. of הָוֵא "being", "existing".

IV.

(De Vogüé, No. 1, p. 5)

(1) בולא ודמס עבדו צלמיא אלן תרויהון

(2) לאעילמי בר חירן בר מקימו בר חירן מתא

(3) ולחירן אבוהי רחימי מריתהון ורחלי אלהיא

(4) בדילדי שפרו להון ולאלהיהון בכל צבו כלה

(5) ליקרהון בירח ניסן שנת ////ב33ב

(*Greek text*, see Waddington No. 2586)

(1) Η ΒΟΤΛΗ ΚΑΙ Ο ΔΗΜΟΣ ΑΑΙΛΑΜΕΙΝ ΑΙΡΑΝΟΤ

(2) ΤΟΤ ΜΟΚΙΜΟΤ ΤΟΤ ΑΙΡΑΝΟΤ ΤΟΤ ΜΑΘΘΑ ΚΑΙ

(3) ΑΙΡΑΝΗΝ ΤΟΝ ΠΑΤΕΡΑ ΑΤΤΟΤ ΕΤΣΕΒΕΙΣ ΚΑΙ

(4) ΦΙΛΟΠΑΤΡΙΔΑΣ ΚΑΙ ΠΑΝΤΙ ΤΡΟΠΩ ΦΙΛΟ

(5) ΤΕΙΜΩΣ ΑΡΕΣΑΝΤΑΣ ΤΗ ΠΑΤΡΙΔΙ ΚΑΙ

(6) ΤΟΙΣ ΠΑΤΡΙΟΙΣ ΘΕΟΙΣ ΤΕΙΜΗΣ ΧΑΡΙΝ

(7) ΕΤΟΤΣ ΝΤ̄ ΜΗΝΟΣ ΞΑΝΔΙΚΟΤ

---

[1] In Bibl. Aram. the participle of the Hophal does not happen to occur, unless we reckon מְהֵימַן (Dan. ii. 45; vi. 5).

(Transl. of Palm. text)

(1) The Council and the People have made these statues, both of them,

(2) to A'ailamī son of Ḥairān son of Mokīmu son of Ḥairān (son of) Mattā,

(3) and to Ḥairān his father, lovers of their city and fearers of the gods,

(4) because they were pleasing to them and to their gods in every respect —

(5) to their honour, in the month Nīsān, the year 450 (*i.e.* 139 A.D.).

(Notes)

(1) תְּרְוֵיהוֹן is a very peculiar form, instead of which we should have expected תְּרֵיהוֹן.

(2) Before מתא the word בר is omitted, as often happens in these inscriptions.

(3) Pron. רַחִימֵי מְדִיתְּהוֹן; מדיתא, or מדינתא, means "city" in Palmyrene as in Syriac, not "province" as in Biblical Aramaic.

(4) בכל צבו כלה lit. "in every thing, the whole of it".

V.

(De Vogüé, No. 123 *a*, II—p. 74)

(1) לבריך שמה לעלמא טבא ורחמנא

(2) מודא מדין בר זבדבול בר מלכו על

(3) חיוהי וחיא אחוהי בירח תשרי

(4) שנת Y∂3Σ///

(*Translation*)

(1) To Him whose name is blessed for ever, the Good and the Merciful,

(2) Madyūn gives thanks, the son of Zebad-bōl, son of Māliku, for

(3) his welfare and the welfare of his brethren. In the month Tishrī (*i.e. October*),

(4) the year 533 (*i.e.* 221 *A.D.*).

(*Notes*)

(1) The formula לברִיך שמה לעלמא טבא ורחמנא is extremely common in the religious inscriptions of Palmyra. רַחְמָנָא " the Merciful", as a name of God, is found also in Jewish writings, but there is no proof that the Palmyrenes borrowed the term from the Jews, as has often been asserted.

(3) חיא is for חַיֵי.

VI.

(De Vogüé, No. 4, p. 8)

(1)   צלמא דנה די יולים אורלים

(2)   זבידא בר מקימו בר זבידא עשתור

(3)   בידא די אקים לה תגרא בני שירתא

(4)   די נחת עמה לאלגשיא ליקרה בדיל

(5)   די שפר להון בירח ניסן שנת 25

(6)   ///Y233

(*Greek text*, see Waddington, No. 2599)

(1) ΙΟΤΛΙΟΝ ΑΤΡΗΛΙΟΝ ΖΕΒΕΙΔΑΝ

(2) ΜΟΚΙΜΟΤ ΤΟΤ ΖΕΒΕΙΔΟΤ

(3) ΑΣΘΩΡΟΤ ΒΑΙΔΑ ΟΙ ΣΤΝ ΑΤΤΩ

(4) ΚΑΤΕΛΘΟΝΤΕΣ ΕΙΣ ΟΛΟΓΕΣΙ

(5) ΑΔΑ ΕΝΠΟΡΟΙ ΑΝΕΣΤΗΣΑΝ ΑΡΕ

(6) ΣΑΝΤΑ ΑΤΤΟΙΣ ΤΕΙΜΗΣ ΧΑΡΙΝ

(7) ΞΑΝΔΙΚΩ ΤΟΤ H̄N̄Φ ΕΤΟΤΣ.

(*Transl. of Palm. text*)

(1) This statue (is that) of Julius Aurelius

(2) Zebīdā son of Moḳīmu son of Zebīdā (son of) ʿAshtōr

(3) (son of) Baidā—which was erected to him by the merchants belonging to the caravan,

(4) who went down with him to Vologesias—to his honour, because

(5) he was pleasing to them. In the month Nīsān, the year 558 (*i.e.* 247 A.D.).

(*Notes*)

(2) עשתור seems to be the masc. form of עשתרת Gr. Ἀστάρτη.

(3) אקים is for אקימו; it would appear that in Palmyrene, as in Syriac, the final *ū* was often dropt in pronunciation. For שְׁיָרְתָּא "caravan", see the Pĕshīṭtā, Gen. xxxvii. 25.

(4) Vologesias is identified by Mordtmann ("Neue Beiträge", p. 12) with the city known in Mohammedan times as Al-Kūfa, in Babylonia.

VII.

(De Vogüé, No. 28, p. 28)

(1) צלם ספטמיוס אדי[נת] מלך מלכא

(2) ומתקננא די מדיתא כלה ספטמיא

(3) זבדא רב חילא רבא וזבי רב חילא

(4) די תדמור קרטסטא אקים למרהון

(5) בירח אב די שנת 3333צ‎Y //

(Translation)

(1) Statue of Septimius Odainat, king of kings,

(2) and stablisher of the city, all of it; the Septimii,

(3) Zabdā, chief general, and Zabbai, general

(4) of Palmyra, most noble persons, have erected (this) to their lord,

(5) in the month Āb (*i.e. August*) of the year 582 (*i.e.* 271 A.D.).

(Notes)

(1) Odainat (Gr. ΟΔΑΙΝΑΘΟΣ, see De Vogüé, No. 21) was king of Palmyra and husband of Zenobia.

(2) Pron. מְתַקְּנָנָא, from תָּקַן "to set in order".

(4) The Greek word κράτιστοι appears in Palmyrene either as קרטסטא (with the Aramaic plural ending ē), or as קרטסטוא (where וא represents οι, pronounced in later times somewhat like the French *u*).

VIII.

(De Vogüé, No. 29, p. 29)

(1) צלמת ספטמיא בת זבי נהירתא וזדקת[א]

(2) מלכתא ספטמיוא זבדא רב חילא

(3) רבא וזבי רב חילא די תדמור קרטססטוא

(4) אקים למרתהון בירח אב די שנת ‏Y‏ ‏//3333//

(Greek text, see Waddington No. 2611)

(1) ΣΕΠΤΙΜΙΑΝ ΖΗΝΟΒΙΑΝ ΤΗΝ ΛΑΜ

(2) ΠΡΟΤΑΤΗΝ ΕΥΣΕΒΗ ΒΑΣΙΛΙΣΣΑΝ

(3) ΣΕΠΤΙΜΙΟΙ ΖΑΒΔΑΣ Ο ΜΕΓΑΣ ΣΤΡΑ

(4) ΤΗΛΑΤΗΣ ΚΑΙ ΖΑΒΒΑΙΟΣ Ο ΕΝΘΑΔΕ

(5) ΣΤΡΑΤΗΛΑΤΗΣ ΟΙ ΚΡΑΤΙΣΤΟΙ ΤΗΝ

(6) ΔΕΣΠΟΙΝΑΝ ΕΤΟΥΣ ΒΠΦ ΜΗΝΕΙ ΛΩΩ.

(Transl. of Palm. text)

(1)   Statue of Septimia, daughter of Zabbai, the illustrious and the just (lady),

(2)   the queen; the Septimii, Zabdā, chief general,

(3)   and Zabbai, general of Palmyra, most noble persons,

(4)   have erected (this) to their mistress, etc.

(Notes)

(1)   צלמת, not צלם, since the statue is that of a woman. At the end of the line an א seems to have been effaced, as Nöldeke has remarked.   Instead of זדקתא we should have expected זדיקתא (pron. זַדִּיקְתָּא); perhaps the ī was pronounced short in the closed syllable.

APPENDIX II.

CHRONOLOGICAL TABLES.

I.

THE EARLIER PTOLEMIES.

		B.C.
Ptolemy Soter	. . . .	306
„ Philadelphus	. . . . .	283
„ Euergetes I.	. . . . .	247
„ Philopator	. . . . . .	222
„ Epiphanes	. . . . . .	204
„ Philometor, *sole king*	. . . .	181
„ Philometor and } *reigning conjointly* „ Euergetes II.	. .	170
„ Philometor, *sole king*	. . . .	164
„ Euergetes II.	. . . . .	146—117

II.

THE EARLIER SELEUCIDAE.

Seleucus	306
Antiochus Soter	281
„ Theos	262
Seleucus Callinicus	245
„ Ceraunus	226
Antiochus the Great	224
Seleucus Philopator	187
Antiochus Epiphanes	175—164

III.

THE PRINCIPAL EVENTS IN JEWISH HISTORY FROM THE CAPTIVITY TO THE DEATH OF ANTIOCHUS EPIPHANES.

INDEX

OF THE PRINCIPAL WORDS AND ROOTS COMMENTED UPON.

The numbers refer to the pages. Roots are marked with the sign √.

For EU product safety concerns, contact us at Calle de José Abascal, 56–1°,
28003 Madrid, Spain or eugpsr@cambridge.org.

 www.ingramcontent.com/pod-product-compliance
Ingram Content Group UK Ltd.
Pitfield, Milton Keynes, MK11 3LW, UK
UKHW010040140625
459647UK00012BA/1513